THE WOODWORKER'S GUIDE TO
FURNITURE DESIGN

THE WOODWORKER'S GUIDE TO
FURNITURE DESIGN

THE COMPLETE REFERENCE FOR BUILDING FURNITURE
THE RIGHT SIZE, THE RIGHT PROPORTION AND THE RIGHT STYLE

GARTH GRAVES

POPULAR WOODWORKING BOOKS

METRIC CONVERSION CHART

TO CONVERT	TO	MULTIPLY BY
Inches	Centimeters	2.54
Centimeters	Inches	0.4
Feet	Centimeters	30.5
Centimeters	Feet	0.03
Yards	Meters	0.9
Meters	Yards	1.1
Sq. Inches	Sq. Centimeters	6.45
Sq. Centimeters	Sq. Inches	0.16
Sq. Feet	Sq. Meters	0.09
Sq. Meters	Sq. Feet	10.8
Sq. Yards	Sq. Meters	0.8
Sq. Meters	Sq. Yards	1.2
Pounds	Kilograms	0.45
Kilograms	Pounds	2.2
Ounces	Grams	28.4
Grams	Ounces	0.04

The Woodworker's Guide to Furniture Design. Copyright © 1997 by Garth Graves. Printed and bound in the United States of America. All rights reserved. No part of this book may be reproduced in any form or by any electronic or mechanical means including information storage and retrieval systems without permission in writing from the publisher, except by a reviewer, who may quote brief passages in a review. Published by Popular Woodworking Books, an imprint of F&W Publications, Inc., 1507 Dana Avenue, Cincinnati, Ohio 45207. (800) 289-0963. First edition.

Other fine Popular Woodworking Books are available from your local bookstore or direct from the publisher.

Visit our Web site at www.popularwoodworking.com for information on more resources for woodworkers.

03 02 01 00   6 5 4 3

Library of Congress Cataloging-in-Publication Data

Graves, Garth.
   The woodworker's guide to furniture design / Garth Graves.
        p.   cm.
   Includes bibliographical references and index.
   ISBN 1-55870-640-2
   1. Furniture design. I. Title.
TT196.G7   1997
684.1′04—dc21

96-29573
CIP

Edited by Adam Blake
Content Edited by Bruce Stoker
Production Edited by Michelle Kramer
Cover designed by Chad Planner

ABOUT THE AUTHOR

Garth Graves has been a woodworker for thirty-five years, designing and producing projects for his home, boat and for woodworking publications. He is the author/illustrator of *Desks You Can Customize* (Betterway Books, 1996) and *Yacht Craftsman's Handbook* (International Marine Publishing/ TAB Books/McGraw-Hill, 1992). He is also a contributor to *Woodenboat, Classic Boat, Fine Woodworking, Popular Woodworking* and *Better Homes and Gardens* magazines.

To Brad, Nina and Jill

Ye who would pass by and raise your hand against me,
harken ere you harm me.

I am the heat of your hearth on the cold winter nights,
the friendly shade screening you from the summer sun,
and my fruits are refreshing draughts
quenching your thirst as you journey on.

I am the beam that holds your house,
the board of your table,
the bed on which you lie,
and the timber that builds your boat.

I am the handle of your hoe,
the door of your homestead,
the wood of your cradle,
and the shell of your coffin.

I am the gift of God
and the friend of man.

Anonymous

TABLE OF CONTENTS

CHAPTER THREE

Applying Standards

CHAPTER FOUR

Committing Plans to Paper

CHAPTER FIVE

Converting to Parts

Introduction

Design standards are a place to begin—to adopt, adapt or disregard.

Why do some designs work, while others do not? What is it that makes the product visually pleasing, comfortably functional? What are those attributes that set off the look of an apple crate made into a coffee table from a finely crafted piece of furniture?

It is a combination of many things—proportion, finish, craftsmanship, detail or nicely shaped legs (which are always a treat)—all in harmony to create a whole, cohesive design. Maybe a past project appeared top-heavy. Maybe the base was structurally sufficient, but visually inadequate in relation to the case supported above. Past designs may have been too clunky; maybe the legs were too heavy, too thin or too short.

Any of these single elements, or the absence of design continuity among components (dissimilar styles), can exaggerate singular distractions.

Custom furniture design is a mix of many things. History, aesthetics, ergonomics, standards, construction methods, joinery techniques, material characteristics and finishes are all brought together to guide the planning and crafting of a project. Of equal importance are your capabilities. As the designer/craftsman, apply your background knowledge and experience and put your mark and your spark into the piece.

Between concept and product, this book interjects the interim, in-process steps before the sawdust flies:

- Scoping the task—that is, assessing the complexity
- Defining and applying the standards
- Capturing your ideas on paper, in models or mock-ups to confirm your approach
- Looking at the mechanics of the part shapes, sizes and materials

This is more of a How-to-*Design* rather than How-to-*Build* book. It is a practical guide to the planning processes, from concept through the design, shop plans and finishes.

A sequence through the custom furniture design process is presented in the following chapters:

1. DEVELOPING CONCEPT—A menu of ideas from what has been done before, or creating in your own style—get the creative juices flowing.

2. DEFINING SCOPE—Temper the concepts with the realities of your resources—time, interest, capabilities and shop space—for the level of complexity.

3. APPLYING STANDARDS—Follow or depart from convention. Look at size and stature of the user, pleasing proportions, style relationships.

4. COMMITTING TO PAPER—Lock in your design, adapting plans and photos, preplanning construction steps.

5. CONVERTING TO PARTS—Select best woods, mill cuts, joinery techniques.

RESOURCES are presented in the appendix
List of Sources and Suppliers
Bibliography

Hopefully the contents will guide the process, providing a logical path from concept to construction. The most important goal in whatever you design and build is to be pleased with the results.

CHAPTER ONE

Developing Concept

Defining your ideas for the next furniture project is the first step in concept development. Whether the furniture will be built for yourself or as a commissioned piece, the design should be a balance of function and form, customized specifically for the intended use and user.

In adopting the form-follows-function precept in custom furniture design, we strive to create a form that fulfills all of the functional expectations of the piece. "Function" in a piece of custom furniture can be aesthetic only, or its appearance may be subordinate to the utility and efficiency of the piece.

But both form and function should be considered in your plan. Your design objectives should strive to balance diverse design objectives into a cohesive whole. You want a design that works, and is both visually pleasing and functionally efficient.

Identifying design objectives early in the creative process is important to the results. Once purpose has been defined as the *objective*, specific interim *goals* delve deeper into all you want to accomplish: How will the furniture be used, where must it fit, what's the desired look, what should it match, what size should it be?

The answers to these, and to more specific questions dealing with your target user and your environs, will further define and prioritize the needs and requirements of your design.

FUNCTION: NEEDS, APPLICATIONS

Whatever you design has a function—a purpose. Whether that role is active or passive, there is some need to be met, even if it is only to fill a space. (See "Define the Function, Need and Application" page 5.)

FORM: MASS, AREA

Whatever you design has form, an assembled whole made up of component shapes and design elements comprised by the piece. Conjure up a mental picture of its size and shape. Is it to be massive and heavy, or small and slight? (See "Envision Form, Mass and Area" page 9.)

ENVIRONS: SPACE, SURROUNDINGS, SETTINGS

Whatever you design will occupy a space, share an environment with the other furniture, surroundings and settings. What form and style will work best, look best? (See "Study the Environs" page 11.)

COMPATIBILITY

How would you like the piece perceived? Whatever you design can complement or contrast its surroundings. It can be designed to dominate or meld, or mix and match. (See "Design to Complement" page 11.)

STYLE: HISTORY, EVOLVING DESIGNS, PERIODS

What you design may be definable only as a one-off custom design, a style-inspired work from the past or a reproduction. (See "A Look at Evolving Styles" page 14.)

CREATIVITY

What you design will come from your own awareness and judgment. The creative process will bring these diverse needs into focus and be met in the custom furniture you design. (See "Beginning the Creative Process" page 33.)

What you, as the craftsman, cabinetmaker or custom furniture designer, bring to the task is your design philosophy, your unique style and your skill based on knowledge and experience. These attributes may not be formally acknowledged, or even recognized, but they are an important part of the cache of "tools" you apply to your projects. And their influence begins at the outset.

Conceptualizing works best with a wide-open mind—a no-holds-barred, freewheeling exercise envisioning the parts, pieces and shapes that make up the whole. At some later point the concepts must be tempered by the realities of function, location and fabrication constraints.

The design process can grow and develop in thought alone, or be recorded and reviewed in written lists. Whichever approach you take, there is a natural order to developing a concept that ensures the initial objectives are not forgotten along the way.

The flowchart on page 6 puts on paper the same type of decision process we go through mentally when designing or designing/building custom furniture, laid out in detail, in sequence, as a flow diagram. Even though these steps may seem obvious, there are some basic questions to ask before you begin, and to continue asking while developing your design.

Each step is expanded on in later chapters, but an overview of the scope will identify and define some important considerations. These definitions, and reiterations, will preserve your design objectives through the entire process, so that your objectives are exhibited in the final product.

The diagram begins with a concept—what is it you're designing, what size do you want to make it and will the standard size meet your custom needs? If not, define why a design decision doesn't meet the criteria. The first loop-back asks why it's not suitable and what change would make it better. Altering the standard size to conform more closely to your application results in a design change, which is then retested for suitability.

In the next step ask yourself, where will this piece of furniture be located? If it is a good fit in the target space, go on. If not, go back and rethink it. Any change can impact an earlier decision, causing you to retest your design approach any time you find yourself in a design loop.

Strict adherence to convention—style, size or any other parameter—is not encouraged, or even suggested. But working from a more knowledgeable base will help justify the direction you take. Any departure made from the norm will be well founded, the results based on an informed decision.

Define the Function, Need and Application

You may be working from a honeydew list: "Honey, do make us a corner display cabinet." Or you might decide the time is right to finally make that game table for the Tuesday night card games. These may be low on your priority list, something you intend to do someday, but the conceptualizing begins the whole design process. When you're finally ready to tackle the project, the list of wants become your design objectives.

At this preliminary design stage, think in more nebulous terms—the gestalt. Many construction decisions will be made throughout the design phase but shouldn't clutter your thinking during conceptual design. You will work out the details, as needed and when needed, as the concept develops.

TEST YOUR DESIGN IDEAS

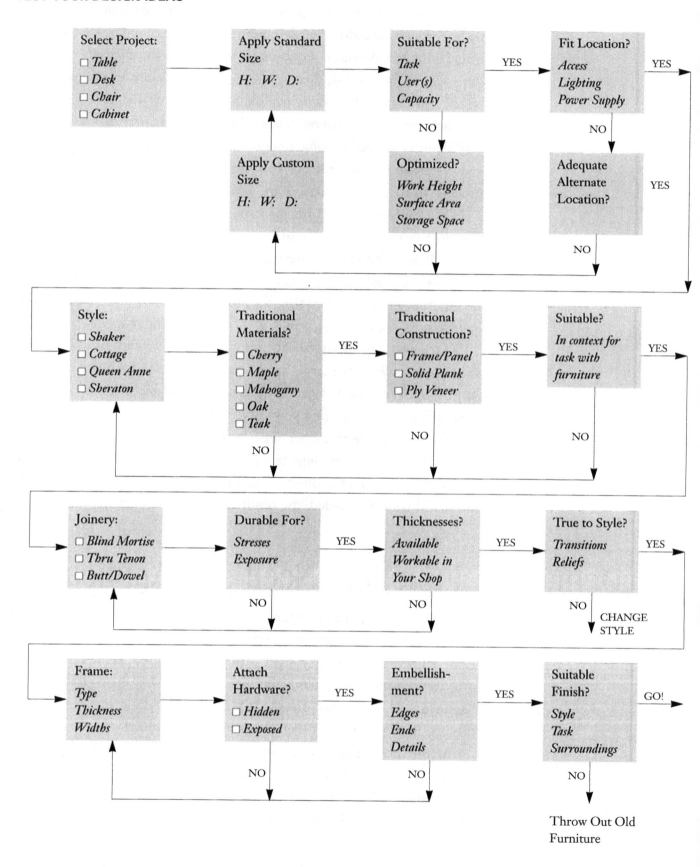

Identify Your Objectives

Your objective is to build a Whatever. Identifying more specific wants and needs early in the creative process is critical to the outcome. Fill in the objectives for the results you want accomplished: Build a cabinet to hold _____, to be located _____, complementing _____ style.

Once the overall purpose or mission has been defined in your objectives, list the more specific functional and aesthetic goals, such as:

- How will it be used (*function*)?
- What size should you make it (*proportion*)?
- Who will use it (*customize*)?
- Where will it be placed (*environs*)?
- What should it look like (*style*)?
- What visual impact should it have (*complement* or *contrast*)?

List Your Functional Goals

To fulfill a need, suit an application and occupy a space are all general objectives. These will expand into more specific detail based on whether you intend to design a piece of furniture to display a collection, a work center customized to a specific user and tasks, or a piece of furniture to fill an area (with an added bonus of adding more storage space). This is where you test the concept against everything you want the piece to accomplish, the objectives you want to meet.

A display cabinet for thimbles or knickknacks will differ from a gun cabinet (aside from a jimmy-proof lock on the latter). This brings up another aspect of design considerations: any legal or social mores to be followed or avoided for whatever reason. In this instance, even though a tier or rack of drawers to hold ammunition would seem a logical design element, common sense tells us to lock guns and ammo in separate compartments, especially where children are concerned.

Identify the Aesthetic Goals

The questions you might ask when focusing on the needs your project is to fulfill will be specific to your project, and may include some of those listed below:

SKETCHPAD 1A
FOR WHAT, FOR
WHOM, FOR WHERE?

Consider both the
functional as well as the
aesthetic objectives when
designing a piece of
furniture.

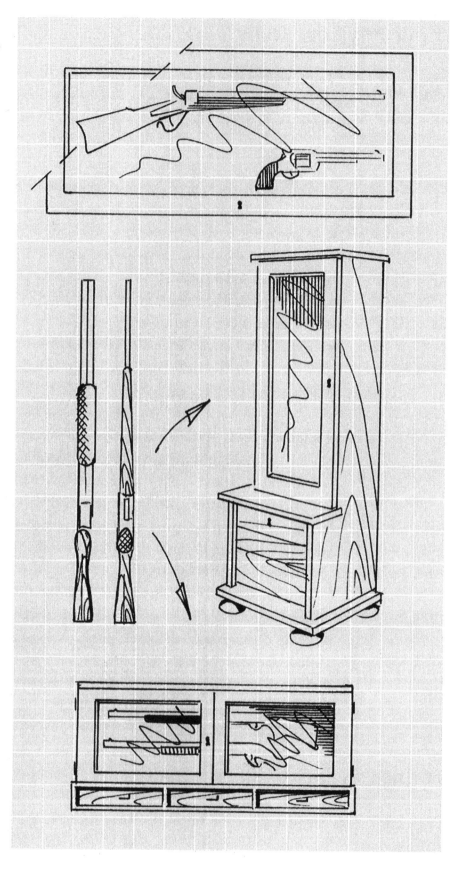

■ How do you want this piece of furniture to be perceived?

■ Should it be a focal piece, or blend in with the surroundings? Will it be an accent or companion piece in the setting?

■ What style and mood will it follow? Is there any precedent set in the location, in the room, in the home?

■ Whose personality and tastes must be reflected? What is most suitable for the user?

■ Should it enclose or showcase its contents? Are you protecting or displaying a collection?

A cabinet or cupboard may be designed to enclose its contents behind solid doors, display the collection through glass or a grille that still protects and envelops, or exhibit contents on open shelves or hung on pins or racks. Assign a level of prominence to both the cabinet and its contents, and make a determination whether they are equal or whether the cabinet or its contents should be favored.

Other aesthetic considerations might come into play where mixed use is a factor. A work desk sharing space in an in-home office doesn't need to look like a desk. Maybe a library table or butcher block might serve as the headquarters. Custom furniture should be suitable with the other furnishings and still meet the small office/home office (SOHO) needs of the user.

Envision Form, Mass and Area

Here, ask yourself whether the piece is to dominate or blend into its designated space. This is a minor consideration at this juncture, but an early awareness of the design direction you might pursue will aid future planning, beginning with this conceptual phase.

The product of your design will take on a three-dimensional mass, a piece of furniture that will occupy an area. The form it assumes should meet an array of functional and aesthetic objectives, including its suitability for the intended purpose or function it provides, the space it occupies and a logical relationship of size to its level of importance. Is it a major piece or an accent piece? An armoire-size bread basket is not within a practical scale for the function, nor is a dining table suitable for bedside.

Defining Size and Shape

Consider function and form. "Form follows function" is a familiar truism from American architect Louis Henri Sullivan. Start with the design standards adopted over time for furniture. Test the norm against your specific needs (content, user, location, scale), and adopt or adapt for those needs when defining the optimum form.

Awareness of Positive and Negative Shapes

Delineated areas, whether filled or void, form a visual shape. A cavity, especially when darkened in shadow, will increase the perception of depth. When viewed face-on, voids form a shape, even though empty or divided by scant parts or contents, and should be looked at as a design element of size, shape and proportion. Even the area between table legs becomes a shape, especially where the legs command more attention resulting from prominent size, shape or mass. Conversely, where legs are slight, they seem only to interrupt a common space that extends beyond the form, so there is less of a demarcation or definition of shape.

Classify as Massive or Slight

Furniture follows some conventions of gender, even though it might not be politically correct to acknowledge that fact. As a designer of custom furniture, you should respect the distinction, and the optimum relationships of product-to-purpose and product-to-user.

When designing replicas, follow conventions of the past. Grandeur from earlier times reflected the society and the social culture of the user, and oftentimes gender was a primary design consideration, as exemplified by the lady's writing desk or vanity table. Even today we design to meet the tastes and wants and needs of the user. Size and form should reflect these differences in size and suitability for the purpose intended and the intended user.

The Clydesdale is massive, the Thoroughbred is slight, but they are both horses, and they both excel at their appointed task. "What does this have to do with furniture?" you may ask. Well, furniture, like horses, has four legs. The legs of the Clydesdale need to be larger to support the weight and to pull the dray. The legs of the Thoroughbred must be strong as well, but slighter to run faster—I could continue this analogy, but you get the point. There is a natural order of sizes and shapes for specific uses.

Regardless of physical size, if furniture you design and build tends to be slight, even a large chest-on-chest can reflect your design trait or signature. You will apply your design philosophy to whatever you design, which will be a distinctive product that satisfies both your design sense and the design objectives of the piece. Find a middle ground that meets everyone's agenda.

That's what custom furniture design is all about.

Study the Environs

Look at the intended location. What form and style will be best in the room? With the architecture? For your lifestyle? Maybe you want your summer cottage to be a complete departure from the New York City town house, or you have a preference for country, nautical, Shaker or period furniture.

You can use an architectural theme for a room's furnishings by studying the design character and detail of the location. Maybe you will get inspired by the look and can include some aspect of the architectural detail in your furniture design.

Design to Complement

Design the piece to complement adjacent furniture in style, size, mass and proportions, and in its details and finishes. Observe the area for dominant shapes, forms and styles you may want to use as possible design elements in your tailored furniture.

Complementary design, however, can easily and quickly be overworked. Too much of the same theme can appear redundant, going beyond the subtle tie-in you may have intended. Avoid overkill. Try to achieve a balance of conformity and contrast, whether in the same piece, or among pieces in the same setting.

Design to Contrast

In order for this to work, you don't have to come up with some off-the-wall design for shock value. A piece of brightly colored furniture in a

SKETCHPAD 1B
ROOM SETTINGS

Look at the architectural surroundings and accompanying furnishings to inspire your design, whether in harmony or contrast.

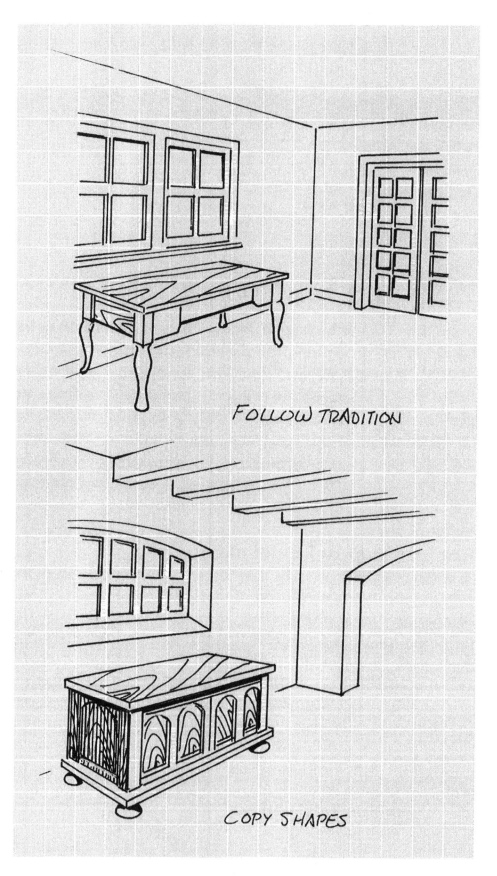

FOLLOW TRADITION

COPY SHAPES

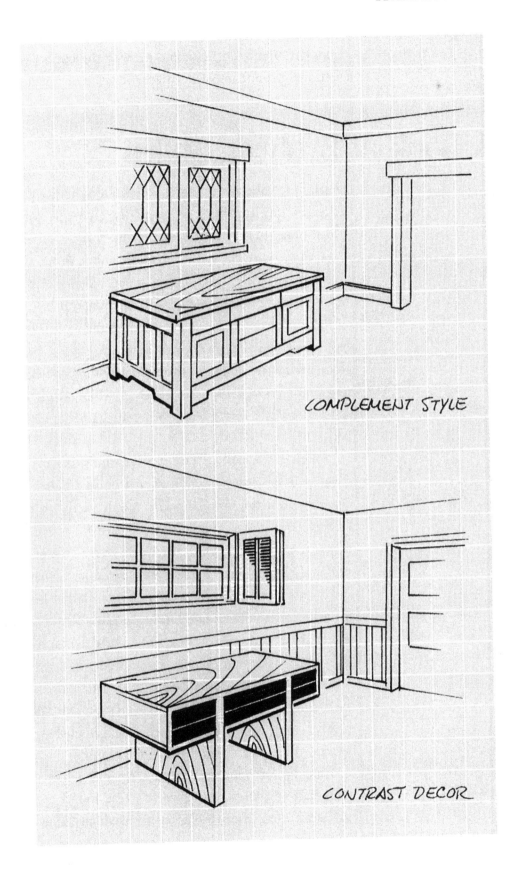

COMPLEMENT STYLE

CONTRAST DECOR

monochromatic setting would provide the contrast, as would using unconventional proportions for an accent piece of furniture.

A Look at Evolving Styles

During the conceptual phase, you can look to the past to guide the present. Egyptian furniture builders went through the same design iterations we revisit today as they produced their wares some five thousand years ago. In their case, however, if the pharaoh didn't deem the results sufficient for comfort in the hereafter, the craftsman could lose face (or more). Fortunately, our efforts are not subject to this drastic level of criticism.

The same process used in designing and crafting today's custom furniture has been applied in every era down through the ages. New trends were sometimes well-funded by influential, and maybe egotistical, rulers employing hundreds of artisans to satisfy a whim, while other movements were expressions of counterdesign, a revolt against opulence, industrialization or politics.

Burchell's *History of Furniture* reminds us that furniture styles did not develop in an orderly progression from a single beginning or follow any orderly path through history. Each culture or era produced its own thing. Historians credit only one region at a time as *the* center of development, even though other significant work was being produced elsewhere. The accepted chronology of these movements may focus on a ruler who died, abdicated or was defeated to put a period on that period of furniture design. As influence waned in one locale, another center would emerge, based on preceding efforts, or skipping to earlier eras, or contributing a whole new look to the evolution of furniture design.

Publishing did a great deal to promote and embed a furniture style of the times. If Betterway Books had been around in the 1700s (and they almost qualify), they would have joined other publishers in compiling the first books of furniture styles for its book club members.

Catalogs of popular furniture designs which were developed by the industrialized guilds of the world, were found by, or found their way to, rural craftsmen who were asked to produce "a nice chair like this one for the mayor."

Country artisans built this furniture using native woods and local joinery techniques. Without the benefit of apprenticing with the Italian guilds, they produced their version of a style based on interpretation, and maybe limited abilities to carve and gild and upholster.

Some of our finer designs came from these humble beginnings, including country (from the provinces of France), provincial and cottage styles. These remain popular, and continue to be what we buy or build for today's lifestyle. Not only is some of the country furniture simpler and therefore easier to build, it has a livable comfort, stripping away the formality of more opulent times.

Early Thoughts on Early Furniture

USE THE BEST FROM THE PAST

Those ignorant of the past are condemned to repeat its worst aspects, or so said George Santayana. Maybe he was referring to custom furniture.

More specific furniture styles you may want to design are described in later chapters, but for now we'll look at the bigger picture of how furniture design evolved, and look at some of the similarities today's designers encounter in an effort to design something pleasing and functional.

Furniture style speaks volumes about the people and the times. Early on, the lack of furniture was characteristic of the Neanderthal (pull up a rock and let's do the male bonding thing), or of nomadic tribes whose persistent cry could be heard on the desert breeze, "Are we there yet?" Early native Latin Americans built spectacular Incan cities, impressive Aztec pyramids and remarkable Mayan mazes, but little or no furniture. It would be centuries until the European influence made an impact, most specifically from the Spanish, who brought their comforts of home with them to the newly conquered land and began the mix of Spanish furniture and Native American interpretation reflected today in our southwestern style of furniture.

The design prowess of five thousand years ago is apparent in the earliest Egyptian furniture. Examples were well preserved in the tombs of kings. Furniture designs from classical Greek and Roman eras are captured in bas-relief friezes or paintings in their architecture. Although this ancient furniture was literally "fit for a king," the aristocracy of the times also shared in these prized possessions.

Byzantine churches and monasteries were adorned with splendid furnishings and were the sole possessors of the art. But that monopoly would soon change.

The Western movement in the 1500s, Henry VIII's edict to secularize furniture for the populace and the Industrial Revolution expanded availability of furniture to the middle class. These events led to a trend toward a more utilitarian style of furniture, of somewhat lesser craftsmanship and ornamentation, to fit the needs, the preferences and the purses of an expanding buyer population.

Pharaohs, kings, queens, regents and emperors, as well as regions and schools, all influenced, or maybe dictated, the furniture style of their eras. A new monarch or a revolt by the masses would bring about departure from preceding styles in protest of political events or political figures. The more faddish the style, the shorter it retained popularity. Styles swung radically, from highly ornate to serene simplicity. Shaker furniture, in its simple beauty, was a statement against secular opulence. And the Arts and Crafts movement was a rejection of the complexity of life and living. These products were, and remain, a reflection on the craftsmen who produced simple, unadorned designs of form and function.

Archeologists, anthropologists and historians, as well as furniture makers, have traced the major movements of design throughout history. They named these movements and identified time spans for the eras of furniture styles. The names and time spans correspond closely with the history of art, which isn't surprising since the craftsmen of the time were considered artisans, creating design expression in three dimensions—and the beat goes on.

Joy's *Connoisseur Illustrated Guide: Furniture* points out that furniture from the continent was often named for rulers (Louis XIV, XVI). The provincial style came from the outlying regions, such as the provinces of France. English and Colonial furniture styles were also given names of rulers; e.g., the style during the reigns of the four King Georges are Georgian. Just to confuse matters, within that same period, styles were also named for the craftsmen, schools or designers, including Chippendale and Hepplewhite.

North America's contribution began, obviously, with the settling of the Colonies, but was largely influenced by heritage, lineage and beliefs carried from the old world. Federal style was named after the new form of federal government in the U.S., so much of the federal symbolism was employed, but the style retained a good deal of its English origins.

The Mighty Chair

Furniture, as a possession, symbolized status. From early Egyptian dynasties, throughout furniture's short history, the finest craftsmen would produce the finest furniture for the finest egos of rulers and aristocracy.

The chair has been a universal symbol of status as either the place of honor or, during some eras, subordinated for use by entertainers or servers of the aristocracy. In early Mesopotamia, the chair was the place for one who entertained or otherwise served the revelers. The esteemed place of honor was the couch, where one could recline while munching peeled grapes. A musician would be seated in the chair while performing. In that culture sitting was subordinate to reclining, but still elevated to a status reserved for those whose talents (or service) were revered by the master.

During the Middle Ages, and still reflected in our customs today, the chair, particularly an ornate variety, was a symbol of highest status for the tush of the most important one in the group. These "chairs of honor" were typically larger, elevated and more ornate for the exclusive use in royal courts, churches and monasteries.

This tradition holds true in today's boardrooms, courtrooms and council chambers. A chairperson is the head of the board, or the committee, or an academic department. Today, the "chair" is the term given to the head or leader, which conjures up some interesting mental images.

Origin of Furniture Detail

Cylindrical chair legs in Mesopotamian design were ringed with metal "bracelets," which were the forerunners of the turned spindles we produce today.

Through the Dark and Middle Ages, furniture was nearly nonexistent for the common masses, and in short supply for those of status. A ruler's summer castle would remain unfurnished in the off-season. When vacationing royalty would retreat to a temporary "beach castle" or hit the road to survey the kingdom, the royal furniture would accompany the entourage.

To meet the portability requirements, artisans produced some of the first knockdown styles, including tilt-top, trestle and drop-leaf tables, X-frame (curule) folding chairs, and beds designed with head and footboards with rails which were easily dismantled, transported and reassembled for a good night's sleep both home and away—not dissimilar to what we build today. There are many other similarities to early designs in today's furniture.

Furniture Time Line

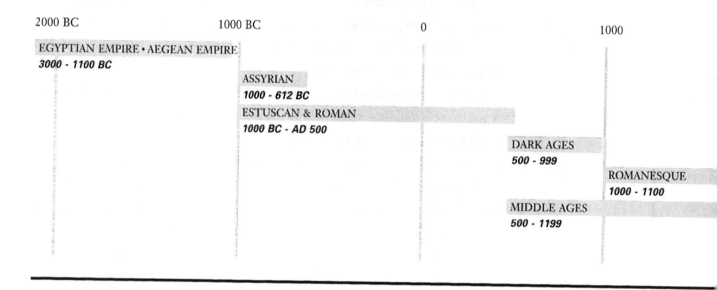

Furniture Time Line

The time line of furniture styles is presented here as a reminder of when and where furniture styles originated, and reinforces the fact that there is very little new in our efforts of today.

Designs were, as is true today, an interpretation of experience and knowledge as a frame of reference (plans not included), a compilation of what we like from the past, an expression of counterdesign in protest of something or someone or just to be different.

Sources differ on beginning and ending dates for furniture styles we group and classify into periods. Style changes were often a blend, a melding and adaptation of current and past efforts. Any attempt to isolate and bracket these periods is subject to interpretation, but the consensus and the time line show an ever-increasing level of activity with technological development and population growth.

This running narrative of the time line gives a broader review of the whos and wheres of historical furniture. Style changes came about, in many instances, based only on a whim or personal agenda of those influencing the change. The same degree of justification exists for today's custom furniture maker to produce what is pleasing, even if only for a population of one.

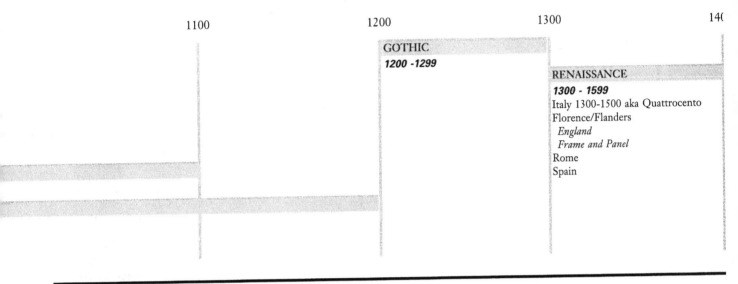

Ancient Egypt, Greece and Rome (3000 B.C.–A.D. 499)

Whatever is used as reference for today's furniture has gone through more recent renewal periods. Renewals of these ancient styles were the mainstay of the Adam Brothers and the Empire styles.

Dark Ages to Middle Ages (A.D. 500–1199)

Somebody lost the recipe for fine furniture, and crude attempts were often gilded to cover the lack of craftsmanship. This was the era when a solitary chest also served as a chair, table or bed.

ROMANESQUE

This era represented the link between the fallen Roman Empire and the beginning of the Gothic style.

Gothic Style (A.D. 1200–1299)

This style, reserved for cathedrals, saw some resurgence when seventeenth-century designers reached back to these times for inspiration. These designers embellished their chair backs, desks and tables with Gothic patterns

Furniture Time Line — continued

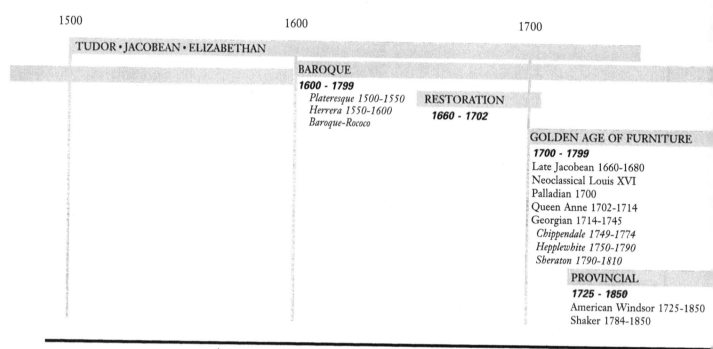

such as carved trefoils, quatrefoils and cinquefoils, and lots of cusps in Gothic tracery—things we would not normally attempt.

Oriental Style (A.D. 1400–1500)

Some of the early Chinese furniture was built for dynasties dating back to 200 B.C., when joinery of the finest quality was developed without the use of pegs, pins or glue. Puzzlelike joints held together for centuries. Around A.D. 1400, their use of what the French later named the cabriole leg became a distinctive element of later Chinese dynasty furniture.

The Renaissance (A.D. 1300–1599)

Coming out of the Middle Ages, the do-all chest was just beginning to be customized for specific purposes. The reign of the Tudors (1485-1603) was the last phase of Gothic style and the beginning of the Renaissance.

1800   1900   2000

CLASSIC REVIVAL

1790 - 1854
Federal 1790-1825
Empire 1804-1815
Duncan Phyfe 1815-1854

VICTORIAN

1800-1850
Biedermeier 1800-1850
Regency 1811-1820
Revival (Neo-Gothic) 1830
Art Nouveau 1875
Arts & Crafts 1876-1916

MODERN

1900 - Present
Functionalist Modern
De Stijl 1917
Bauhaus 1919-1933
Art Deco 1920-1930
Organic 1930s
Contemporary
Scandinavian
Eames 1946
Saarinen 1950s
Maloof
Krenov
Castle
Bennett
Osgood

ITALIAN/FLEMISH INFLUENCES

Fifteenth-century Florence was the center of Renaissance influence. The de'Medici family sponsored all forms of art, including furniture. Venice was a close second to Florence in Renaissance art. When Florence lost ground, this center of influence moved to Venice and Rome, and into the High Renaissance era.

Early Renaissance design was simple in line, with emphasis on the horizontal, based on ancient Roman design. In the early sixteenth century, High Renaissance evolved into excesses, including highly lavish furniture.

Frame and panel construction was used and forgotten in earlier times, but revived in Flanders around the fifteenth century because experience once again exhibited the impractical practice of joining large solid planks to build large cabinet furniture. The wooden planks would shrink and expand, causing the same problems as in the past. Frame and panel was adopted by the Flemish to relieve these stresses and allow for seasonal changes in wood. The heavier frame and panel furniture would become the style of English furniture with its multipaneled design.

Arabesque designs (used widely in Italian work until 1527 when Holy

Roman Emperor Charles V's armies took Rome) featured much ornamentation, using floral, foliage, fruit, animals and figural outlines to produce an interlaced pattern of lines.

THE AGE OF OAK (A.D. 1500-1660)

The "age" periods are retrospective designations based on the furniture style of the era and the wood selected for the design characteristic of the time. Designations changed with the changing centers of influence and were renamed for the species best suited to produce the furniture style, whether light or dark, carved or uncarved, highly figured or not, or whatever. The other "age" periods are Walnut (1660-1720), Mahogany (1720-1765), and Satinwood (1765-1806).

ENGLISH INFLUENCES

Italian Artisans—have tools, will travel! Louis XII (reigned 1498-1515) imported Italian artisans to France.

Henry VII (reigned 1495-1509) used Italian artisans in England as well, to work alongside English tradesmen, primarily for the Italians' contribution in ornamental detail.

Henry VIII's (reigned 1509-1547) split from the church expanded the markets of furniture crafters previously dedicated to meeting the needs of the church, to a broader, secular populace. The pope and the people had to share.

FRENCH INFLUENCES

France was the site of two styles under the rule of Francis I (reigned 1515-1547) and Henry II (reigned 1547-1559). In 1522, Francis I extended the contract Louis XII had with the Italian artisans and employed their skills in remodeling the palace of Fontainebleau, which turned into a showcase of columns, scrolls, carved bands (to replicate tooled leather) and carved figures.

When Henry II entered the scene in 1547, he appreciated the carved figure work, but relegated the columns and arches below the case as legs, supports and other underpinnings, giving this version a lighter look. The heavier chest-on-chest design, however, was a product of this era.

SPANISH INFLUENCES

Spain, during the Renaissance, combined Spanish, Italian and Moorish designs. Their claim to fame, in addition to the fun names to spell for Art

History [Plateresque (1500-1550), Herreran (1550-1600) and Churrigueresque] was the vargueño, a cabinet-desk with fall front made during the sixteenth, seventeenth and early eighteenth centuries, according to Aronson's *Encyclopedia of Furniture*.

Early records are unclear on the origin of the Spanish desk, but classified it as a *mueble escritorio* to describe a writing desk. It is believed to have originated in Vargas (Toledo) around 1600, but according to *Antique Spanish Furniture*, no carpenter or workshop is recorded as its producer. But they had to assign some origin.

The vargueño design lends itself to a stylized Spanish or completely contemporary upright desk of many drawers and pigeonholes.

The Unofficial Age of Transition (A.D. 1600–1699)

With the passing of the earlier furniture styles that few of us would want to tackle, we arrive at a time in history that began producing furniture or details we might duplicate or modify.

Furniture styles began popping up with greater and greater frequency. Obviously the chair was just a part of the ensemble, but its design displays the characteristics, discipline and design features for the style. Chairs from the Furniture Time Line are presented to depict the era, times, movements and the direction of furniture design.

JACOBEAN STYLE

Jacobean (1603-1629) is the Latin name for James, as in James I. This style is known for its applied carvings. The style continued under Charles I to the mid-1600s, replacing the Gothic look with lighter, straight-line furniture. This period gave us the gateleg table.

BAROQUE STYLE

Elaborate ornamentation was in style during the seventeenth and eighteenth centuries. The best examples of the era, produced in Holland and Germany, were built for nobility and the church. Flanders was isolated and remained untouched by European conflict of the times and continued to develop new furniture designs with details incorporating inlays of exotic woods and mother-of-pearl.

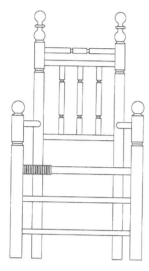

FIGURE 1-3A
The Carver Chair

BREWSTER AND CARVER CHAIRS

Brewster chairs, brought to America in the early 1600s, were highly carved and ornate. An offshoot of these was the Carver chair, differentiated by the lack of ornamentation on solid panels and no detail on turned posts or leg segments beneath the seat. Carvers were generally turned spindles and posts—spindle, slat or ladder-back chairs.

RESTORATION (LATE JACOBEAN)

"Restoration" refers to the restoration of the monarchy under Charles II of England in 1660. This period produced a revitalization of baroque designs in less portable, heavier furniture with lots of frame and panels, influenced by Flemish design and adorned with French decoration. Sir Christopher Wren (1632-1723) led the Restoration movement as the chief architect charged with rebuilding both furniture and buildings after London's Great Fire of 1666.

"William and Mary" was named for William of Orange, of Dutch origin, and Mary II, who jointly ruled England from 1689 to 1702. This style brought an end to Late Jacobean and introduced the prevalent use of veneers and Flemish carving.

The Golden Age of Furniture
(A.D. 1700–1799)

The Golden Age of Furniture is a classification that overlays the Golden Ages of Woods. This term refers to late baroque, rococo and neoclassical styles. The Colonial classification covers almost everything built in the early beginnings of the American Colonies.

Much of the furniture created by today's production crafters comes from this design era of the 1700s and 1800s, the era of elegance and "traditional" design.

FRENCH NEOCLASSICAL

These designs (aka Louis XIV) were based on the furniture of ancient Greece and Rome. Louis XIV became king in 1643 (at four years old) and took over the reign in 1661. It was this era, from 1661 to 1708, that produced the opulence of the Palace of Versailles and the Louvre. This style remained popular and continued, albeit in smaller scale, to influence the Regency style.

French guilds thrived. Joiners, carvers, gilders, polishers, upholsterers, cabinetmakers, casters, glaziers organized into guilds, which were then abolished during the French Revolution (1789).

REGENTS/REGENCY

France's duke of Orleans was appointed regent, awaiting the accession of Louis XV, who was only five years old when his great-grandfather, Louis XIV, died in 1715 with no (legitimate) male heirs. The duke was not enamored with the formality of Versailles, and moved the operation to town houses in Paris. With this relocation into smaller accommodations came smaller, simpler furniture that retained the now French innovation, the cabriole leg. (But we know it originated in China.)

William Kent (1685-1748), an English architect, artist, landscape gardener and furniture designer, was the first (recorded) architect to treat furniture as an integral part of interior design.

PALLADIAN STYLE

Palladian style (England 1700) included highly decorative chests and cupboards with bonnets and skirts, moldings, cornices and pediments. The style was named for a 1500s Italian architect, Andrea Palladio, who used Roman arches, pediments and cornices in his designs.

QUEEN ANNE STYLE

Queen Anne (reigned 1702-1714, style to 1749) was known as a "Poor Man's Palladian." Queen Anne was still somewhat decorative, but stripped of overembellishment. The cabriole leg was, and is, an efficient structural design suited to the style. The cabriole's shape provides mass and strength at the top for solid joinery, and graceful curvature to the broad feet or bulb at the base to resist wear. The products of the period also included some classic secretary desks.

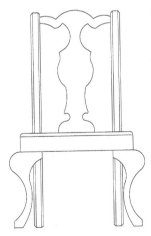

FIGURE 1-3B
Queen Anne

ROCOCO STYLE

Rococo (1730-1765) was named for the French *rocaille* (rockwork) and included shells, *C* and *S* scrolls, ivory inlays and carvings. Home of the claw-foot table, this period is also known as Louis XV. The movement reembellished the Regency style, which was looking too plain and simple.

FIGURE 1-3C
Georgian Style

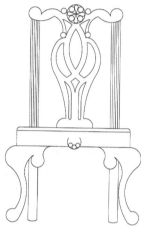

FIGURE 1-3D
Chippendale

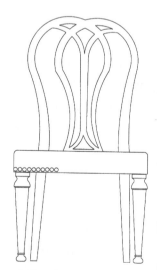

FIGURE 1-3E
Hepplewhite

PROVINCIAL STYLE

Provincial (1750-1850) was a country version of French court furniture. French provincial, named for the influence from France's provinces, simplified furniture lines. The outer reaches of France were adapting and interpreting the more classic styles for utilitarian purposes.

GEORGIAN STYLE

Georgian (1740-1810) was named for the four King Georges who reigned during the period. They were not particularly patrons of the arts, so the styles were fairly simple, with little or no ornamentation. Styles of this period were concurrently named for the designers and craftsmen of the time: George Hepplewhite, Thomas Chippendale and Thomas Sheraton (who moonlighted as a Yorkshire preacher).

CHIPPENDALE STYLE

Thomas Chippendale (1718-1779, prominent from 1749-1774) was perhaps a better publisher than cabinetmaker, but was credited with being a master carver. His furniture styles were design derivatives from Louis XV (1723-1774). In 1754 he published *The Gentlemen & Cabinet-maker's Director*.

You will note that Chippendale was the first to discover (or to state on record) that "Cabinet-makers" were not necessarily synonymous with "Gentlemen," but we already knew that.

ENGLISH NEOCLASSICAL STYLE

English Neoclassical (late 1750s), aka Louis XVI, dropped the Versailles influence and went way back to classical Greece and Rome's geometric forms. Influenced by a visit to Pompeii, Robert Adam found design inspiration in the furniture and furnishings buried under volcanic ash from Mount Vesuvius since A.D. 79.

HEPPLEWHITE STYLE

George Hepplewhite (1750-1790) published *The Cabinet-maker and Upholsterer's Guide* in 1788, featuring his Grecian designs with their tapered legs and spade or brass-capped feet.

FIGURE 1-3F
Sheraton

SHERATON STYLE

Thomas Sheraton, Jr. published the four-volume *The Gentlemen and Cabinet-maker and Upholsterer's Drawing Book* (1791-1794), wherein the French influence showed in his work, such as his sofa (coffee) table.

WINDSOR CHAIRS

The original Windsor chairs were products originating around and about Windsor Castle. It is believed these were made by wheelwrights rather than cabinetmakers; thus the spokelike spindles and splats. The design was popular in the U.S. around 1725-1825 with many variations, including two-tier comb backs. The classic design is still appreciated in today's homes.

FIGURE 1-3G
American Windsor

SHAKER STYLE

FIGURE 1-3H
Shaker

In 1784 the Shakers immigrated to the U.S. and set up their communities of simple living, surrounded by simple things. Shaker furniture was, and is, a study in design simplicity with distinctive character (sounds like a wine critic's description). The purity of design was a statement of the Shakers' puritan ways—a rejection of the opulent lifestyles and ornate material possessions embraced by the not-so-puritan outsiders. Family members, recruited for their skills, applied the talent for the benefit of the community. Benches were made to seat the family at worship. Furniture was simple and Spartan, designed for work, worship or their stark dwellings.

A forerunner of the office work module, a "workstation" was designed for two or more members to work together on community projects, each having common access to the needed materials and tools.

Style remained true as the family expanded (through recruitment, not procreation) to different regions and as different tradesmen were attracted to their flock. There were no appreciable differences in the product, except for the use of materials local to the region. Shaker furniture style had, and has a great influence on what we know as modern, and especially on Danish and Scandinavian design.

FEDERAL STYLE

Federal Style (1790-1825) was named for the new Federal form of government in the U.S. It was America's interpretation of English furniture styles (Hepplewhite and Sheraton) with a great deal of symbolism, which most likely included an American Eagle motif.

The Nineteenth Century (A.D. 1800–1899)

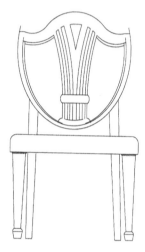

FIGURE 1-31
Federal Style

EMPIRE STYLE

This was a product of Napoleon I's reign (1804-1815). Also known as Napoleonic, the Empire style was a complete departure from the furniture of choice before Napoleon crowned himself emperor. This furniture was heavy on Grecian influence, and uncharacteristically large in scale (since he, himself, was fairly small in stature). The style is also known as neoclassic.

ART NOUVEAU STYLE

Art Nouveau (1800-1900) evolved as a contrarian statement against the Industrial Revolution. It provided an artisans' playground for free-form, free-flowing lines derived from nature as its whiplash curves formed highly sculptured shapes. The movement influenced almost every art form of the time and was soon so overworked that it fell out of favor.

BIEDERMEIER AND RESTORATION STYLES

The Biedermeier style (Germany, 1815-1848) and Restoration style (French, named for the restored monarchy after the Napoleonic Empire collapsed in 1815) resulted in solid, comfortable designs for the upper-middle class. These styles are considered provincial as well, because they stripped away the ornamentation of the neoclassic style and produced basic utilitarian designs.

During this same period, North America was being served by three major players in the country's northeastern region: Duncan Phyfe—New York; William Savery—Philadelphia; and the Townsend-Goddard family—Newport, Rhode Island.

DUNCAN PHYFE

This American furniture designer produced American furniture in the English tradition. From 1800 to 1818, he followed (copied?) trends from Sheraton to Grecian to Federal and Empire. Phyfe was a chaser of fads, a proponent of mechanized production. He kept his shop busy.

WILLIAM SAVERY

William Savery (1740-1787) produced Philadelphia Chippendale, highly ornate furniture of high quality, for the local market.

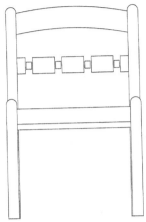

FIGURE 1-3J
Duncan Phyfe

TOWNSEND-GODDARD

The Townsend-Goddard families exported much of their wares to India and, based in Newport, Rhode Island, kept the local mansions furnished as well. These two furniture-building families began in the mid 1700s, and the descendants of both Goddard and Townsend carried on through the late 1800s, producing fine cabinetry, most often embellished with their trademark carved shell motif.

HITCHCOCK STYLE

Maybe it was a statement against the American Fancy (1820-1840) that prompted Lambert Hitchcock to design and build simpler (by Sheraton standards) cane-seat chairs, often painted with floral motifs.

FIGURE 1-3K
Hitchcock

Victorian Age (A.D. 1830–1914)

HISTORIC REVIVAL

The Historic Revival (1830-1880) included Gothic Revival, rococo and Renaissance, used together in the same household to furnish different rooms, or mixed in a potpourri of Victorian furniture (named for England's Queen Victoria, 1840-1901).

BENTWOOD

Michael Thonet, Vienna (1840-1900), produced and mass-produced unique, distinctive furniture made from laminated ply to create a design we all recognize and appreciate, and some may want to duplicate.

FIGURE 1-3L
Bentwood

CRAFTSMAN STYLE

The Arts and Crafts movement (1876-1884) was Gustave Stickley's crusade. He was an inventor, publisher and furniture manufacturer. Among other things he was an avid follower of William Morris, head of the Arts and Crafts movement in England.

Stickley published (edited, printed and distributed) his magazine *The Craftsman* from 1901 to 1916. It included all nature of topics on the simplification of life, including architectural plans in the Craftsman style. Architects Irving Gill and Charles and Henry Greene (Greene and Greene) found California a warm and ripe climate for the bungalow style of design. Our area of interest is Stickley's mission furniture, so named because the "mission," or role, was so obvious in its simple, straightforward style.

FIGURE 1-3M
Craftsman

CONTEMPORARY DESIGN

Near and beyond the turn of this century, some forward-thinking designers, most of them minimalists, reflected on the history we have just reviewed and decided there must be a better way. Artisans of the past applied their trade fulfilling the wants, needs, desires and directions of commerce. Shaker, Arts and Crafts, art nouveau and other contrarian movements kindled a free-thinking atmosphere. Art, form and function melded into a singular design objective, each requiring individual attention, yet combining to achieve a cohesiveness of design.

The bibliography at the end of the book contains only a few of the works that deal with philosophies, design styles and products of past and present artisans.

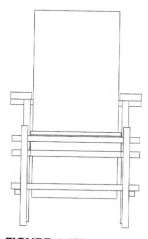

FIGURE 1-3N
Red-Blue Chair

Modern Furniture (A.D. 1900–Present)

DE STIJL (THE STYLE)

Dutch architect and furniture designer Gerrit Rietveld was known for his abstract, rectangular forms painted in primary colors, as in his famous Red-Blue Chair, 1917.

The Bauhaus

The Bauhaus (1919-1933) produced many fine designers and classic modern designs, including:

- W. Gropius (architect/educator)—Tubular steel, simple, non-ornamental style
- M. Breuer, 1925—Tubular Steel Chair
- A. Aalto, 1935—Cantilevered Chair (bent plywood)
- M. Breuer, 1936—Long Chair
- L. Mies van der Rohe, 1925—Barcelona Chair presented at World's Fair, Barcelona, in 1929

FIGURE 1-3O
Swedish

Walter Gropius headed the Bauhaus from 1918 to 1928. Ludwig Mies van der Rohe was its director for the final three years before Hitler closed its doors in 1933 because its work was "decadent" (not to mention that many of the five hundred graduates were Jewish).

ORGANIC DESIGN

Frank Lloyd Wright designed structures and their furnishings expressly for the setting. Some of the furniture was built-in, but built-in or separate, he strived for a sense of belonging. Organic design was a move away from the linear, geometric forms of the modern movement.

ART DECO

The Art Deco style (1920s and 1930s)—art nouveau-influenced but without the curves and carvings—is a more streamlined design, placing more emphasis on decoration than on substance.

INTERNATIONAL INFLUENCES

International styles of the early to mid-twentieth century have characterized what is now considered modern or contemporary furniture. That is, the design of most of today's contemporary furniture is based on the work done in Germany, the Netherlands and Scandinavia from 1900 through the 1950s. The Functionalist Modern (1920), as its name implies, and Danish Modern (mid-1900s) styles were among the newer designs which focused on function. These styles used a variety of new materials, with the widespread use of plastics and other synthetics in the late 1940s, and also employed traditional materials in innovative ways. Other examples of this broad category of style include the work of Charles Eames and his Eames chairs (1946) and Eero Saarinen and his Tulip Suite (1957).

FIGURE 1-3P
Tulip Chair

REALLY, REALLY CONTEMPORARY

Artisans and craftsmen are doing interesting adaptations and producing creative furniture. Some of the free-form, flowing cabinetry has become an expression of freethinking on the part of the designer and the buyer. A decade or so ago, there were excellent examples of contemporary furniture in a West Coast collection presented as California Design. The pieces were well crafted, with flowing lines, and not at all the "off-the-wall" characterization usually assigned to California. Other regions and locales offer similar exhibits and competitions, providing a forum for what we produce today.

WHERE DO WE GO FROM HERE?

History has recorded furniture styles through the ages as they were Created, Restored, Revived, Neo'ed, Nouveau'ed, Provincialized, Functionalized, Minimalized and Organicized. How will future historians characterize today's custom-crafted furniture? Maybe this current phase will be known as Craft Faire Fare, or maybe Personalized.

What's in store for the twenty-first century? Furniture of the future may be laid-up composite filaments, or molded plastic with its unmatched strength, durability, low maintenance and pop-out manufacturing efficiencies.

Wood will continue as *the* premium material for fine furniture, prized for its rich and warm beauty. Due to some serious shortcomings that may include a scarcity of wood brought on by environmental pressures, and a decline in crafting skill, however, perhaps the designer/craftsman will go the way of the shipwrights of the early twentieth century.

Even if these shortcomings don't materialize, the quality of wood might decline, with the milling of only culled trees, or the harvesting of hybrid, genetically altered wood from tree farms.

The former gives us fine spalted wood for bowl turning, but wood that is not always suitable for fine furniture. As for the tree farm crop, fast-growing conditions don't bring about the natural cycle of good and adverse conditions that add character (and characteristics) to the wood, resulting from a natural cycle of lean and bust years that produce the most interesting growth patterns and figuring for our furniture.

History may record the twentieth century as the end of the wooden furniture era, but we custom furniture designers/makers can prove them wrong.

Beginning the Creative Process

With a sense of the past offerings and a wide-open mind, we set out on the journey to conjure up a design concept, maybe based on the origin and originators of the furniture type and style we want to produce today.

"Standard" to you is what you or the recipient like. You may want to stay with the simpler forms developed for a simpler lifestyle, or reach back to the still popular 1700s and 1800s for some grandeur in an attempt to keep up with the Vanderbilts. You have a wealth of resources to draw on, whether you are building a replica of a period piece we now know as Early American, or the anti-Industrial Revolution era of the Arts and Crafts movement including Stickley's Craftsman, the more ornate art nouveau or the products of the Bauhaus.

Develop Cognitive Awareness

To begin the creative process, you need to be cognitively aware of what you want to build. That is, you must come to know what you want in both awareness and judgment. In a nutshell, you have to think about your project. Decide what you want and weigh it against what you need. Don't throw anything out just yet; just think.

The creative process takes form in many different ways, sparked by a variety of stimuli. To a chosen few, creativity (or talent) seems to be a natural gift. The rest of us have to work harder at it.

Mozart, as in Wolfgang Amadeus, it is said, envisioned his compositions while in peaceful thought and composed his work, complete with full orchestration, in his head. Only when it was complete would he pen the notes, bars and stanzas on paper.

Few of us are that gifted. Most of us must work out the design on paper and in the workshop, as well as in our head, in whatever combination comes most naturally. Ingenuity, inventiveness and resourcefulness are part of our skills. How, when and where we apply these attributes differ with each person.

What works for you? Do you get your inspirations while on the links, while fishing, jogging (you have to be thinking about something), reclining in your favorite chair or in the shop while in the throes of building? Wherever the creative juices flow, an innovative thought may pop up, so keep your pad and pencil ready. You never know when inspiration will strike.

In-shop development is especially practical when working with wood, since its physical characteristics seem to have a mind of their own. Bending a thin, arced batten will form a pleasing curve more naturally than drawing one on paper or lofting the shape on the selected stock.

Even if you can't draw, you can design as you build. Test your theories in the shop using scrap wood. It is readily available, handy and less expensive to experiment with a particular joint, form, fit or process.

A few well-placed rungs (or square sticks) can be arranged and rearranged to satisfy your sense of design. Place them in parallel or splayed, with equidistant or diminishing spacing, to find the most pleasing arrangement.

Just as you wouldn't go into surgery without a second opinion, it's good to bounce your idea off someone—get a second viewpoint. You may agree, or ignore, or compromise, but the design process gets yet another set of eyes, from a different frame of reference, from a different base of knowledge and experience.

Using the Creative Process in Design

We are familiar with the standard components of furniture and the traditional construction methods tested and proven in the past. These accepted norms can always be made more interesting, or you can begin anew, asking yourself what other form could serve as legs, seats, backrests? Why are cabinet openings typically along the face? Is there a design possibility for the sides? Don't close off radical concepts—you don't know where they might lead.

Frank Lloyd Wright's credo was that architecture should be in harmony with its surroundings. His architecture showed this, as did his Organic-style furniture. Harmony is an objective equally important in furniture design. Wright designed furniture for one space, one setting. Predating Wright by 150 years, William Kent, an architect, artist, landscape gardener and furniture designer, is credited as the first architect to treat furniture as an integral part of interior design. Today, it still remains a lofty, but achievable goal.

What inspired Saarinen to design the Tulip Suite, when his past work with furniture was more along the lines of upholstered forms on tubular or laminated frames? These earlier works were and are pleasing to the eye and body. The Tulip was a complete departure, equally pleasing to the eye, if not the body.

Charles Eames, along with his brother, had a thing for molded plywood, and carried it off in a number of classic Eames designs we recognize today.

Other well-known designs were products of expositions and calls for designs, such as the Barcelona Chair by Ludwig Mies van der Rohe, and the Red-Blue Chair by Gerrit Thomas Rietveld (before he joined the De Stijl group). New York's Museum of Modern Art sponsored furniture-above-design competitions that netted some famous work. Ideas, and ultimately trends, from schools such as Bauhaus, De Stijl and the architectural movements of Le Corbusier, or Frank Lloyd Wright's Taliesin and Taliesin West, provided forums to focus creative energies into lasting design forms (or maybe it was the talent they attracted).

Mixing or Matching Styles

A piece of furniture can complement its environs by emulating the surrounding style, or be a complete departure used as an accent piece. Such contrast can verge on retro- or antidesign.

Accents can be contrasting wood or solid color, disproportional overall size or the sizes of its components, dissimilar styles or an unconventional treatment of a familiar style. Even a subtle design difference can create an effective impact. Going overboard with contrast, however, can become comical, which is fine if this is how you want the piece perceived.

Keep It Simple

We've all heard the story of the keynote speaker who, just before he began addressing the assembled group, was handed a note by his wife with the word *KISS* written on it. It wasn't a term of endearment or encouragement, but a reminder to *Keep It Simple, Stupid.*

Sometimes, innovative furniture of truly simple lines is far more difficult to design and to build. Added detail has its place, and may be a required characteristic of the furniture style you like.

"Simple" may mean designing a piece with a minimum number of parts hewn into natural flowing forms, devoid of superfluous braces, brackets and unnecessary appendages. Joinery, master-crafted to form a strong joint well concealed within the thin lines of the piece, is part of the art of custom furniture design and building.

This isn't to say that design needs to be simple to be good. Any embellishment or complexity that reflects your style, or a style from an earlier period, is good design if it hangs together. Complexity is bad when it is used to cover flaws, weaknesses or faulty joinery. To use added parts and pieces to cover or support a form that might be better left unadorned is one of the designer's Seven Deadly Sins. (There must be seven, but I haven't counted.)

Shaker is a good example of a minimum of shapes assembled in a pleasing, unpretentious form that is both viewed and used with a deep appreciation of its simplicity. The Windsor chair is another product of design simplicity, although somewhat more complex with its bow back, slightly splayed spindles and the decorative turnings on rungs and stretchers. Scandinavian furniture (Danish Modern) has the same simple lines, but is slightly sculptured to create more comfort and more flowing transitions, and therefore a bit more bond area to the joint.

Craftsman is a study in simple, linear construction. Heavier in mass and more geometric in form than the turned forms of Shaker or the turned and sculpted forms of Scandinavian, this style represents a basic design we also call Arts and Crafts, or Stickley. The embellishment you might see in Arts and Crafts furniture, an offshoot of the architectural Craftsman style, would be the bullnosing of the members, or maybe, in the case of Greene and Greene, nice exposed lap joints or through tenons, pegged and wedged in place.

Cottage has given us the Adirondack chair. This is one design from that region that is widely accepted because it is comfortable to sit in on the porch on a late summer's eve sipping your favorite beverage. Not too much sipping though, since these chairs can present a challenge when you stand up again, even after a glass of lemonade.

Applying an Idea

Chapter three contains thoughts on developing a design, taking shell ratios and blocking in different parts of the whole. Then we talk about a ten-step process, building on a design in conceptual terms initially, and gradually developing more and more detail as the shape, form and style evolve. But sometimes a detail can drive the whole.

By way of example, the sample design sheet on page 37 is intended to illustrate how you might expand on a concept.

We are accustomed to a desktop fastened directly to a leg frame, and the areas between filled with a drawer case. What are the design possibilities when all parts "float"? The top is raised, and the drawer case is suspended between leg braces.

Experiment with a theme
or concept without regard
for how it might be
executed. The realities will
be worked out later.

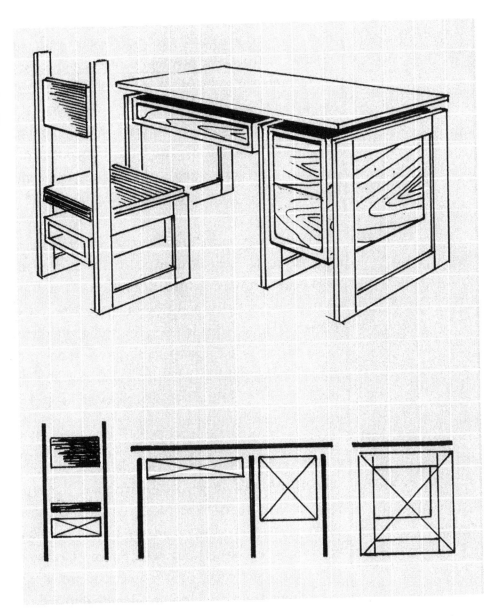

Long before drawing the details, think in terms of shapes, their relation-ships to adjacent and opposing shapes and of the whole. Worry later on how this can be made to work. Conceptually the leg braces could be joined with half-lapped corners, or mortise and tenons, or dowels or biscuits, which will provide a rigid square or rectangle on the diagonal. Drawer cases serve as spreaders and aprons, holding the leg braces at the vertical.

Options for standoffs include (1) fastening the frames to the cases for a frame-and-panel look, (2) insetting a riser well back from the face planes or (3) using standoffs of large dowels (the only round things in the design) or short rectangular blocks, maybe the width of the leg frame material, as separators between assemblies.

The chair concept follows the design theme. The chair seat and back float between a similar leg brace design, with the back length higher to capture the backrest, playing on the nested look. An alternative would be to float the seat and chair back atop and in back of the leg frame, more like the desktop.

All materials could be similar, or you might accentuate the design by making the drawer cases in a contrasting wood or of prefinished composition material. If so, a solid top could give way to a contrasting (or similar) inset to play on the open space of the leg frame and maybe a different color drawer case.

Whichever comes first, the concept or the need, the custom furniture designer should begin to develop that preliminary idea much like an architect begins, by defining the needs, preferences and lifestyle of the client, the setting, the materials and type of construction. Collect these needs. Rank them by their relative importance, and apply them to your concept.

A review of the history of furniture soon reveals that this disciplined approach to furniture design and building wasn't always followed, or maybe the designers' priorities were a bit skewed. Past furniture styles went beyond creature comfort and pleasing design just to satisfy the egos of the aristocracy, the church or the kings (Gothic, baroque, Louis, Empire). Some styles pared down and simplified these elaborate designs, striving more toward a utilitarian form (Queen Anne, Georgian, Biedermeier). Other designs or styles evolved from different trades, tools or skill levels (provincial, Windsor, Shaker, country). Contrarian furniture resulted from various "anti" or "retro" movements (art nouveau, Shaker, Craftsman). Modern, as we perceive it, is a statement against opulence and complexity, and a movement toward minimalizing furniture design into its most basic form for the function.

Examples from the past can be replicated, copied, suggested or rejected. A custom design, the product of the custom furniture designer, by the nature of its function, is not new. It is just a different twist in a developing history of furniture styles. The concept can be uniquely yours, but the design is added to the time line of furniture development.

This chapter offered some places to begin—from replicas of classic furniture design to concepts known only to you. The following chapter brings real-world reality into what is required to bring off your design, and some compromises that may satisfy both your design instincts and your craftsman skills.

CHAPTER TWO

Defining Scope

Just a few thoughts on scoping your project. If you are both designer and craftsman, can what you design be produced with your skills and the tools at hand?

- TIME—Is this a weekend or extended project? Furniture projects are time consuming.
- TALENT, SKILLS, INTERESTS, AMBITIONS—Design within these parameters or constraints.
- TOOLS AND EQUIPMENT—Base your design on what you have to work with.
- SPACE—Is your workshop a dedicated area or do you share it (basement, garage, etc.)? Can you commit the area to a long-term project?
- BUY OUT—Buy what you need if you have no time, interest or equipment. Wide-belt sanding, beveled glass, cabriole legs, whatever—some things you just cannot or do not want to do. Hire someone else to do it or buy the pieces outright.

As a designer/craftsman, design furniture that will be producible within your span of interest, equipment capacity and work space. Or maybe stretch the envelope to include a new technique, but be aware of what will be needed to accomplish this. You need not personally build every component. It's okay, for whatever reason, to buy parts and pieces from commercial sources or collaborate with other woodworkers. But use the opportunity to challenge your abilities; try something new to expand your enjoyment and level of accomplishment.

When assessing your abilities, there are no prerequisites for designing custom furniture, except for your desire to just do it. Your interest in and knowledge of woodworking qualify you to design a piece of furniture, whether your experience is building toys or building houses. We all know what we like to build, and will design it to meet various objectives along the way toward the final product, including the interim steps and processes we make part of our design.

Checklist of Personal Resources

Defining the scope of what we design deals with many topics and many disciplines we should address before taking on a project that may be beyond our skill level.

Time

Busy life. Busy family. Are you long on ambition but short on time? Design a project that will fit into your schedule. Instant gratification and furniture building are not synonymous, and probably shouldn't appear in the same sentence.

Completing each phase in sequence may take a bit longer, but resources and space won't be committed for extended periods. A comprehensive design package that has been checked and double-checked can be completed before you begin the shop phase.

By working out all of the details at the outset, you can design a furniture kit. Complete design plans, bills of material and cutting lists will allow the cutting and kitting of pieces for later assembly in the shortest time span. This approach is the best for the most efficient use of your shared time and shared space.

Talent, Skills, Interests, Ambitions

Assess your levels of interest, ambition and skill, and design within those parameters. You most likely will design what you enjoy building.

Talent denotes a gift, a bent, a natural or nurtured ability or skill. For the designer/craftsman, talent encompasses all of these attributes directed toward the innovation and creation of a design and the building of the piece, using the knowledge of what it takes to make it happen.

If asked to quantify the percentage of interest, ambition and skill necessary, the answer would be in whatever combined levels you bring to the project. Obviously there is interest or you wouldn't be reading this book, or have a desire to spend your time designing and building custom furniture.

Ambition, an extension of interest, will dictate the level of involvement in the scope of the project: its size, complexity, what enjoyment and challenge you expect.

Skills you bring to the table (pardon the pun) can always be further refined, polished or expanded to meet the challenge of creating a craftsman-like piece. Getting into and working out a process is the best way to learn and to grow.

What may be lacking in one area is overcome by another, so the resulting design and product will be your interpretation of design and construction. Such limitations, if indeed they are limitations at all, add another interpretation to what you build. A variation of style, a simplified detail or a departure from traditional lines or techniques gives a new interpretation to a style. Whole movements began and thrived under similar conditions.

Tools and Equipment

A new project is a good excuse to buy those tools you've been eyeing, but you probably can't justify an entire workshop. Design the piece so it can be produced with the cache of equipment and tools in your shop.

Look at what tools you will need to produce the design and the accompanying details. You are well aware of what you are equipped to build, and will design accordingly. To some extent, how you normally treat edges, surfaces, turnings and everything else with the tools at hand becomes a part of your style, your signature.

Space

Can you commit the work area to a long-range project? Will its size be manageable and emerge from its place of origin when completed? A workshop is often too small or poorly laid out, or any other perceived shortcoming, but many craftsmen are working in much smaller spaces, under more adverse conditions than our own. We can complain, but we should still *do*.

Buy Out

You might want to buy out the cabriole legs, the beveled glass or upholstery you include in your design. Talk with the providers of these items early on, and heed their suggestions, requirements and tips in what you design.

Typical Production Schedule

FIGURE 2-1

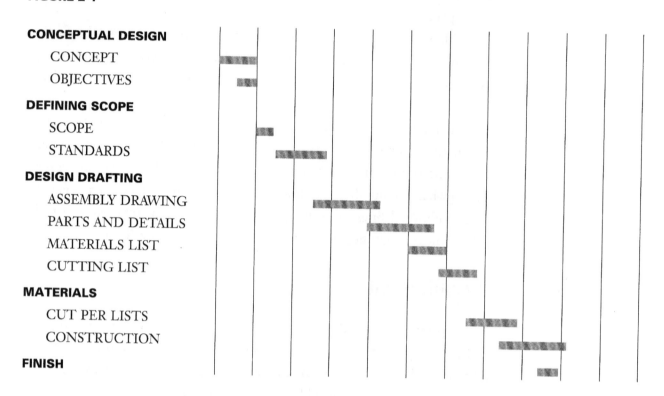

CONCEPTUAL DESIGN
    CONCEPT
    OBJECTIVES

DEFINING SCOPE
    SCOPE
    STANDARDS

DESIGN DRAFTING
    ASSEMBLY DRAWING
    PARTS AND DETAILS
    MATERIALS LIST
    CUTTING LIST

MATERIALS
    CUT PER LISTS
    CONSTRUCTION

FINISH

The bar chart above shows the major steps and their relative durations—in other words, demands on your time. Just how long this stretches out will be based on the size and complexity of the project and the time you have to devote.

The time span for a project may be three days, three weeks or three months, depending on its complexity and the hunks of time you can devote.

What Piece? In Which Style?

Designing and building a generic desk, table, cabinet or chair may well be within your capabilities, but scope changes with increasing ambition and complexity. Even the most seasoned craftsman might pale at the thought of reproducing an ornate Louis XIV chair.

Custom-built furniture can be a one-of-a-kind design, or an adaptation of past styles tweaked to your liking. If drawing from the past, look for the elements that characterize a certain design style, and decide whether they should be duplicated or simply be indicated in a stylized approach to achieving the look.

Reducing the elements of style to simpler forms has gone on throughout the history of furniture, and many times these interpretations marked the beginning of a new look, a new movement and a departure from earlier times. For example:

■ As the design pendulum swung from ornateness to simplicity, lavish furniture for courts and cabinets was pared down (maybe they were better forgotten) in provincial and country styles that produced furniture rural artisans were able to build with local skills and native woods. In a less drastic example, but retaining a little less of the formality, the Palladian style was made more producible and more widely available than the Queen Anne style.

■ The Industrial Revolution brought about change through mechanization, which was immediately countered by the Arts and Crafts movement.

Mechanized furniture manufacturers (many of which are still producing today) went for productivity and efficiency, a balance of old-world craftsmanship and mechanization, to produce the popular furniture of the last two centuries. Today these manufacturers are working in somewhat simpler lines, stylized to suggest a heritage from the real McCoy.

Much of today's commercially produced furniture is a continuation of combining mechanization with the handcrafted works of many talented artisans. No one person can or needs to conquer that many disciplines. As somebody once said, "We are all smart, but about different things."

Determine Where to Begin

Not only do we learn from the past—the origin—but we can also appreciate how others interpreted past designs in a contemporary or customized environment.

A good source for assessing the complexities of the piece you want to build are books published to promote today's furniture manufacturers. Although somewhat self-serving, these tomes are a helpful resource to determine the scope of a given project and to provide a good basis for your custom design. These companies have remained in the business by producing and reproducing the more popular styles, and they have certainly done their homework on the origin of these pieces. We can appreciate these accomplishments and take note of the interpretation of shapes and joinery they employ.

Early furniture designers/manufacturers Chippendale, the Adam Brothers and Sheraton, published catalogs of their wares beginning in the 1700s, which were instrumental in perpetuating their respective styles. Some of these first books on furniture are available in reprinted editions; others are in the dank, dark corner of the rare book lockup, maybe in your local library.

More recent collections of work we can use include Sam Burchell's *History of Furniture*. This work was published as a promotional piece commemorating Baker Furniture Company's 100th anniversary.

More specific, and containing more detailed plans, is a book produced by Thomas Moser, *Measured Shop Drawings for American Furniture*. This collection presents clean, nice Early American furniture, presented in clear, easy-to-follow plans for construction or insight into the details of your own design.

Ethan Allen, a purveyor of Early American-style furniture, interprets traditional furniture from the Colonial period as it was interpreted from the Old World. Contemporary furniture is the niche market of Knoll International, a company that duplicates some of the more modern twentieth-century designers.

Custom Interpretation

Look at published plans as a resource for ideas in your search for pleasing furniture design. The easy way out would be to produce your next project from such plans, which is totally acceptable if the design meets your needs. It is more likely, however, that you will adapt and style the design to fit your objectives.

List at the outset what will meet your objectives, and consider that which is doable and functional and will fit into the scheme of things.

The bibliography at the end of this book includes a sampling of books available on many styles, from many eras, that could be of help and interest. These may have been written as a guide to antique furniture collecting, or as a tribute to the artist or artisans who not only carved out a nice piece of furniture, but a place in history as well.

Portrayed in this book are the more popular styles which have originated or have been revitalized over the past couple of centuries. Other work is mentioned as examples of innovative design, but the kudos to the designers and the attributes of their designs are left for others to explore. The omissions here are not out of a lack of respect for the designers and their products, but the practical reality of the types of furniture you are most likely to design and build for your home.

What Has Survived and Endured?

Whether your mansion is furnished in authentic period style or you share your dwelling with a mix of Early Cost Plus, a potpourri from the unfinished-furniture store or just hand-me-downs, a room's personality has blossomed (even though it may not be your favorite flower). A theme has developed which can be complemented, contrasted or changed by your efforts.

Why Some Designs Still Work

Maybe "standards" have survived because they are functional, well proportioned and pleasing to both eye and body. A standard style might fit our lifestyle or our personality, or suggest visions of some past grandeur. Or what pleases us might be the richness and warmth of the wood and an appreciation of the skills and talent that have gone into the piece. The style you consider "standard" may be the look of furniture you were brought up with. Certain styles or types of furniture provide a link to the past, and you just feel comfortable (or maybe uncomfortable) surrounded by it.

Looking beyond all these warm and fuzzy feelings, we like furniture that meets our personal objectives. We like to be around nice things, take pride in our surroundings and maybe showcase our environs for guests. No matter whether our reasons are based on the design or what the style represents, we continue to like and therefore perpetuate our own "standard" style in our surroundings.

The chronology of chairs shown in chapter one depicts styles by era. A chair exhibits a fairly complete picture of a particular furniture style and the required disciplines of the period. Treatments of legs, seats, backs, rungs, spindles and splats typify the style, era and region that produced the chair. The Carver (it would be a Brewster if the legs were ornamentally turned below the seat level) may be a good plan for a child's chair. The Queen Anne (or a Louis, Sheraton or Hepplewhite) may be a perfect addition among more traditional furnishings. The Windsor is classic, as is the Shaker ladder-back chair.

As a custom furniture designer/craftsman, you have the advantage to do what you please. However, classic styles shouldn't just be pulled from a bag of historical parts. Consideration for the preceding work is suggested. You can adapt and adopt the design to your style, to your own signature or hallmark, but unless you are launching a whole new design movement, the design will be more cohesive if it conforms, even remotely, to a classifiable style.

What we think of as classics are the more popular styles that survived generations of critics and collectors. Some styles have endured, are being revived or are being reinvented by today's woodworker. Styles listed as "standards" may not be your cup of tea. If so, you have the incentive to research and build your personal heirloom. In this discussion of scope, we'll skip over the Gothic, baroque and rococo. If you want to be the first king or queen on your block, however, go ahead and build, carve and gild your very own coronation chair.

Heirlooms can be replicated or modernized retaining the ornateness or simplicity that typifies the style. Furniture design has flip-flopped between ultrafunctional and ultradecorative, and each still appeals to someone's tastes in home furniture.

Where the Market Is

Commercial furniture producers concentrate on the traditional designs in the styles of past centuries, while custom furniture designers, the artisans of today, may strive for something unique and different. The designer/craftsmen's design philosophy may solidify into a signature style over time, or the objective with each new project may be to be different just to be different. Sometimes this antidesign approach is successful, and other times—well?

In some design circles, inspiration is found in past furniture. In the more artistic camps, inspiration is sought in everything *except* furniture, which results in a piece of art or sculpture first, doubling as furniture.

Think about your design philosophy (and you have developed one, whether or not it is formally acknowledged). Just putting together pieces doesn't create a design. It can just as easily create a disaster. Design what is needed, enjoyed and appreciated, whether for yourself or the commercial market.

Continuing Evolution

In 1840, in *Democracy in America*, Alexis de Tocqueville wrote, "[Democratic nations] will habitually prefer the useful to the beautiful, and they will require that the beautiful should be useful."

The evolution in furniture styles deals with more than the physical appearance and advances in the craft. Furniture was a symbol of the stature and wealth of privileged kings, clergy and aristocracy. As the Industrial Revolution begat furniture for the common folk, the privileged maintained the differential between the haves and the have-nots in the form of furniture styles from the utilitarian to the grotesquely ornate.

Throughout more recent history, countermovements by individuals, religious groups and whole nations used their furniture design to protest a particular ruler, past aggression or the world and life they left behind. Whatever the movement is titled—anti, retro, counter—there have been political undertones in the evolving furniture styles.

Functionality and usefulness have been a part of furniture design for the past one hundred years, and the marketplace will accept the beautiful, especially if it is functional and useful.

We reviewed the history and the distinguishing characteristics of certain style standards in order to associate various projects with the types of tools and skills you may require. You may throw all that out in favor of a style that fits your personal objectives, not unlike what has gone on down through the history of furniture.

List the objectives you are trying to satisfy. What is the ultimate function, and what does it take to get there? Include those processes and operations you want to undertake in building the piece. For example, your objectives might be to:

1. Begin a new workshop project.
2. Design and build a _____.
3. Make it the focal point of the room.
4. Depart from the predominant style.
5. Use contrasting woods.
6. Incorporate laminated forms.
7. Superscale the joinery.

Your personal list of objectives can be as conservative or outlandish as you choose. It may contain tools, processes or materials you wish to use. The list is nothing more than the thought process we all go through when launching a new project. By committing these objectives to paper, we focus our attention and efforts toward the overall objective.

Today's Conventions

Commercial offerings, as mentioned earlier, are an impression or, in some cases, a replica of furniture that has a market. They provide a good product of matched pieces to fill your dining room, or an upholstered wing chair, a chaise or a bedroom suite for your home, and a thousand other homes like it.

You have no particular agenda to follow, other than to design a piece of custom furniture that suits your needs and tastes. It is said that a surgeon can bury his mistakes but an architect has to live with his. You are like the architect of furniture.

Some custom furniture design is unconventional, one-of-a-kind (and sometimes off-the-wall), attempting to make a statement for statement's sake. But custom furniture can be made more familiar, more compatible with the furniture we live with.

Evaluate the Complexity of the Project

You may want to review and redesign popular styles in terms of their identifying characteristic and the type of tools and equipment required to undertake each style. Characteristics of components and operations should be considered when designing custom furniture. An authentic detail, or maybe an embellishment, can make or break your project. Whichever of these you employ to meet your design objectives must be within your limits of time, tools, talent and inclination.

The ability to flute, or vein, or run a quarter-round bead along an otherwise Spartan edge, adds an artisan's touch. But be careful not to overwork details. A Craftsman-styled piece should not be adorned with decoration or too much detailing. Some furniture demands simple, straight geometric shapes and nothing more.

Design Features: Production Requirements

Staying with the more popular styles presented in chapter one, here are a few of their characteristics and some of the required tools and techniques.

**SKETCHPAD 2A
EARLY CHINESE**

Some fine designs and craftsmanship evolved over thousands of years in the Orient. The S-curved leg (forerunner to the cabriole) supported heavy chests, while other furnishings were slight, yielding a good example of intermixing weights and shapes.

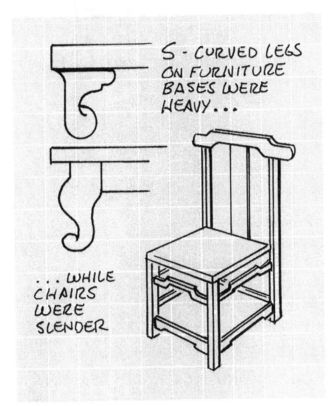

S - CURVED LEGS ON FURNITURE BASES WERE HEAVY...

...WHILE CHAIRS WERE SLENDER

ORIENTAL—This style was evident as early as 200 B.C., but what we like originated around the 1400s to 1500s. Oriental design brought to the world S-curved legs and highly lacquered finishes. Low tables with S-curved legs (later named cabriole) are good projects for the lacquered (or japanned) look. We're mixing cultures, but the results are pleasing. This furniture was originally joined in puzzlelike joints, assembled durably without pegs or glue. You can buy cabriole legs, or cut and form them using a band saw, drawknife and shaves.

BREWSTER, c.1600—This style featured lathe-turned legs, stretchers, backs and beaded spindles below seat level.

CARVER, c.1650—This design included turned spindles and usually plain cylinders below the seat. Both styles lend themselves to playroom furniture. Having lots of beaded turnings, maybe painted in bright primary colors, they are a natural for a child's use. The open-spindle seat frame is perfect for a woven rush seat. Early ladder-back or rung-back chairs require lathe

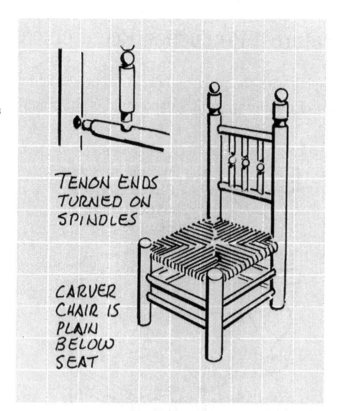

TENON ENDS
TURNED ON
SPINDLES

CARVER
CHAIR IS
PLAIN
BELOW
SEAT

work for cylindrical legs (Carver) and lots of beaded spindles and stretchers (Brewster). In addition, there is a lot of lathe work on spindles and tenons, and drilling of sockets.

AMERICAN WINDSOR, 1725-1825—Spindles form the back, armrests and legs, which all peg into sockets on the seat. This chair is a refinement of the turned stool. Always appreciated for the flowing lines, thin splayed spindles and a certain homeyness, this chair seems to say, "Come and sit, take some comfort, bring a book." The Windsor chair was actually a middle-class style designed and crafted by wheelwrights and was popular in country homes. A thin arced back of bent ash curves gracefully into seat braces, or is raised on shorter spindles as arms. The seat is solid, hogged out in a saddlelike shape to conform to the bum. If you are up to the wet-wood bending procedure, there are books on the subject. Otherwise, resaw strips on a band or circular saw to laminate the bowed form. Turn the spindles, stretchers and rails on a wood lathe.

QUEEN ANNE, c.1750—Defining features include cabriole legs between straight or curved aprons, and a seat back comprised of a curved frame and pierced or plain splat. Furniture in this style is good as accent pieces in the right setting. Simpler than its forerunner, Palladian, Queen Anne is less ornate but comprises complex parts that come together to form an instant

SKETCHPAD 2C AMERICAN WINDSOR CHAIRS

Years of product development, starting with the wheelwrights around Windsor Castle, produced a lasting design of ageless beauty. American Windsor was a continuation of this style, which continues today.

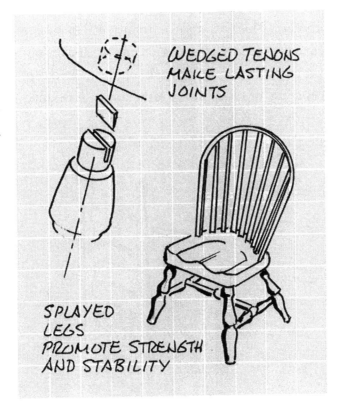

WEDGED TENONS MAKE LASTING JOINTS

SPLAYED LEGS PROMOTE STRENGTH AND STABILITY

SKETCHPAD 2D QUEEN ANNE CHAIRS

Cabriole legs are the hallmark of this style. The leg has limited application, but is shown for its functional shape for chairs, chests and tables. The thickness at the top can be solidly attached to aprons (between or from behind), the S-sweep lightens the look of the piece and the wider foot rests solidly at the floor.

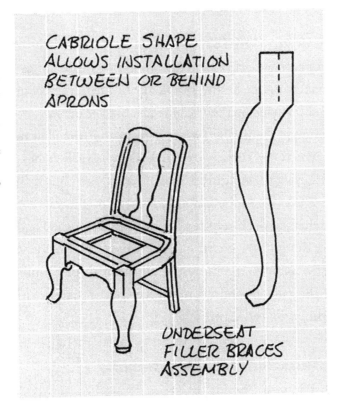

CABRIOLE SHAPE ALLOWS INSTALLATION BETWEEN OR BEHIND APRONS

UNDERSEAT FILLER BRACES ASSEMBLY

heirloom. This furniture is traditional in design, with many curves and turned spreaders. This is a chance to make (or buy) those cabriole legs, long, gracefully sweeping back supports and a bent splat back. You will need a band saw or saber saw, a lathe and a drawknife.

SKETCHPAD 2E
SHAKER STYLE

Many good design ideas come from the Shaker movement. Simplicity in construction, use of common materials and a distinctive yet simple charm have inspired many fine designers.

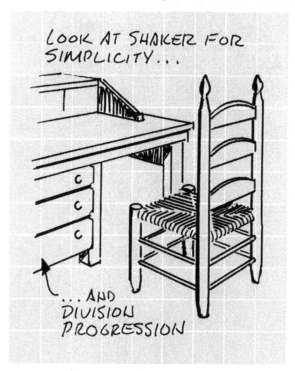

LOOK AT SHAKER FOR SIMPLICITY...

...AND DIVISION PROGRESSION

SHAKER, 1784-1850—This style is uniquely simple, extremely well-proportioned, rural and ultrafunctional. Attributes to be emulated from the Shakers might be the simplicity of form, the economy of style or the level of craftsmanship they attained. A Shaker dresser, with its linear construction of simple shells, filled with nicely proportioned drawers, typifies other things at which the Shakers excelled, like chairs, benches and hat boxes. Whether designing to duplicate a Shaker piece, or simply using their highly developed style for your contemporary chest of drawers or a small bench for the kitchen, look closely at what they accomplished and build upon it to achieve the design you envision. The Shaker furniture style influenced what we know as modern, and especially Danish or Scandinavian, and a good deal of the custom-crafted furniture from today's workshops. You will need a lathe, drill and scroll saw.

COMMERCIALIZING FRENCH DESIGNS

Chippendale, Hepplewhite, Sheraton—most of what this trilogy did was to adapt classic and popular styles and produce them for mass marketing.

Their publishing efforts helped to establish them as furniture purveyors. Even though they were not on the cutting edge of new design, they built on the Louis look, reminiscent of formal dining occasions.

SKETCHPAD 2F CHIPPENDALE STYLE

Chippendale was a carver, which is evident in the style attributed to his philosophy. Simple was not in his vocabulary. This style is included here as a warning of what you might encounter when asked to build something in this style.

CHIPPENDALE STYLE, 1749-1774—He liked open fretwork on chair splats, maybe with Queen Anne legs, or a ladder-back with open rails, or his more Gothic offering of geometric framework and open splats, but carved in more Gothic forms. In addition to publishing catalogs of furniture and building chairs, Chippendale produced the English secretary desk, chests, table and beds that were made in simplified style in the U.S., resulting in the block-front secretary. Bring out all the tools: *Everything is needed.*

HEPPLEWHITE, 1750-1790—His signature was his shield-back chair, an assembly of curved pieces that didn't curve in any human direction. Legs were usually square, occasionally with a slight taper. Accompanying pieces, such as a sideboard or desk, had similar leg treatment. You will need a band saw to cut the shield design, as well as a table or radial arm saw and a jointer/planer.

SHERATON, 1790-1810—These designs are ornately carved, with an open fretwork splat lyre back. Turned legs were detailed with veining in the vertical planes. You will need a lathe, maybe with a routing attachment for ribbing the legs, a saber saw or jigsaw for cutting the fretwork, a bench saw and a drill.

SKETCHPAD 2G HEPPLEWHITE STYLE

Influenced by the Italian design, Hepplewhite kept it fairly simple with clean lines, but couldn't resist adding a bit of decoration to his pieces, which is something you might consider as an inlay, a coving or simple veining.

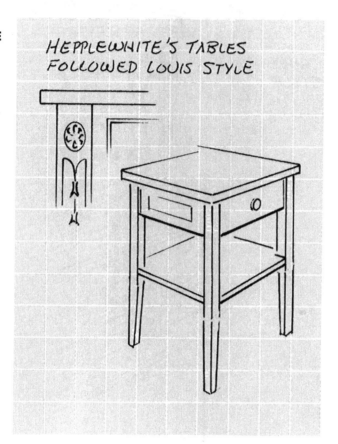

TRANSITIONAL STYLE CHARACTERISTICS

BIEDERMEIER, 1815-1848—This style was named for Papa Gottlieb Biedermeier, a Viennese comic character depicting the commoner vs. Austria's middle class. Furniture styles include Georgian, English frame and panel, or German Biedermeier. Leg posts and corners can be solid or angled, either mitered or butt-joined to achieve the massive look without placing undue strain on your back or your wallet. Where the corner brace is exposed, such as at the extended feet, design a block to fill in the square. Highly figured veneers are a possibility here. Major shop tools are required to build these.

AMERICAN FANCY, 1820-1840—This furniture featured elaborate turnings and scroll work, and was often decoratively painted. Just before the Victorian era was the period known as American Fancy. Lambert Hitchcock emerged from a small shop to become a full-blown manufacturer of slat-back/ladder-back chairs. Seats were usually faced with a sculpted edge, falling away in a caning pattern at the chair back. If you want to do some tole painting, this style may be a good candidate, for many of the original chairs were decorated with a painted motif. A combination of English and American Windsor, the legs are pegged in a heavy seat frame. Most of your shop tools will be required, especially a lathe and a scroll saw.

**SKETCHPAD 2H
SHERATON STYLE**
Fluting and ribbing on round or square legs, and spade feet, were distinctive features of this style. Both characteristics may have a home in a future project.

SHERATON LIKED RIBBING AND SPADE FEET

MODERN STYLE CHARACTERISTICS

The influence of major design schools in the early twentieth century remains evident in the contemporary furniture we design today. Chrome and foam might be replaced by natural wood, solid or laminated for flowing curves, molded ply or padded platform, but the simple, contemporary look of Bauhaus and De Stijl continue to fit in with our furnishings and lifestyles and satisfy our sense of design.

ARTS AND CRAFTS/CRAFTSMAN/MISSION, 1876-1916—The early definition of Mission style referred to simple lines and ultrafunctional furniture that clearly depicted its mission, its role in the scheme of things. Straight,

Look to the Craftsman style for simplicity in design and handcrafted procedures. Fine furniture can be built with a minimum of shop tools.

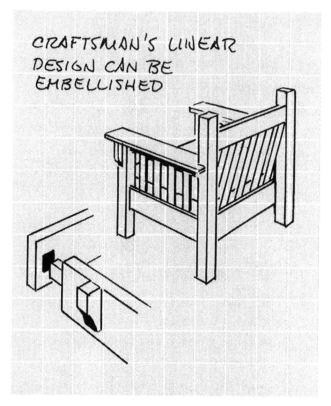

CRAFTSMAN'S LINEAR DESIGN CAN BE EMBELLISHED

geometric shapes can be cut with a table saw and assembled using a mortising bit or a sharp chisel. A jointer/planer is optional if you use a good hollow-ground blade to cut the parts.

DE STIJL GROUP, 1917—Gerrit Rietveld's Red-Blue Chair is a familiar geometric design, very linear. Straight, linear frames used as stretchers for canvas or a strung seat and seat back can be produced with few tools other than the basic shop complement. A table saw and drill are required to produce similar designs.

THE BAUHAUS, c.1920—This school included many styles, but perhaps was best exemplified by the Barcelona Chair, designed by Ludwig Mies van der Rohe. It was Germany's offering in their country's pavilion at the Barcelona World's Fair in 1929. This chair characterizes the "form following function" precept.

CHARLES EAMES, c.1940—Eames began working with laminated plies, collaborating with the government to produce a lightweight litter for rescue work. The Eames brothers later applied the technique to furniture in both mass-produced molded "pop-outs" of commercial appointments to limited-production easy chairs and ottomans, all in a characteristic style.

**SKETCHPAD 2J
EAMES-TYPE
MOLDED FORMS**
Much of the task is in the preparation of molds and forms to shape laminated plies into comfortable contours. Have lots of glue or epoxy, clamps and Carnauba wax as a releasing agent over the male or male/female molds.

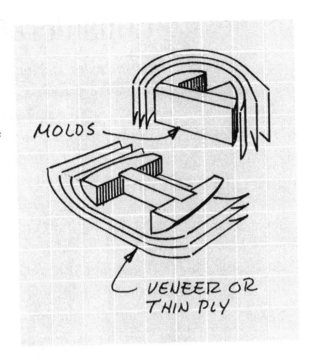

If laminating forms is in your future, plan to spend as much time fashioning the molds to form the shapes as you will spend in finishing the piece. Devise fixtures to apply pressure, and have plenty of Carnauba wax as a releasing agent and epoxy to imbed and set the plies into the desired shape. Consider using veneer sheets, or maybe veneer strips, for the core where the molded form has abrupt changes, but thin ply will suffice if the molded form is more subtle.

CHARACTERISTICS OF TODAY'S MODERN STYLES

Some of us have been around so long that we are seeing the furniture of the 1950s being revived. Some of the lean-years styles of the post-Depression era are even being collected as "antiques." These styles feature lots of chrome and linoleum, as well as country-style cupboard work. Almost anything goes. Late-twentieth-century furniture is a mixture from the distant and not-so-distant past. What is new is the custom furniture efforts of designers and craftsmen, interpreting or rejecting these past offerings.

We see art forms in today's furniture. We see artisans stretching the limits of conventional design, and we see chairs that aren't chairs, but racks to brace the knees and the buttocks in a semi-standing/sitting position. They look torturous, but for someone with back problems, they might be pretty comfy.

Additional Complexity Considerations

We have highlighted a few furniture styles, and some processes that characterize the styles, that may become the genesis of your next design, or be the design itself. There are more general requirements that span periods and furniture styles that need to be considered in your design.

Moldings, Covings and Carvings

Some of the more complex parts you may buy to reduce scope require some preplanning for size, scale and fit with the other parts you produce yourself. Identify the family, color and figuring of the wood at the outset so you can match color and grain pattern in the lumber you buy.

For example, the size of covings and trim you select will have a bearing on how to design a top or base, which must be wider and deeper to integrate an extra wide cabinet cove. Tops that overhang the chest or frame may need to be beefed up for the same reason. In your design, go heavier on top or base thickness in a pleasing proportion to the coving. For example, a ¾"-thick top to be supported by heavy coving or corbels would be too slight.

Also, when buying carved wood trim for your project, it needs to be matched to your construction material (or vice versa). So the shortcut of buying premilled parts may reduce the scope to some degree, but it increases the preplanning and material selection requirements.

Curved Forms

Anything designed with curved parts will require more shop tools and time. There is an inherent complexity in designing and building a table pedestal with curved legs, or a chair with a curved seat, a curvature in the backrest or any form requiring staving or segmenting. If these parts are designed as a laminated curve, plans should include a forming jig for controlling the laminated bend—especially critical when duplicate pieces are required.

Preplanning your material is important when carrying out any type of segmented assembly. A cutting diagram will offer guidelines on planned thicknesses for various radii to make a curved chair back, or seat frame, or whatever you are building. Arcs, segments and tangents all figure into the formula.

The ability to produce true angles, both simple and compound, is required. Proper wood clamps are needed to glue up the assembly.

Compound angles and other fun subjects are expanded on in chapter four, "Committing Plans to Paper," but for now just consider the requirements when scoping a potential project.

The Complexities of Joinery

Classic joinery adds more than a craftsman's touch to the project. It provides strong, lasting joints for your table or chair, chest or bed.

TENONS AND SOCKETS

Sockets for spindles, stretchers and legs may be drilled to the diameter, depth and angle of the turned tenon. These can be tightly fit and glued. Some of the old-world approaches included using seasoned wood for the tenoned piece. This piece would be inserted into sockets drilled into green or unseasoned wood, which dries and shrinks tightly around the tenon. Another approach was to blind-split the tenon. The wedge is inserted only part way in the split, to be driven home when the spindle is inserted, thereby expanding the tenon in the socket. Through tenons can be split and then wedged tight after insertion. A lathe and drill are required.

MORTISE AND TENON

Mortise-and-tenon joints are the accepted method for constructing wooden chair frames. For the typical joint, you can get by with drilling a line of holes, then chiseling the sides flat to open up a blind or open mortise (exposed on one end). Matching tenons can be cut by hand or with power tools. A router is another means to cut both the mortise and tenon. More substantial power tools make the task easier, quicker and more precise. Through tenons can be used on Craftsman-style pieces, maybe square-pegged in place, or on a trestle table to fasten the stretcher for a quick knockdown. Add a mortising bit/drill press for making quick work of the mortise pockets.

Scoping Generic Furniture Parts

The scope described above deals with design characteristics of specific furniture styles. There are some more general guidelines for crafting traditional furniture parts, regardless of style.

**SKETCHPAD 2K
GENERIC PARTS
AND PIECES**

Styled in the look you want
to achieve, there are some
common elements in the
things that make up a piece
of furniture. Here are but
a few of the designer's
options.

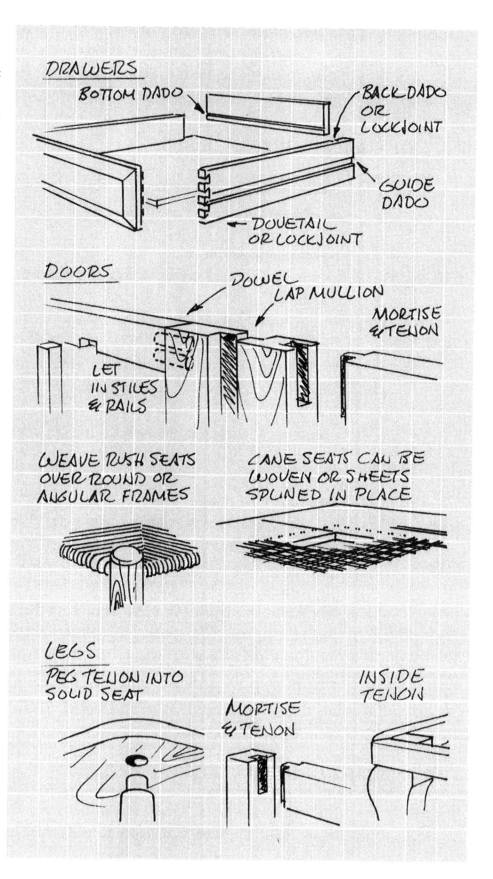

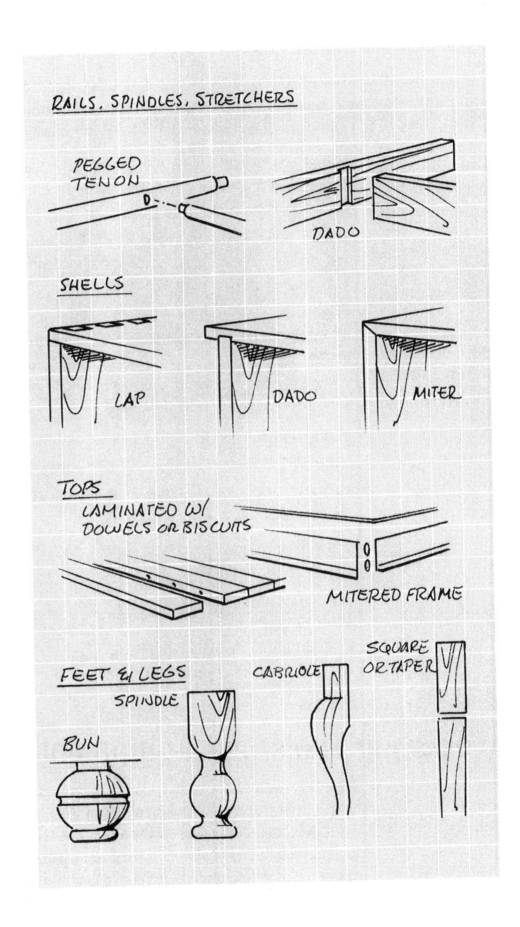

RAILS, SPINDLES, STRETCHERS

PEGGED TENON

DADO

SHELLS

LAP   DADO   MITER

TOPS

LAMINATED W/ DOWELS OR BISCUITS

MITERED FRAME

FEET & LEGS

SPINDLE   CABRIOLE   SQUARE OR TAPER

BUN

GENERIC PIECES

DRAWERS—Dovetailing sides to face, dadoing for drawer bottom and slides and guides, rabbeting laps and clearances, shaping face. Dovetail guide, router (portable or shaper table), dado setup on table saw or radial arm saw.

DOORS—Dadoing mullions and muntins, rabbeting frames, mortise/tenon or dowel/biscuit rail and stile corner joints. Router, dado setup on table or radial arm saw.

SEATS—Solid, rush, cane, upholstered. Research what you will need to accommodate the seat type: a dadoed slot for caning, a frame for rush seat weaving, hole pattern for stringing, etc.

LEGS—Attaching to frame or seat:
- ROUND: Drill. Lathe, drill press or power hand drill.
- SQUARE: Mortise/tenon, dowel or biscuit, threaded metal. Router, drill press/router, shaper table, mortising bit on drill press (or portable power drill and chisels), dado setup on table saw.

RAILS, SPINDLES, STRETCHERS, POSTS—Lathe, drilling jig (drill press or portable drill).

CASES—Shells, carcasses. Table or radial arm saw (with hollow-ground finishing blade).

TOPS—Solid plank or frame with center inset. Table or radial arm saw and everything else in the shop.

FEET/LEGS—Building various styles:
- BUN FEET: Lathe
- CABRIOLE: Band saw, drawknives
- TAPER: Bench or radial arm saw, jointer/planer

Workshop Tools and Equipment

Here is yet another cut at what scope your project might require. This list is by type of tool and which operation you will most likely use.

A discussion of required tools early in the design book is intended to help identify the types of furniture you are equipped to build. This is not meant to thwart lofty ambitions, but to group workshop operations by tools required, or suggested, and maybe allow you to focus on the project you want to design and produce.

A few of the following portable tools might suffice for some of the larger tools listed above. Having these portable tools available, even if the bench model is up and running, makes the building process more efficient: Smaller tools can generally get into tighter spaces and produce tighter, finer results.

Standard Hand Tools

- Squares—framer's, combination, bevel, try square
- Depth gauge/marker
- Rulers—long straightedge, yo-yo (tape measure)
- Planes—bench, rabbet, jack, finger
- Handsaws—crosscut, rip, coping, keyhole, fret
- Files/rasps—including Surform, needle, rifler
- Clamps—C-, pipe-, bar-, web-, furniture-, spring
- Calipers—inside, outside
- Compass
- Protractor
- Straight chisels
- Carving chisels
- Lathe chisels
- Bench vise
- Mallet(s)—wood, leather
- Brace and bits—augers, mortising bit

Purchased Pieces

In addition to the obvious mechanical parts including drawer guides, hinges, hardware, brackets and other specialty products to make the project easier, there are some wood products available through the resources listed in the back of this book (and others I probably overlooked).

Candidate items to buy:

- Legs—cabriole, tapers, bun feet, spindles
- Bedposts and robe rungs
- Chair seats—rush, woven rattan, leather, padded
- Glazing—especially leaded, beveled or stained glass

Standard Power Tools of the Basic Home Workshop

OPERATION	TOOLS	ACCESSORIES
STRAIGHT-CUT PARTS	Table or radial arm saw	Combination, hollow-ground, dado and veneer blade
DRESS SURFACES	Jointer/planer Belt sander (with disk attachment)	Variety of grades/grit
WOOD TURNING	Wood lathe	Turning chisels (Gouge, round nose, skew) parting tool; size based on project—long and strong for big projects, for miniature lathe turning
SHARPENING/HONING	Bench grinder	Wire brush, stone wheel, Carborundum abrasives (honing)
SHAPING	Router table, shaper table, drill press	Router bits, feed table
FRETS AND FRILLS	Band saw Jigsaw or scroll saw	3 tpi (coarse), 12 tpi (medium), 24 tpi (scroll) Various coarseness

There are also some services you might consider, including wide-belt sanding and thickness planing to bring your planked tops to a flat surface.

The scope of the project as envisioned in the early stages needs to be well planned. Some variation and adaptation will likely occur during the detail design and building, but you'll want to avoid major surprises.

During the design process, many ideas gel at once, and they all come together when working out the details. Don't get too hung up on detail before it is needed. A disciplined approach might be to use a ten-step method in developing your concept within the chosen standards.

The Ten-Step Conceptual Design Approach (see Figure 2-2) adds detail only after the more general concepts are locked in. With each step comes added detail. Initially, you identify what you want to design, then which style, model, hardware, color, finish, etc.

Standard Portable Power Tools

OPERATION	TOOLS	ACCESSORIES
CUTTING—Straight —Scroll	Circular saw Saber (jig-) saw	Combination, hollow-ground, veneering blades Coarse, medium and fine blades
JOINING	Drill (⅜″ chuck) High-speed router	Spade bits, twist drills, Forstner bits, chisel point High-speed bits: veining, round nose, straight shank; biscuit cutter
DRESSING/SHAPING	Sanders—disk, belt, palm, orbital, profile	Various grits/grades
GRINDING	Grinder (disk) Grinder (rotary) Hobby-size rotary grinder (Dremel, Mototool)	Rasps, grinding wheels, sanding drums

A detail, a technique or a process may be the inspiration for the design, however, and the steps will lead the design toward these objectives, but before you spend too much time on developing an accent, you must determine what it should accent.

BEGIN AT THE BEGINNING:

STEP 1. Determine the rough shape of the project and its proportions.

STEP 2. Block in the forms. Allocate space devoted to function based on the use, efficiency and convenience.

STEP 3. Apply dimensions to the shell. Make sure the allocated areas will suit the application—hold legal files, hang a wardrobe, hold your library of books or whatever.

STEP 4. Settle on the desired style of the piece.

STEP 5. Define the configuration of the whole and the parts. Assign relative areas, spaces and locations of the components.

THE TEN-STEP CONCEPTUAL DESIGN APPROACH

STEP 1.
ROUGH IN CARCASS
PROPORTIONS
Cube or rectangle, high or
low—Depth/Width/
Height

STEP 2.
BLOCK IN SPATIAL
RELATIONSHIPS
Allocate areas of major
shapes. Symmetrical or
asymmetrical

STEP 3.
ASSIGN OVERALL
DIMENSIONS
Overall size to house target
spaces

STEP 4.
SELECT DESIGN
FORM
Floor-based or raised

STEP 5.
CONFIGURE SPACES
Subdivide component
shapes, quantity and sizes;
equidistant or progression

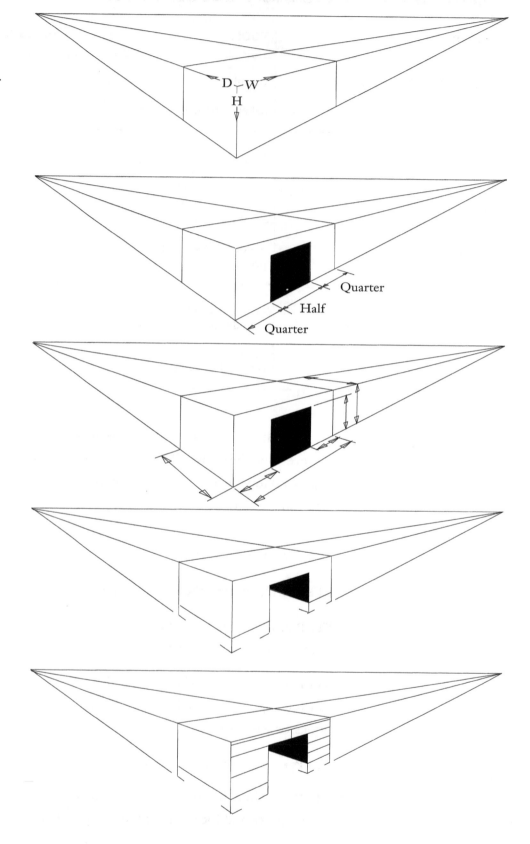

**STEP 6.
CHOOSE
CONSTRUCTION
METHOD**
Solid, frame & panel,
veneered ply

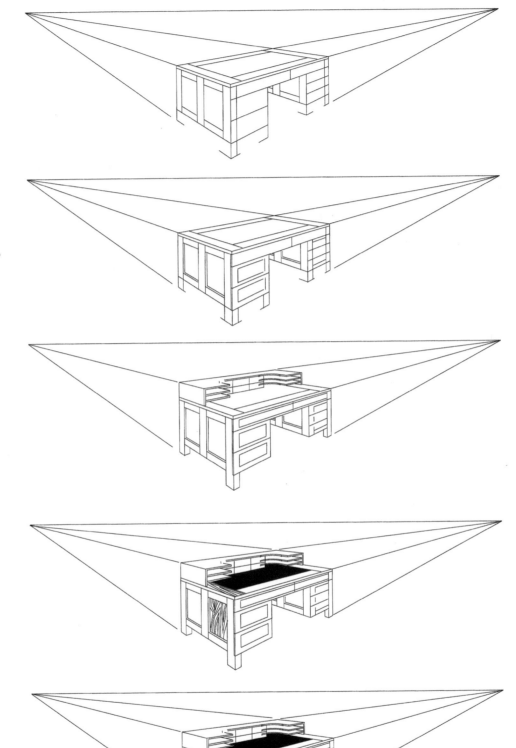

**STEP 7.
ASSIGN
COMPONENT
RELATIONSHIPS**
Thicknesses of top, frames,
facings in proportion to
whole

**STEP 8.
CONSIDER DESIGN
DETAIL AND
EMBELLISHMENTS**
Added elements,
treatments, decor

**STEP 9.
DECIDE ON COLOR
AND FINISH**
Confirm original
finishing plan

**STEP 10.
SELECT
COMPLEMENTING
HARDWARE**
Confirm original hardware
style/size selection

STEP 6. Based on the style you selected, choose a compatible construction method—solid plank, frame and panel, ply/veneer.

STEP 7. Determine how much and what design detail you want to add to the piece. Stay true to the style and avoid adding detail that doesn't belong.

STEP 8. Embellishments can include using special treatments for integral handles, adding compartments or a rack of interior drawers, or carrying through the uniqueness of the design to the less prominent, infrequently exposed areas.

STEP 9. Reconfirm the selected finish. Do you really want to candy the overcoat and hide the natural beauty of the piece?

STEP 10. Select or design handles and knobs, hinges and stops that complement the whole.

Through a step-by-step exercise similar to the one described above, you won't lock yourself into a detail at the outset that might not be suitable for the outcome. Let the preliminary decisions, which have been based and built on the developing design, guide the process to determine forms, sizes and methods that will ultimately become the designed parts that make up the whole.

Plan the project around your capacity, but broadened to an ever-widening scope of tasks and techniques. Design within your scope, but extend yourself a little with each new project.

CHAPTER THREE

Applying Standards

In the act of reaching for a doorknob you should be able to turn it comfortably, with a natural motion. Stairs should be consistent in both height and depth of riser and tread. While standing at a pullman sink, you expect a place for your toes. If the designers and manufacturers followed the book of standards, your newly installed dishwasher should match the height and depth of the kick plate aligned to the cabinetwork. Likewise when the 6′8″ door assembly or the 4-0/6-0 window is popped into place, the framer has allowed for these sizes. These are design standards.

Some standards are based on margins of safety, some on physical characteristics, while others evolved from a more efficient use of common material sizes. Design standards for furniture are not quite as structured, but some of the same concerns apply. An undersized lintel may be incapable of supporting the overhead weight above the opening in both a house and the furniture that goes into it. You want the house and the furniture to stand straight and true, to be strong with no lateral or torsional flexing. Concentrate on the basics, and the details will follow.

Furniture Design Standards

Standards apply primarily to the relational design and, in a more subjective way, to the style and the aesthetic qualities which are all elements of design.

To paraphrase Charles Eames's thoughts (according to Charlotte and Peter Fiell's *Modern Furniture Classics Since 1945*), design is the act of combining *parts* of selected *materials*, well proportioned to the piece and the *use*, forming a cohesive *whole*.

PARTS: Combine parts, pieces, forms and shapes for the use and user in the style, size and proportions that, when brought together, meet the defined functional, aesthetic and structural objectives.

MATERIALS: The selected organic or processed materials should be suitable for traditional design, or you may take the medium to the limit in application and expression.

USE: The intended use can be actively functional to a task, such as sitting in relaxation, while dining, at work or at play, or visually functional, in that its only relationship with the user is viewer admiration, appreciation and pleasure, providing a prominent object, storage or display.

THE WHOLE should be a cohesive unit, comprising parts fashioned from efficiently utilized and effective materials which are singly pleasing and singularly assembled into a lasting union to satisfy the designer's objectives.

As your mental image of the parts, materials, uses and the whole develop, there are other equally important design considerations that should become a part of your objectives as well; that is, design with people in mind, and design in scale with the surroundings.

It is within these latter objectives that design standards are applied.

Standards differ with the culture and stature of a group and what that group may be accustomed to—what is acceptable, fashionable and worthy of our purchase (or our time designing and building) and deserving to be part of our surroundings.

Certain standards have been adopted for furniture. Heights of a dining table, its accompanying chairs, and the clearance between the table apron and the seated figure should be a comfortable distance for dining, crossing legs, or whatever else may go on under the table. The optimum height of a desk chair is the height that is comfortable at seat level and at its position relative to a computer keyboard or typewriter (you remember those keyboards without a monitor) and the writing surface. These standards are reflected in manufactured parts you buy for the project, such as 27″ cabriole or turned legs for dining table height, or an assortment of 12″ legs for a coffee table.

In addition to work-surface height, consider the kneehole: How wide, how high, how deep? Consider the chair, which should not be so low that knee strength is tested in lowering the bum to the seat, nor so high the feet don't rest comfortably on the floor (or on rungs for taller stools), nor so wide it doesn't fit with the companion furniture. Also consider the relationships of seat to well, seat to desktop, seat to keyboard and seat to extended reach.

Consider the Environs

Once you know what you want to design and where it will be placed, you need to consider the environs—the surroundings.

Compatible Furniture

Compatible furniture can be whatever pleases your individual taste or design sense. Design a mass that is visually capable of fulfilling its task, whether it is a chest-on-chest, a library ladder or a buffet/sideboard. Its size, scale and style are part of the design, and each individually and collectively contributes to the design.

At the outset, realize the need may arise to compromise the size selected for the user (ergonomics) and the location (environs). If your abode is a small bungalow or condominium, an upstairs flat or studio apartment, the entire scale of furniture might be cranked down a notch, not only to allow maneuvering within the room it occupies, but to achieve a better visual balance of furniture with its surroundings.

Style

From the first spark of an idea, you probably locked in the style you wanted to build. Maybe it is to complement existing furnishings or accent a contemporary setting with a period piece (or vice versa). Maybe your setting is all contemporary and you want to go a bit off-the-wall, either harmonizing or contrasting with the surroundings.

Design with style in mind:

- Period
- Contemporary
- Off-the-wall
- In harmony with surroundings
- In contrast with surroundings

Other design considerations are based on the architecture; whether the home you are designing furniture for is a 1930s bungalow, a 1970s modern or today's Italian villa, take note of its character. The type of house you are in now and the type you may buy next will probably be similar in feel. Your furniture will follow suit as well.

Consider the role of a picture frame. It should complement, not compete with, the painting it surrounds. You may emphasize or de-emphasize the presentation with a mat the color, width and shape of your choosing. These considerations hold true in your furniture design as well.

With respect to finishes, a monochromatic color scheme might be effective in some settings and monotonous in others. Extremes can exhibit good design qualities. Totally stark white or all dark motifs connote sameness, which can be used to highlight a focal piece designed to contrast with its setting.

Study the Location

There is a good chance the ceilings in your dwelling are 8' off the floor. And odds are that more square footage is allocated to the living area than to the kitchen, and the master bedroom is larger than the others. "Your Old House" may have a huge dining room where large families once congregated, a parlor for informal gatherings and a study for some peace and quiet.

Furniture scale remains about the same from room to room, but quantity varies by living area based on access, activity, room size and traffic pattern.

Be sure to consider wall openings: doors and windows. Door or archway size differs with the purpose and prominence of the room and style of the architecture. Wall space is interrupted by a window or two. While these openings also provide natural light and ventilation, they represent prominent design elements with their own character and form, and devour usable wall space. In looking at prospective furniture for the setting, window size is a consideration, as is any unique shape, form or treatment. Study the size and appearance for possible design elements to consider in your design. Then, within a year, you'll probably move to a home with a completely different look and feel, so don't get too literal or specific with the emulation.

The illustration on page 73 shows a progression of furniture heights and their relationship in a lineup, with a fairly standard 32″×80″ or 32″×84″ doorway and a 3′×4′ window set 40″ off the floor. Light switches and outlets, ducts and access panels should be considered when planning the perfect piece for the intended location, and for alternate rearrangements or relocation.

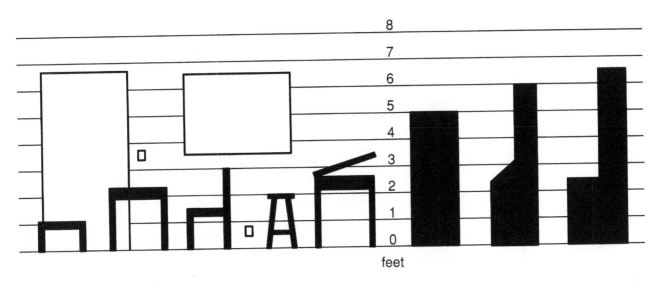

FIGURE 3-1
Lineup of Furniture Profiles

Environs

Whether the furniture you design will complement or contrast its setting, a close look around its new location could have some positive influence on the design. Note these and other attributes in your mind, on a list or in a sketch under "other things to consider" in your design effort:

Architectural style

Furniture style

Colors

Textures

Lighting

Square footage

Volume

Heights

- *Ceiling*
- *Wainscot*

Windows

- *Quantity*
- *Area*
- *Sill heights*

Wall space

Set your *functional* objectives to design and build furniture to a practical height for the intended use and user, and your *aesthetic* objectives to optimize size, style, materials and finish.

FUNCTIONAL FACTORS to consider in your design process include asking if it will fit under a window and still be high enough to use for its intended purpose. Look at the sill, moldings and window dressings (shades, drapes, blinds) to arrive at the optimum height. Then, if you must go over or under a more standard height, stay within a functional range.

AESTHETIC QUALITIES might include a piece pleasing in proportion and design detail, with some relationship, whether in harmony or counterdesign, with its surroundings. A nice piece of work needs to belong or contrast, and not invade other furniture in the room.

The table on page 75 contains a range of furniture heights by location. The norm falls somewhere between the minimum and maximum heights (in inches). Values are for typical settings used by a person of average stature. These are for guidance only. Begin here, but adapt these heights to meet your composite design needs. Furniture heights will vary by function and location.

In a living room, the coffee, occasional and end tables are typically low, to be reached when hunkered down on a cushy couch.

Dining table heights (with ethnic exceptions, such as an Oriental table ringed with floor cushions) should be designed close to expected heights, suitable for comfortable dining, writing or game playing.

In a great room or family room, anything goes—casual.

In the bedroom, the most prominent piece of furniture is obviously the bed, so its height should influence the design of bedside tables, side chairs, vanity, valet, armoire and blanket chest. And a new head and footboard should be designed to a height and proportion based on bed height and the style of the addition.

For the home office, apply some "away-from-home" office standards based on industrial engineers' studies on efficiency, fatigue and safety. The conclusions need not result in a plastic and fiber cubicle. Sharing home office space with your living space might require a little compromising, as noted earlier; maybe a library table is the CEO's desk and a butcher-block table the Accounts Receivable Department. Design the heights and proportions to meet or balance any of your dual-use objectives.

Standard Furniture Heights by Room (Inches)

ITEM/ROOM	LIVING	DINING	FAMILY	BED	OFFICE
CHAIR: (SEATING)	Sofa *15-17* Easy *15-17* Side *17-18*	Dining *17-18* Bench *16-18*	Casual *15-17* Game *17-19* Dining *17*	Vanity *16-18* Valet *15-17* Bench *16-20*	Desk *16-17* Drafting *24-30* Waiting *Too Low*
(BACKS)	32"-42", proportioned to style/usage Perpendicular (some Shaker) to 6°-8° slant				
TABLE: (SURFACES)	Coffee *12-14* End *17-23* Hall *27-30*	Dining *29-30*	Game *26-32* Serving *28-32* Dining *27-30*	Vanity *27-30* Bedside *18-26*	Desk *25-30* Layout *36-42* Drafting *32-42*
ACTIVITY CENTER	Secretary *27-28* Desk *27-28*	Server *27-30* Tea Cart *27-29*	A/V Center *[Open]* Bar *30-36*	Sewing *27-30*	Keyboard *25* Desk *27-28*
CABINET: (STORAGE)	Bookcase *[Open]* Display *[Open]*	Welsh *68-72* Buffet *27-32* Sideboard *68-72*	Cupboard *[Open]*	Armoire *58-60* Dresser *27-32* Blanket *22-24*	Letter File *[Open]* Flat File *[Open]* Storage *[Open]*

(Open = Your choice based on usage and space)

Customize: Tailor to User, Usage and Space

Scaling furniture for the setting is only half the design equation. It is equally, if not more, important to scale furniture for the "sitting," to make it comfortable and livable.

Customize for the Target User

Leonardo da Vinci's drawing of the human form is possibly the best known depiction of human proportions. His lesser known cousin, Victor da Vinci, couldn't draw the human form, so he used ellipses instead. (Note: In the world of Ellipsedom, his model was considered one handsome dude. And his wife, Ellie, was known in some circles as a "real fox.")

The human form is an efficient machine, but has limited movement in both range and motion, which vary by height (more appropriately known as stature) and whether seated or standing. When designing a piece of furniture, start with the standard, or average, then adapt to your intended users.

Exceptions would be children's furniture, where scale is substantially reduced, or specialized furniture for the physically disadvantaged. For example, you should throw out all standard height recommendations and position the keyboard at the height where the operator can type, or place the work surface at the height where the artist or sculptor can work. This presents a whole different set of design problems, but the solutions are most rewarding.

When designing a piece for a target range, remember that very tall people adjust to subscale furnishings, and shorter than average people are accustomed to up-sized furniture. So, unless you are commissioned to furnish an NBA lounge or a meeting room for the Center for International Lilliputians, stay close to standard sizes.

The graph on page 78 depicts the distribution of U.S. population by stature. These are the types of data used by commercial furniture designers and builders, who must produce a single size to meet the needs of all but the most extreme upper and lower fifth percentile of the population group. Because it is more feasible for a taller person to function with a smaller piece of furniture than is true for the opposite scenario, furniture tends to be built for the mid-height range. Furniture for women is built for the majority (88.9 percent) who range between 5'2" and 5'8", whereas furniture for men targets the 82.7 percent of men who are between 5'8" and 6'2". For unisex furniture (one size fits all), the average used is in the 5'8" range.

Stature changes with age. The data shown (See figure 3-3) are for the maximum-height years for both men and women, age thirty-five to forty-four. As we age, we shrink. There is no such thing as "average" physique. Even though stature is identical in 30.6 percent of men in this age group, arm, leg and torso lengths vary within the group, so the average population

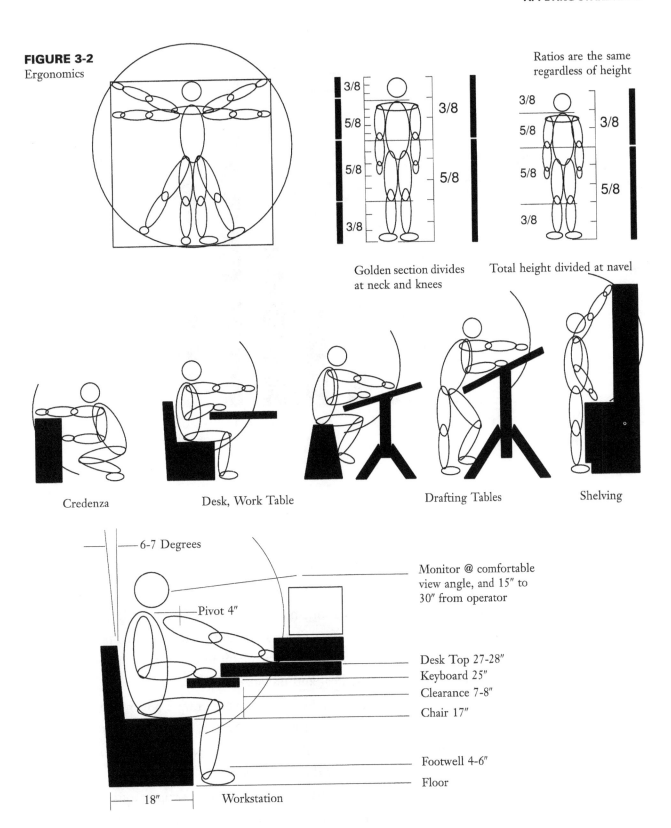

FIGURE 3-2
Ergonomics

Ratios are the same regardless of height

3/8
5/8
5/8
3/8

3/8
3/8
5/8
5/8

3/8
5/8
5/8
3/8

3/8
3/8
5/8
5/8

Golden section divides
at neck and knees

Total height divided at navel

Credenza

Desk, Work Table

Drafting Tables

Shelving

6-7 Degrees

Pivot 4"

Monitor @ comfortable
view angle, and 15" to
30" from operator

Desk Top 27-28"
Keyboard 25"
Clearance 7-8"
Chair 17"

Footwell 4-6"
Floor

18" Workstation

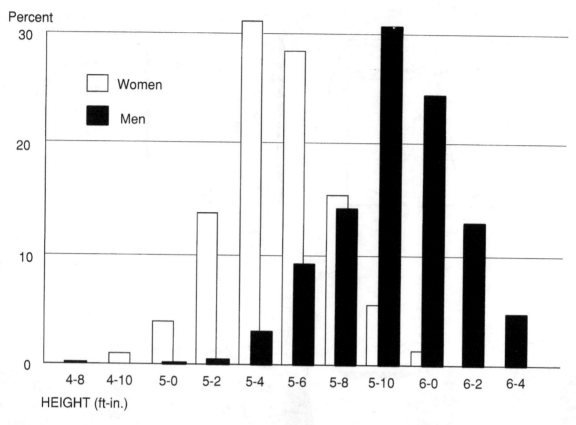

Percent

FIGURE 3-3
Stature of U.S. Population

is further reduced when additional parameters are considered. Except for identical twins (maybe) no two bodies are exactly the same in all respects.

The "Cumulative Percent Distribution of Population" table contains a more complete breakdown on the distribution of stature. Each update of these data points out the fact that the height of the world's population is substantially increasing over time, especially in countries with warmer climates and improved medical and dietary advances.

As a custom-furniture builder, you have a unique advantage in making the piece truly custom-tailored to the user's stature. But when designing for the masses, a "one size fits all" design approach must be taken to accommodate 90 percent of the population.

You can build for a population of one, where proportions of the piece are tailored to the user. Nothing stays the same, however: As that person ages, some decline in stature will occur. What is perfect in midlife will require a little longer reach in the golden years—perhaps not enough to matter, but it does highlight the role of furniture designers in trying to

Cumulative Percent Distribution of Population

MALES

AGE	18-24	25-34	35-44	45-54	55-64	65-74
HEIGHT						
% UNDER:						
4'8"	0	0	0	0	0	0
4'10"	0	0	0	0	0	0
5'	0.18	0.05	0.27	0	0.27	0.24
5'2"	0.34	0.42	0.87	0.70	0.92	2.66
5'4"	2.37	1.55	3.66	2.55	5.28	10.53
5'6"	8.24	9.51	12.39	11.39	17.54	29.42
5'8"	26.68	26.69	26.40	33.56	43.53	57.75
5'10"	53.66	55.35	57.01	63.38	71.51	81.95
6'	80.14	81.58	81.15	85.83	90.99	94.52
6'2"	92.74	9.57	95.05	98.01	97.66	99.17
6'4"	98.40	99.23	99.19	99.70	99.79	100

FEMALES

AGE	18-24	25-34	35-44	45-54	55-64	65-74
HEIGHT						
% UNDER:						
4'10"	0.94	0.64	0.95	1.22	3.02	4.25
5'	4.22	3.65	4.56	8.88	11.40	17.20
5'2"	17.75	18.11	18.24	27.68	31.71	44.34
5'4"	41.81	47.43	49.90	57.21	63.89	76.46
5'6"	74.75	74.92	78.07	84.54	88.91	94.63
5'8"	92.30	93.28	93.43	96.28	97.70	97.66
5'10"	98.34	99.49	99.19	99.58	99.78	99.81
6'	100	100	100	100	100	100
6'2"	100	100	100	100	100	100
6'4"	100	100	100	100	100	100

Source: *Statistical Abstract of U.S., 1994*

accommodate the range of sizes, shapes and lengths for different target populations.

If you are designing for the masses, refer to studies such as Julius Panero and Martin Zelnik's *Human Dimensions and Interior Space* for the predominant population and average measurements for the commercial designer. Your local library will have other books under the subject of *ergonomics* or *interior design* that will be similar in content. Measurement data for a complete range of stature include:

- Eye level, standing and seated
- Midshoulder height seated erect
- Shoulder breadth
- Elbow-to-elbow breadth
- Hip breadth
- Waist height
- Elbow-rest height
- Thigh clearance
- Knee height
- Buttock-knee length
- Buttock-toe length
- Buttock-heel length
- Vertical reach—sitting
- Vertical grip reach
- Side arm reach
- Maximum body depth and breadth
- Weight by height

A less scientific, but hopefully helpful table is presented on page 81. Based on the golden section in nature, and more specifically the proportions of the human body, the theoretical measurements of the body in various positions are offered as a place to begin.

This data can be used to begin locking in your design parameters based on the stature (or height) of the user. Derived from the golden section values shown in Figure 3-3A, the "Table of Theoretical Heights" on page 82 contains cumulative heights of a figure in a standing and seated position, and includes maximum reach extension to optimum seat height. If your subject falls between the heights listed, you can extrapolate the values or multiply the target height by the factors listed in the figure.

Looking specifically at a seated figure to determine chair height and

Calculations for the "Table of Theoretical
Heights" may be applied to a known height by
multiplying height by factors shown. The subject
can be measured as shown in Figure 3–4A.

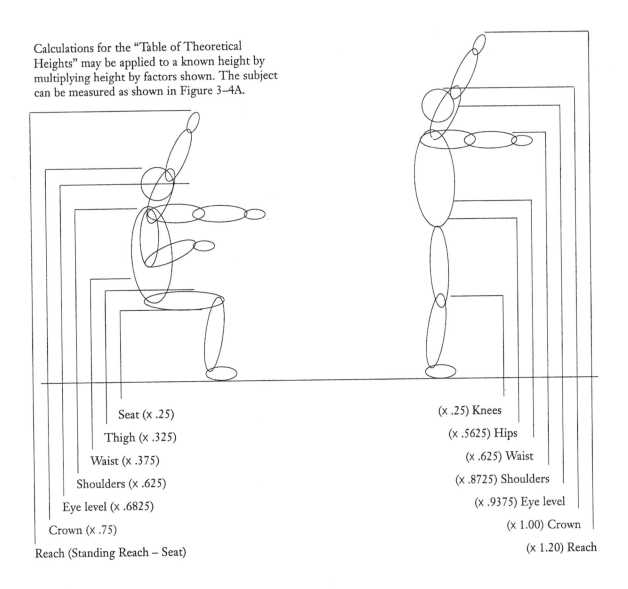

Seat (x .25)
Thigh (x .325)
Waist (x .375)
Shoulders (x .625)
Eye level (x .6825)
Crown (x .75)
Reach (Standing Reach – Seat)

(x .25) Knees
(x .5625) Hips
(x .625) Waist
(x .8725) Shoulders
(x .9375) Eye level
(x 1.00) Crown
(x 1.20) Reach

FIGURE 3-3
Factors Used in Theoretical Height Calculations

everything relative to that height, you can use the numbers in the table as
your guideline. For more tailored results, measure your target population
of one (or take the average stature of the potential users). Remember, a
taller person can adapt better to smaller furniture than the opposite scenario.

When designing a chair, use two views of a seated person to capture
the dimensions. First is the elevation. For the height, measure the distance
from a foot flat on the floor to the underside of the thigh. The angle can
vary depending on the task or function. The depth of the seat varies based
on activity as well, but should be sufficient to support the entire seated
figure from the lumbar to inside the bent knee.

Table of Theoretical Heights

HEIGHT (Inches)	48	52	56	60	64	68	72	76	MEASURE	MEASURE
STANDING*										
REACH	57.6	62.4	67.2	72	76.8	81.6	86.4	91.2		
CROWN	48	52	56	60	64	68	72	76		
EYE LEVEL	45	48.75	52.5	56.25	60	63.75	67.5	71.25		
SHOULDERS	39	42.25	45.5	48.75	52	55.25	58.5	61.75		
WAIST	30	32.5	35	37.5	40	42.5	45	47.5		
HIPS	27	29.25	31.5	33.75	36	38.25	40.5	42.75		
KNEES	12	13	14	15	16	17	18	19		
BASELINE	0	0	0	0	0	0	0	0		
SEATED*										
REACH	45.6	49.4	53.2	57	60.8	64.6	68.4	72.2		
CROWN	36	39	42	45	48	51	54	57		
EYE LEVEL	33	35.75	38.5	41.25	44	46.75	49.5	52.25		
SHOULDERS	30	32.5	35	37.5	40	42.5	45	47.5		
ELBOW	18	19.5	21	22.5	24	25.5	27	28.5		
WAIST	18	19.5	21	22.5	24	25.5	27	28.5		
THIGH CLEAR	15.6	16.9	18.2	19.5	20.8	22.1	23.4	24.7		
SEAT	12	13	14	15	16	17	18	19		
BASELINE	0	0	0	0	0	0	0	0		
Adjust for Seat**	5	4	3	2	1	0	-1	-2		
REACH										
HORIZONTAL	21	22.75	24.5	26.25	28	29.75	31.5	33.25		
*CUMULATIVE HEIGHT FROM FLOOR										
**VARIATION TO STANDARD SEAT HEIGHT OF 17 INCHES										

FIGURE 3-4A
Measuring the Seated Form

FIGURE 3-4B
Extended Reach and
Motion of a Seated Figure

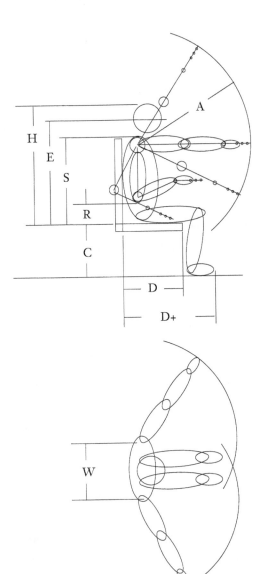

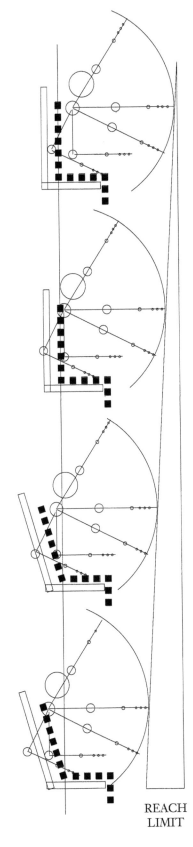

Seated upright
at 90°, 4"
shoulder pivot

Seated upright 90°

Seated at 6°
recline with 4"
shoulder pivot

Seated at 6° recline

Note: Chair back or
armrests may limit
elbow retraction

REACH
LIMIT

A = Arc
C = Chair
D = Depth
D + = Toes
E = Eye
H = Head
R = Rest
S = Shoulder
W = Width

For relaxed seating, the level can be lower and somewhat angled to nestle the buttocks into the sofa. For a workstation, this angle should be flatter, the body more erect or slightly reclined, but the leg-to-seat height should be sufficient for the seated figure to have support against slippage forward and away from the back lumbar support.

All other dimensions can be based on this chord or baseline, including the distance from the elbow to seat height (armrest location), seat to shoulder level (backrest height), seat to work top (desk, table) and seat to eye level (monitor or task focus).

Shown in figure 3-4B are the reach extensions, including a shoulder pivot distance of 4″ from an erect seated position, to a reclined seat with no shoulder pivot. Although no values are given for these lengths, be aware of the decreasing reach capacity as a result of the chair configuration, and place drawers and pigeonholes within reach of the user.

Body Parts

Whatever limits your furniture design may place on the user's motions, the body's capacity to function in cramped or awkward quarters is boundless. If you've ever played with a robotics demonstration at a science museum, it soon became obvious just how complex the motions are for what we call dexterity.

Duplicating the actions of extending, rotating, grasping, lifting and carrying requires masterfully engineered hinges, pins, balls and sockets driven by hydraulic or mechanical "muscles" activated by electrical power and controlled by programmed motor sensors or your own attempts to control the motions with buttons or a joystick. The physiology of the upper body, specifically the opposable thumb, dexterous fingers, articulating wrists, torsional rotating forearm, bendable elbow, movable shoulder, rotating torso and articulated spine—the whole "dis bone connected to da . . ." routine— is capable of a multitude of tasks, which eases the furniture design process.

Reach isn't limited to a static torso, but using that assumption in this example, a person seated erect ("sit up straight," remember?) has a lateral reach of one-third the body height. Reach can be extended another 3″-4″ when the shoulder pivots forward—which is not a particularly uncomfortable motion if done infrequently, but should not be required in the normal course of activity.

If the chair back reclines, which the user might prefer as a more natural position for the task, the reach shortens with the reclined angle of the torso, both with and without the shoulder pivot.

Excessive chair width can inhibit the range of close-up motion, such as opening an adjacent desk drawer. A wide seat back may limit the distance the arm can be retracted, and the seat width might block the opening of drawers or doors.

A desk front will impede bending at the waist while seated, but a break-front design—maybe for sitting at a vanity, or standing at a drafting table or at a podium-height work top—will allow more bending and therefore greater reach distances. Design changes can extend the reach envelope for a higher top drawer or shelf, or a deeper drawing board.

The user will position a chair relative to the workstation where it is most comfortable or efficient, but only if you design clearances to match chair width, kneehole width and chair arms, if any. Generally, the distance from the front of the seated figure to the desk face should be at a comfortable distance for the task.

A comfortable seat height can be the beginning parameter on which all other heights are based. If this is your starting point, and the chair is to be customized for a single person, measure the distance from the heel to knee, reduced by the thigh thickness for seat height. Add a clearance of 6″ above the chair seat, maybe a 3″ drawer face and a 1″ top, and you have a theoretical design height for an accompanying work surface. If this is too low, look again at the chair to see if it could be higher, with a front stretcher placed strategically as a footrest.

The keyboard height in a computer desk is a critical dimension and should benefit the operator. Conversely, an improper relationship in heights can, over time, be detrimental to the tendons (tendinitis) or cause carpal-tunnel-type problems.

In addition to keyboard position placed at the optimum height to the chair seat and operator, include in your design parameters vertical placement of the monitor, mouse pad and work area for reference or source materials. These height relationships were shown in figure 3-2.

In an overhead plan view, consider the distance from chair back, through the torso, to the facing edge. Then look beyond to any drawers, racks or pigeonholes planned for the top to arrive at how close or far from the user these should be placed for the frequency of use and the intended purpose. They should be within reach for fetching postage, a paper clip or a notepad.

A plan-view sketch can guide the design's length, width and depth by determining what will surround the computer and monitor. Plan a place for the keyboard (pullout drawer or desktop), maybe with an accompanying wrist pad, a right- or left-handed mouse pad, a digitizing tablet and other components, plus an adequate, well-lighted work area required for the task.

These distances were covered (see table 3-3), but can be measured to ensure the fit of the user to the use.

Maximum extension is of little value unless there is a button to push or a switch to flip. However, within the span from shoulder to wrist, a knob can be pulled, a paper clip can be fetched, a notepad can be retrieved. This maximum distance is splayed in an arc based at a radius from the shoulder to the wrist from eleven to three o'clock for the right shoulder, and from nine to one o'clock for the left, with the two arcs separated by the offset width of the shoulders. Studies show women have a greater range of motion through such an arc than men do.

Other Considerations for a Seated Figure

Man does not live by desks alone. Among the other types of furniture a designer/craftsman might undertake, certain relationships, although fewer and less critical than those for a desk, are worthy of consideration.

■ BENCH —Width should be elongated if designed for public seating, but can be narrower and cozier for home use.

■ COFFEE TABLE —Consider the height, width and breadth and the distance relative to the seat level of the sofa and chairs surrounding its perimeter.

■ END TABLE —Consider the height, width and breadth relative to the sofa's armrest.

■ DINING TABLE —Determine the number of guests you plan to accommodate comfortably for normal occasions and squeezed at those special gatherings. Sketch a seating chart that avoids human leg interference with the table legs, unless designing a pedestal table.

Allow an area 16″×24″ minimum for each place setting, and at least a 12″ swath in the center for shared space. Chair width should fit within the place-setting allocation.

■ GAME TABLE —A game can be played at any table, but if you have the space and the inclination, a game table can be a gathering place for chess masters, firehouse checkers, backgammon or other board games, and can offer an opportunity to apply your marquetry skills for the game board.

Tables are usually small in size for access to attacking game pieces, or designed for a rousing card game of four or more players.

■ VANITY —With flattering lighting (to bolster the ego of the user), this well-mirrored piece can be small and personal, with drawers and shelves and trays nearby for easy access to the magic powders and potions.

■ TASK TABLES —Sewing centers, for example, should be designed to accommodate man (or woman) and machine. Consider the activity, tools and processes related to the task; whether it is assembling models, stringing beads or collecting stamps, coins or butterflies, each has storage and work area requirements unique to the activity.

Comfort Zone Seating

Instead of launching right into another discussion about workstations and work heights, let's look at some comfort zones. When designing furniture for the home, these are not that critical, but for commercial, public use, they become very important.

Studies have defined personal comfort zones that vary with our degree of familiarity with the person in or near our space, which then defines whether their presence is an intrusion.

INTIMATE ZONE—This is obvious, and makes an intriguing title for a future book: *The Joy of Intimate Furniture Design.*

PERSONAL ZONE—This is a close-in envelope where the relationship with the close person does not intrude personal space until it begins to enter the intimate zone.

SOCIAL ZONE—This widens the comfort zone to between 3′ and 4′.

PUBLIC ZONE—This zone definition is wishful thinking at 25′, but the message is to provide some space, some barrier, some demarcation.

In a small restaurant one recent evening, a table for eight was quickly broken down to a table for six and a table for two. The waiter brought in a frame, similar to a freestanding mirror but completely open, and separated the two groups with this "barrier" without moving the tables apart. For public seating, some type of demarcation helps to define impersonal zones.

Most designer/craftsman's work will deal with personal and social space, but there may be a commissioned piece for a reception area or a conference

FIGURE 3-5
Comfort Zone Seating

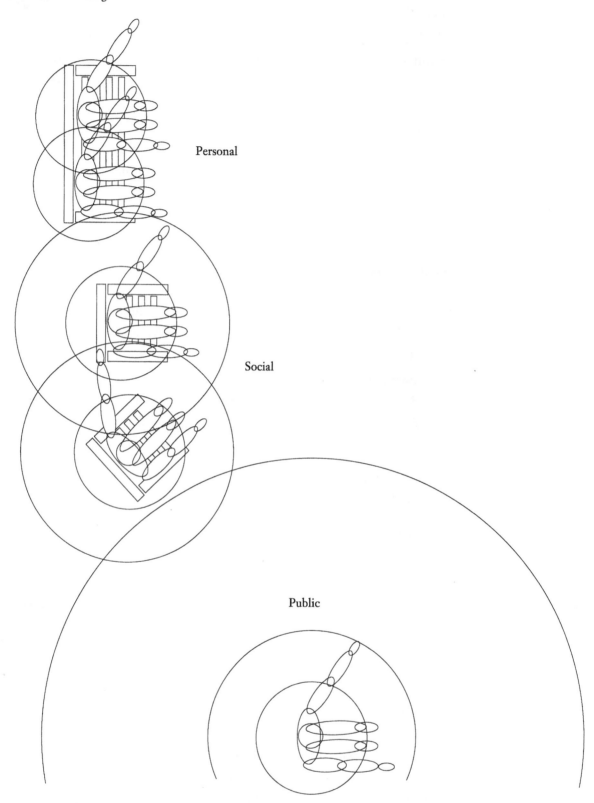

Personal

Social

Public

room or some other commercial application for custom furniture. Garner as much information on the accepted standards as you can to form a basis for your industrial or commercial design efforts.

Other Personal Considerations

Furniture design includes more considerations in addition to providing clearances between body and furniture, optimum height relationships and comfort zones in both commercial and custom design.

Frustration sets in when door and drawer pulls can't be grasped both naturally and comfortably, or when the pulls snare, snag, catch or otherwise mutilate clothing or flesh.

If true to your design, maybe finger pulls can be integral with the case, routed along a drawer-face edge atop, below or along either side, or can share access and clearance with the drawer bearers along the drawer casings. For doors, the push-release latch circumvents the need for any type of grip or interruption of your design lines.

Maintain a pleasing proportion between exposed hardware, the parts and the whole. This can be a challenging design exercise. Hidden or imbedded hardware does not conflict with the design lines. Conversely, fully exposed hardware must complement the look and proportion in its style, color, size and configuration. Some trade-offs may be made in order to provide a handle or knob in both an acceptable scale and theme and in a practical size.

Users expect to use a light touch when pulling out a delicate drawer, whereas workbench drawer handles should be hefty. An obvious analogy, but the point is to combine all of the design attributes—form, function, size, clearance, strength—when designing or selecting pulls and handles for your project.

Discomfort can result if stool stretchers are too high or too low to comfortably rest a foot, or the chair back doesn't conform to the lumbar of the spine, or the solid seat you carefully formed doesn't conform to the tush (that is, the buttocks and coccyx). Maybe the chair seat is not deep or wide enough to fully support the seated figure, or it is too high or too slanted, causing the legs to dangle and inhibiting blood circulation.

If a pigeonhole organizer is placed just beyond the reach of a seated figure, or the pigeonholes are too narrow or too deep for the user to fetch its contents without some implement, it will be awkward to use. The placement of a monitor just outside the normal viewing range, distance or angle can also be described as awkward. Consider eye level when designing a workstation—and when designing cases and display shelving also.

More on Viewing Angles

DISPLAY CABINETS—Keep these cabinets low or shallow, aligned with normal viewing levels and hopefully at the most favorable angle to the items displayed.

PERSPECTIVE—Adjust thicknesses based on the normal viewing angle. A perceived reduction in part size occurs the farther away it is from the viewer; therefore, an equal thickness used for the top and the base will appear slightly smaller along the base. You can increase the thickness to compensate for this illusion.

MONITORS (COMPUTER AND TV)—Monitors should be at a comfortable viewing angle while seated at the computer. A TV viewed from an easy chair will be lower than one viewed while reclining on the bed.

LOUVERS—Louvers used for airflow or decor need to be angled and spaced to prevent peering through at the normal viewing angles. Where the louver panel is viewed from well above or well below, design so the set angle is oriented properly. Where viewed straight on, the louver rails will need to be broader to the face and spaced more closely to fill the opening.

MODESTY PANELS—Not a normal consideration for a home desk, a modesty panel may be needed for a reception area, a workstation or included as a structural or aesthetic element of your design.

Furniture Proportions

The task would be simple if we could state: "If a desk is x wide, its height and depth should be ⅔ of x," but rule of thumb may not apply to what you envision. However, there are some general guidelines that might put you in the ballpark.

Webster says: "Proportion is the relation of one part to another or to the whole with respect to magnitude, quantity or degree: ratio. Harmonious relation of parts to each other or to the whole: balance, symmetry. A statement of equality between two ratios in which the first of the four terms divided by the second equals the third divided by the fourth (as in 4/2 = 10/5): size, dimension.

"Ratio is the indicated quotient (the number resulting from the division of one number by another) of two mathematical expressions. The relationship in quantity, amount or size between two or more things: Proportion." These terms are sometimes used interchangeably, and apply to the whole as well as to the parts of a design.

Proportions of Basic Furniture Shells

Figure 3-6 contains blocks of whole-number (integer) values that have been applied to height-to-width-to-depth. A ratio of 1:1:1 (a cube) could be considered as the starting proportions for a chair base, stool, grouped tables, lamp table or bedside table.

To arrive at the three dimensions, the dimension assigned as the target height, width or depth is multiplied by the remaining ratio values to begin blocking in the form. For example, a carcass with proportions of 2:3:1 forms a shallow horizontal shell that could be a bookshelf, the upper shell of a Welsh dresser or a wall-mounted display cabinet in these proportions. If the depth (ratio of 1) is equal to 11″, the height (ratio of 2) would be 22″ and the width (ratio of 3) would equal 33″. The same shell with the same dimensions but oriented vertically would be expressed as 3:2:1 (H:W:D).

Where a ratio of 1 is not one of the factors in the proportion, reduce the value assigned to the guiding measurement to a factor of 1. A shell of 2:4:3 may be a table to be built to a height of 30″. The height (ratio of 2) would be assigned the value of 30″. To reduce that ratio to 1, take half the height, yielding 15″. Then the width and depth ratios (4 and 3, respectively) are multiplied by 15, resulting in a width of 60″ (15×4) and a depth of 45″ (15×3). Another way to express this is: 30 is to 2, as W is to 4 and D is to 3. If a large desk is planned, you might use a ratio of 2:5:3 (30″×75″×45″) to begin your design.

A selected set of shell proportions is an opportunity to expand a known or desired dimension to the remaining two dimensions. These are still preliminary figures in the iterative process on the way to developing your design. Use these hypothetical carcass proportions as a launching pad if you find yourself staring at a blank sheet of paper wondering where to begin.

FIGURE 3-6
Proportions of Basic Furniture Shells

H:W:D

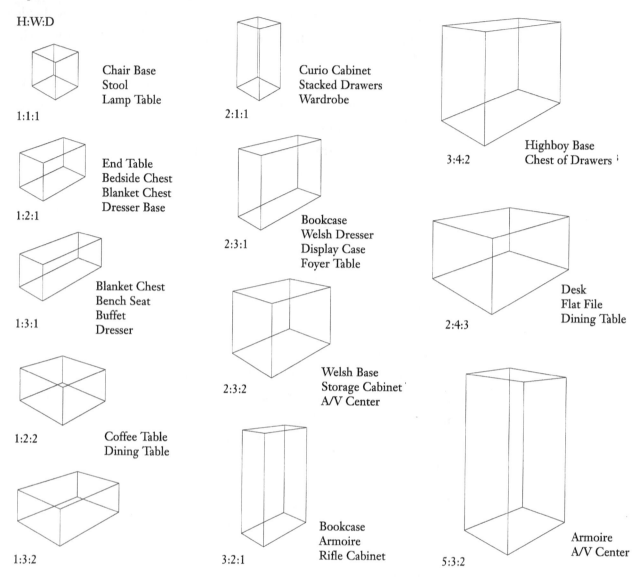

Chair Base
Stool
Lamp Table
1:1:1

Curio Cabinet
Stacked Drawers
Wardrobe
2:1:1

Highboy Base
Chest of Drawers ˀ
3:4:2

End Table
Bedside Chest
Blanket Chest
Dresser Base
1:2:1

Bookcase
Welsh Dresser
Display Case
Foyer Table
2:3:1

Blanket Chest
Bench Seat
Buffet
Dresser
1:3:1

Welsh Base
Storage Cabinet ˀ
A/V Center
2:3:2

Desk
Flat File
Dining Table
2:4:3

Coffee Table
Dining Table
1:2:2

Bookcase
Armoire
Rifle Cabinet
3:2:1

Armoire
A/V Center
5:3:2

1:3:2

There is nothing magic about the ratios or rules—they are guidelines.

Some standard proportions, however, are associated with certain types of furniture, based on contents, style, function and location. A bookcase, for example, needs to enclose tiers of shelves, which are thick enough, deep enough and spaced wide enough apart to support, hold and display the sizes and number of books in your library. An upper cabinet of a Welsh dresser should have enough height, width and depth to present the Wedgewood china, and its base should be both visually and structurally capable of supporting the upper china cabinet. Figure 3-7 shows how these shells might be visualized, either singly or in combination, to further define your design concept. You can even cut a quick three-dimensional paper model of the shape, as shown in figure 3-8.

Furniture Size

Make a bold statement. A rectangle should be recognizable and visually pleasing. If the width is too similar to the height—even though it is, by

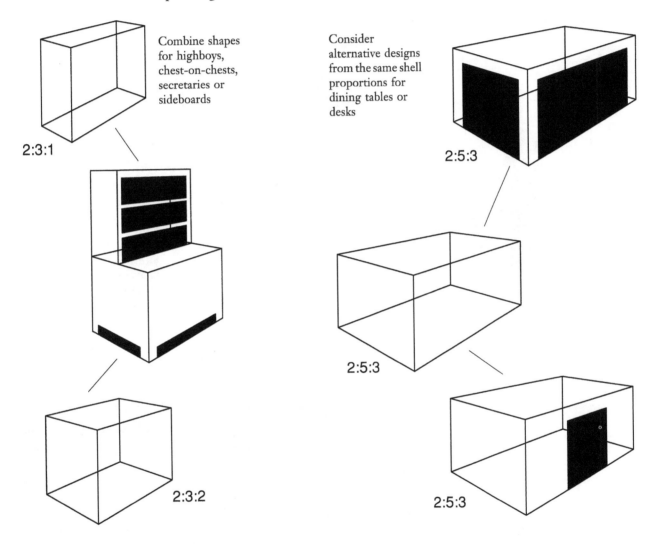

Combine shapes for highboys, chest-on-chests, secretaries or sideboards

2:3:1

Consider alternative designs from the same shell proportions for dining tables or desks

2:5:3

2:5:3

2:3:2

2:5:3

FIGURE 3-7
Blocking Out Faces

definition, a rectangle—it might appear that you missed the mark in designing a cube. But don't go too far the other way. An exaggerated length, too long for the width and height, could produce a nice sarcophagus or slop trough, even though you were targeting for a cedar blanket chest.

FIGURE 3-8
Visualize Through Modeling

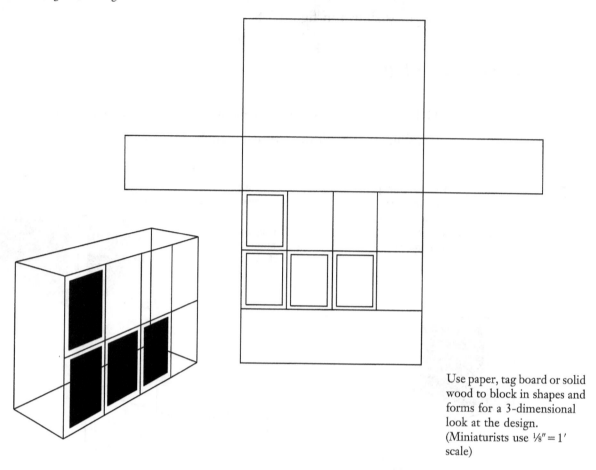

Use paper, tag board or solid wood to block in shapes and forms for a 3-dimensional look at the design. (Miniaturists use $\frac{1}{8}'' = 1'$ scale)

Whatever shell proportions you adopt, they must be translated into suitable physical dimensions.

Height and vertical relationships within that height are probably the most critical dimensions in functional furniture, especially chairs, desks and work surfaces, but these dimensions are also important relative to adjacent furnishings and environs.

Work surface heights—desks, secretaries, drafting tables, sewing centers, potter's benches—should be designed within the natural, comfortable ranges of the human form for the writer, seamstress, illustrator or potter.

When building a case with a retractable work surface (as a pullout work table, keyboard tray or layout/cutout table), the working height for the intended activity is the critical dimension.

Width considerations include (1) providing a large enough work area for the intended task (or derriere when designing a chair), (2) fitting within the available space and (3) using a pleasing proportion to height and depth.

Here, use the golden rectangle method (described a little later), or whatever works and looks best to your mind's eye.

Depth is aesthetically important to visual proportions and ergonomically important to staying within the limits of motion of a seated or standing figure. Depth should also provide an adequate footprint, both structurally and visually, to support the design height and width for the piece alone and any element it is designed to support, such as an upper cabinet or shell or seated body.

In reproportioning any or all of the suggested ratios, be sure this doesn't place the size of your design beyond a range of practicality. You need to provide an adequate work area, not too small to do the job and not so large the user can't reach a shelf or tool along the back.

The same approach can be used to resize the vertical sides, but again preserve the critical height while maintaining the relational width and depth.

You can proportion surfaces mathematically as well. If dimension A is reduced to x, then B (being in the same scale as A) will be proportional when you apply x, the percentage of reduction.

For example, a source drawing of a desktop measuring $32'' \times 48''$, when reduced by 25 percent will be $24'' \times 36''$ (multiplying each dimension by .25 and then subtracting that from the original dimension). If you want the length to be $40''$, 48:40 is a reduction of 16.67 percent, so the $32''$ side reduced by 16.67 percent becomes 26.667 (or 26 5/8 for woodworking purposes). This can also be expressed as:

$$\frac{48}{40} = \frac{32}{x}$$

$$48x = 40 \times 32$$
$$48x = 1280$$
$$x = 26.667$$

Apply the Golden Section Proportions

Architects, artists and custom furniture designers use the golden section as a general guide for drawing, as well as designing environs for people. It is of particular interest to the custom furniture maker, as it can be used to size interior spaces and furniture to human proportions.

While the golden section was developed to define man-made structures, natural forms occur in the spiraling chambers of a nautilus, a snail or a sunflower head. Its origin dates back to early structures, such as the Parthenon, designed on this principle. These eye-pleasing ratios have been defined and used by master painters and architects, and employed when designing smaller structures such as furniture.

FIGURE 3-9

Golden Section and Golden Rectangle

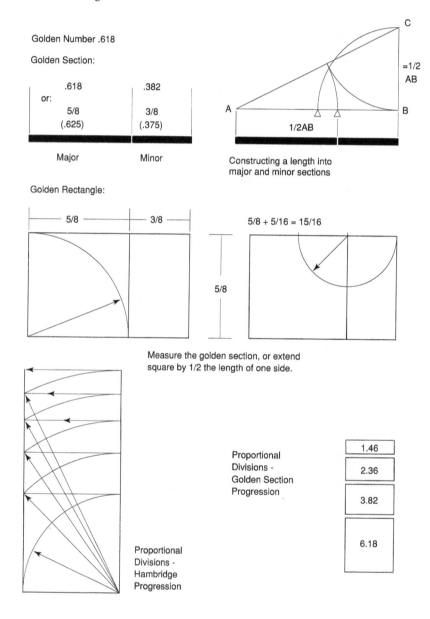

The golden section is a line segment divided into a larger and a smaller section, so that the ratio of the short section to the long section is the same as the long section is to the whole. The golden number is 0.618. (0.618 is to 1 as 0.382 is to 0.618). To simplify matters, architects and almost everyone else have adopted a ⅝:⅜ ratio (0.625:0.375) to represent the golden section. Close enough.

Division of the human form into the golden section (see figure 3-2) was derived from early applications in Greek and Roman architecture. Leonardo da Vinci in the fifteenth century and Le Corbusier in more recent times applied these divisions in their studies of the human form. These same ratios are critical in furniture design.

When the human form is divided into the golden section, the major segment (⅝) is located from the feet to the navel. (From the feet to the crotch is about half the total height.) The minor segment (⅜) extends from the navel to the top of the head. Within the major and minor segments, the neck and the knees are located ⅝ of the way above and below the navel forming yet another set of golden sections.

As shown in figure 3-9, you can apply the golden section to a line segment either by measuring off the ratio values or by constructing the golden section geometrically. (See "Constructing the Golden Section Geometrically" for the step-by-step geometric process.)

A golden rectangle (see figure 3-9) adds a second dimension to the form. The height (when talking furniture) of a rectangle equals the length of the major ⅝ section of the width. This forms a square before the shorter ⅜ section is tacked on the width. A quicker ratio of pleasing proportions is to add a minor section half the width of the major section to the adjacent square to form the long side of the rectangle. In this approach, using the ⅝″ square shown in figure 3-9, one half that distance tagged on to the length would result in the addition of ⁵⁄₁₆″, or a total length of ¹⁵⁄₁₆″. The sum ¹⁵⁄₁₆ is not quite 1, but it's close enough to qualify as a (tarnished) golden rectangle.

If you have a target height, say 27″, you can begin with that as a given. We then know the height, or short sides, of the rectangle, and we know that it is equal to the major segment of the long side. Still with me? We can calculate the width (the long side) of the golden rectangle.

If the height is 27″, the major section of the width must be 27″. This means that the 27″ segment is ⅝ of the width. If 27″ = ⅝ width, then

$$\text{width} \quad = \quad \frac{27}{⅝} \quad = \quad \frac{27}{0.625} \quad = \quad 43.2.$$

CONSTRUCTING THE GOLDEN SECTION GEOMETRICALLY

STEP 1:
Draw line segment AB.

STEP 2:
Determine the midpoint (m) of AB. Open a compass to slightly more than half of segment AB and draw arcs above and below AB from both points A and B. Connect the intersections of the arcs above and below AB. The midpoint (m) is where the line crosses AB.

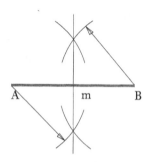

STEP 3A:
Construct a perpendicular line segment. Extend AB beyond B and mark two points the same distance from point B with a compass.

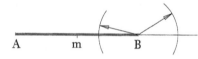

STEP 3B:
Next, open the compass wider than half the distance from B to the arcs drawn in step 3a, and draw an arc from both sides of B, crossing above B. Draw a line through the intersecting arcs down to B.

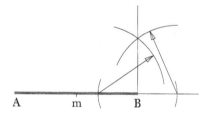

STEP 3C:
Then, open the compass to the length of mB and draw an arc across the vertical line segment from B; this will be point C.

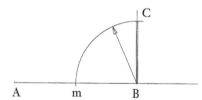

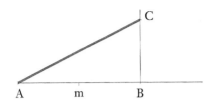

STEP 4:
Draw the hypotenuse. Connect points A and C. This (AC) is the hypotenuse of the triangle.

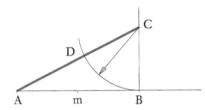

STEP 5:
Divide the hypotenuse. From C, drawn an arc across the hypotenuse with a radius equal to the length of BC.

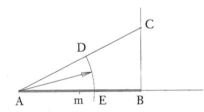

STEP 6:
Mark the major and minor sections. Open the compass to the length from point A to the new point (D) on AC, and draw another arc across AB from point A. This is point (E) that marks the major (AE) and minor (EB) sections of AB.

Use whichever dimension you deem critical to your design to determine the other ratio values.

The Golden Carcass

If there were such a thing as a golden carcass, it would take into account the third dimension to form a shell. Its dimensions might be 24″ high and deep (length of the larger segment) and 38″ wide.

We know the golden section divides a line segment into ⅝ and ⅜ section lengths, and the golden rectangle adds the ⅝ section length as the height of the form.

For a golden carcass consider any logical combination that fits your design. Maintain a balance of the most functional and most pleasing proportions for your project. Apply these segment lengths however you please. For example, the depth of the shell could be equal to the height of rectangle

FIGURE 3-10
Golden Carcass

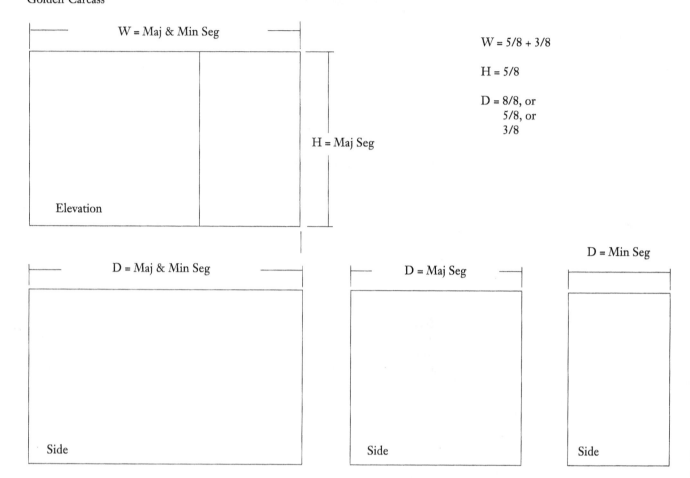

W = 5/8 + 3/8

H = 5/8

D = 8/8, or
    5/8, or
    3/8

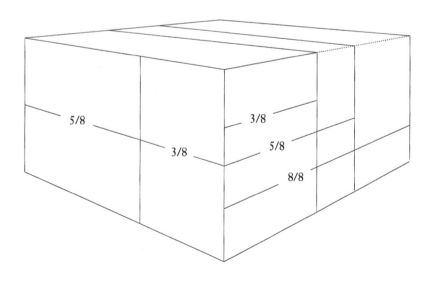

(h = 0.625, w = 1.0, d = 0.625) or the length of minor section (h = 0.625, w = 1.0, d = 0.375).

If the calculated depth is different than desired, experiment with subsections of the major or minor values. For example, a depth of 0.375 the length could be reduced or enlarged by another golden section factor that will net pleasing and functional proportions.

There is magic in the golden section. It works both mathematically and visually, but too much of a good thing can soon become monotonous. Don't hesitate to mix things up a bit.

But whatever shape you design, make an unmistakable statement in the form you present.

Dividing Areas Within a Frame

If the shell face surrounds shapes of equal size, divide the area into as many spaces (doors, drawers) as you want. Just how these and other examples translate to the real world of fit are described in chapter four. But if your project will involve some pattern of proportionally changing divisions, here are a few approaches you might consider.

PROGRESSION—INCREASING OR DECREASING

Suppose you want progressively smaller heights for a set of drawers. You can use the golden number, 0.618, to calculate these heights into golden sections (see figure 3-9). Multiply the largest height by 0.618 to get the next smaller height. Multiply this new height by 0.618 to get the next one, and so on.

So, if your first height is 10″, the next will be 6.18″, then 3.82″, 2.36″, etc. This method reduces heights fairly rapidly, and you soon reach an impractical segment for a drawer.

THE HAMBRIDGE PROGRESSION

Also shown in figure 3-9 is the Hambridge Progression, which can be used to expand a rectangle into a stack of diminishing proportions of drawers, doors or shelves. The diagram shows how divisions can be drafted.

The Hambridge Progression produces a pleasing reduction in height, which can be applied to designing drawers or shelves for a chest or display cabinet. You could consider the initial square as a lower cupboard, or

BUILDING THE HAMBRIDGE PROGRESSION

STEP 1:
Draw a square which is the width of the shell you are building.

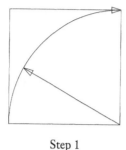

Step 1

STEP 2:
Draw vertical lines extending the sides of the square.

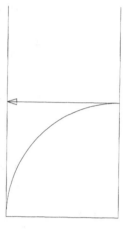

Step 2

STEP 3:
Draw diagonal AB.

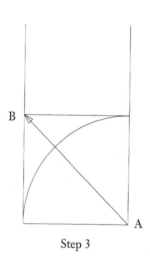

Step 3

STEP 4:
Opening a compass from A to a radius equal to diagonal AB, draw an arc connecting B to the vertical from point A.

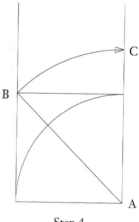

Step 4

eliminate the first division from your plans and begin the tiers using the second and subsequent rectangles.

There are other arithmetical and geometric progressions that all seem to come back to the golden section. The Hambridge approach is superior in that it includes a relationship of heights based on the width of the carcass, so the vertical spacing changes with a change in shell width.

FIBONACCI SEQUENCE

According to the *Encyclopedia Britannica*, Leonardo of Pisa, or Leonardo Fibonacci, was the son of a Pisan merchant. As a youth, he was sent to

STEP 5:
Draw the new side. From the new point (c), draw a perpendicular line to the vertical from point B to form point D.

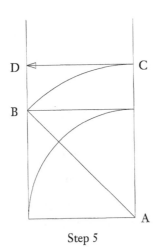

Step 5

STEP 6:
Draw Diagonal AD.

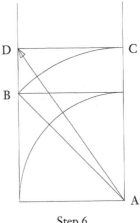

Step 6

STEP 7:
Opening a compass from A to a radius equal to the diagonal AD, draw an arc from D to the vertical from A.

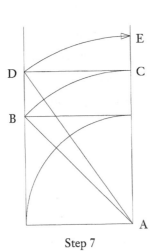

Step 7

STEP 8:
From the new point (E), draw another perpendicular to the opposite side. Continue drawing diagonals from A and drawing arcs with the new radius to form the new side for each progression, as is shown in figure 3-9 (page 96).

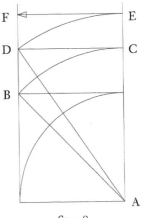

Step 8

different parts of the Old World to study mathematics. His works, published in 1200, set the tone for the Arabic numbers we use today. He also theorized on proportions, and developed a problem for one of his books relating to rabbits: how many to start with, how many after one year. He was right. The world is now knee-deep in rabbits.

The Fibonacci sequence deduced from that solution includes a rise in value based on the sum of the two preceding values, or:

1, 1, 2, 3, 5, 8, 13, 21, 34, 55, . . .

Fibonacci was a visionary, able to prove his theories by using deduction and logic; later those theories were tested and proven more rigorously as the science of mathematics became more complex. Fibonacci numbers are used today in technical analysis of the stock market. His rules of ratios and progressions can also apply to furniture design. Within a practical range, progressions using the Fibonacci sequence might be 8, 5, 3 and 2 when dividing an area progressively within 18″.

Progressions Within a Fixed Height

You can use other approaches to determine satisfactory progressions. Knowing two or more values, you can calculate the unknowns, such as the first division height, the last division height or the number of divisions.

What you are working with here is a set of parameters for drawer-height progression within a known distance. These are:

- First division (F) = height of first drawer
- Last division (L) = height of last drawer
- Number of divisions (N) = number of drawers
- Common difference (D) = amount added or subtracted from each
- Sum of divisions (S) = aggregate height

You can start with any value, select a common difference and see how it looks on paper. For example, if for five divisions, the first drawer is 6″ and the common difference is 1″, the progression would be 6″, 5″, 4″, 3″, 2″, for a total height of 20″. If the first drawer is still 6″, but the common difference is changed to 0.75″, the progression would be 6″, 5.25″, 4.5″, 3.75″, 3″, for a total height of 22.5″. The sum of the progression values dictates the shell height you need.

My trusty *Machinery's Handbook* tells us how to calculate progressions within a predefined shell size, as opposed to adding the values in the example above and building the shell to suit.

Say we want four drawers of a decreasing progression within an opening of 24″, and we want the top drawer to be 3″. We know F = 3, N = 4 and S = 24. We can solve for the last division height.

To find L, the last drawer height, when given F, N and S:

$$L = \frac{2S}{N} = -F = \frac{48}{4} - 3 = 9.$$

To find D, the common difference, when we now know that L = 9:

$$D = \frac{L-F}{N-1} = \frac{9-3}{4-1} = \frac{6}{3} = 2.$$

Now we know:

F = 3	First drawer
L = 9	Last drawer
N = 4	Number of drawers
D = 2	Common difference per drawer
S = 24	Sum of distance filled

or 3 (First) + 5 + 7 + 9 (Last) = 24.

That was too easy, resulting in a progression you might logically assign without working within a specific height. Here is a second example, a bit more obscure and using another set of "givens."

Suppose we have a shell opening of 31½" (S = 31.5), with a lower cupboard of 12" (F = 12), and we want the top drawer to be 4" (L = 4). We want to find D, the common difference.

$$D = \frac{L^2 - F^2}{2S - L - F} = \frac{4^2 - 12^2}{2 \times 31.5 - 12 - 4} = \frac{16 - 144}{47} = 2.723.$$

The progression is 12, −D (common difference of 2.723) = 9.277, −D = 6.554, −D = 3.831, = a lower cabinet plus three drawers within 31.7". As a woodworker, you'll round off these values to 12", 9¼", 6½" and 3¹³⁄₁₆" for a total height of 31.5625". The extra 0.0625" can be taken from the first division or distributed among them.

The various methods described above produce different mathematical results, but the idea—and the message—is to produce a pleasing progression.

Component Proportions

If x is to y, then z is to. . . . There should be a catchall formula for designing the case, the frame, the legs, the moldings and so forth. Much of this, however, is left to the designer to determine the most pleasing size for each component and to compare those components to the whole.

We have spent paragraphs describing the shell, its proportions and its divisions, but it is your call to describe what fits best with the look you want, the style you have chosen and the proportions, mass and all of the other design decisions. Look at past interpretations similar to your design. Conduct the Three Ws test: *Why* is it that specific shape? *Where* (and for what reasons) did the design originate? *What* can I do to improve on it— to tailor it to my design, to imprint my style on it?

Learn from the past but apply that knowledge to your custom design. Certain furniture components are individually unique, such as the unadorned simplicity of the Shaker style or the sharp-edged Mission style, or the ornate sweep of Queen Anne cabriole legs. Most other components are combinations of common shapes and detailing.

Furniture Components

MOLDING

Moldings are usually used as a transition between parts from one plane or thickness to another, and may be decorative only or structural and decorative. In furniture, waist molding can be used to cover the joint of a two-piece cabinet, while top and base molding obviously can finish off the top and base horizontally or may be positioned vertically as corner or face molding, maybe terminating at rosette corner blocks.

Different passes in the sticking process produce varied cross sections which may include ogee, reverse ogee, fillets and the simpler quarter-round, veining edge.

Some of the more traditional sticking profiles may not suit your contemporary design, but the illustration on page 108 serves to show the basic cutter designs available for your router or shaper setup. Some of these profiles are suitable to detail the edge of a table, to reed or vein a leg or to round over corners.

Any frame-and-panel work you plan will employ some combination of these sample shapes, and a period piece might require the waist moldings and covings to serve as a cover or a transition between shapes.

Carved molding can be very ornate, including the egg-and-dart, the enriched talon or any number of bead-and-reel, pearl or symmetrical patterns turned on a lathe. Forming a helical pattern in lathe work results in the rope, the cable or the twining stem. Routed or saw-cut molding produces patterns such as the key.

Furniture Components

PROFILE	SURFACE	SHANK	HEAD	FOOT	EDGES
Legs Square					
Straight	Smooth	Square	Square	Run-out	Break
Tapered	Smooth	Taper all	Square	Run-out	Break
	Smooth	Taper inside	Square	Run-out	Break
Other Options	Fluted	Fluted	Veining	Spade	Chamfer Bead
Legs— Round					
Cylinder	Smooth	Round	Square	Run-out	Square Head
Tapered	Smooth	Tapered	Square	Run-out	
Double Taper	Smooth	Double Taper	Run-out	Run-out	
Spindle	Smooth	Spindle	Square	Square	
Other Options	Faceted	Ocatgon	Square	Spade	Break
	Spiral	Helix		Ball	
Aprons					
Straight	Smooth				Sharp
Contoured	Smooth				Break
Scalloped	Smooth				Beaded Quarter-round
Other Options					Bull-nosed
Profile	Surface	Shank	Head	Foot	Edges
Rails					
Flat	Smooth			Tenon	Break
Contoured	Smooth				
Cylinder	Smooth			Dowel	
Tapered	Smooth			Dowel	
Spindle	Smooth			Dowel	
Posts					
Faceted	Straight				
Cylinder	Straight	Smooth Fluted Spiral			
Tapered	Smooth				

FIGURE 3-11
Moldings and Coving Profiles

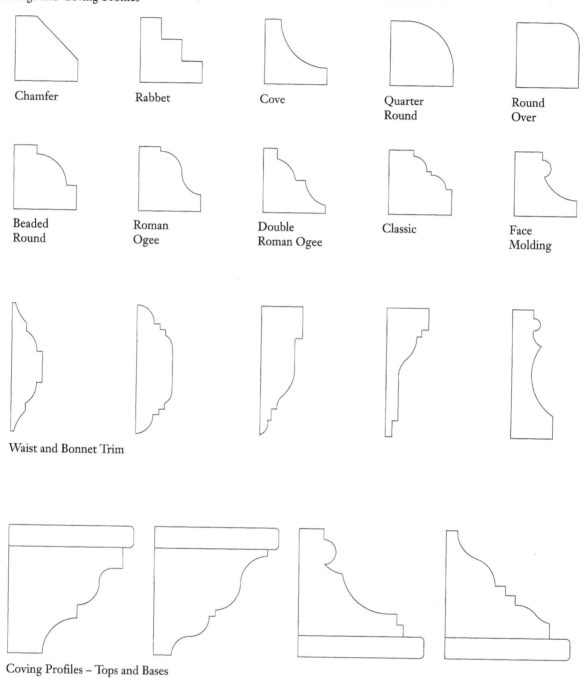

Chamfer   Rabbet   Cove   Quarter Round   Round Over

Beaded Round   Roman Ogee   Double Roman Ogee   Classic   Face Molding

Waist and Bonnet Trim

Coving Profiles – Tops and Bases

FRETWORK

Period furniture may be known for its pierced-splat chair back. Even contemporary furniture may need some open fretwork which is usually executed in thin material to maintain a pleasing proportion of the depth to the face. Fretwork is also the forerunner to inlays and marquetry.

FRAMES AND PANELS

In the dictionary of frames and panels, the perimeter of each unit is the frame, the horizontal divisions are known as rails and the vertical members are stiles. Panels are panels in either orientation. The stiles at the center opening are neither stiles nor frames, but mullions.

Look at the face view of the parts (frames, panels) and their relationship to one another and to the case. The pieces comprising a paneled door can be visualized as shown in figure 3-12. Play with the combinations of widths and heights. Horizontally, assign dimensions or relational values to the surrounding case or shell, the doorframe, preliminary panel width, a stile, another panel and the mullion. Vertically, envision the target panel height and sketch the shell, frame, rail, panel, rail, panel and frame.

From a layout such as this you can get a good idea of the look you want, while quantifying the panel width and height, rail and stile widths and spacing.

You can continue this exercise by deciding what complementing edge routing or applied molding will surround the panels (and be designed to capture the panel to the frame). Sketch in any raised panel treatment you want to apply to the design.

CASES

Shells made from ¾″ wood can be made to look a bit heftier by applying a facing or wide molding around the perimeter. An extremely tall or large shell with only ¾″ thickness on the face would need very delicate lines of whatever is planned for the face to complement the thin case. The larger the piece, the heftier the frame should be.

Design Symmetry

Details selected for any of the parts listed above fall into some pattern of design rhythm.

REPETITION—Repeating a pattern or a shape, either a positive or a negative, usually results in some form of symmetry. Repetitive shapes include repeating sizes.

MIRRORING—Opposing shapes repeat the left to right sides in proper proportions and diminishing patterns. Mirrored or balanced shapes need to be on par with one another.

FIGURE 3-12
Frame-to-Panel
Proportions

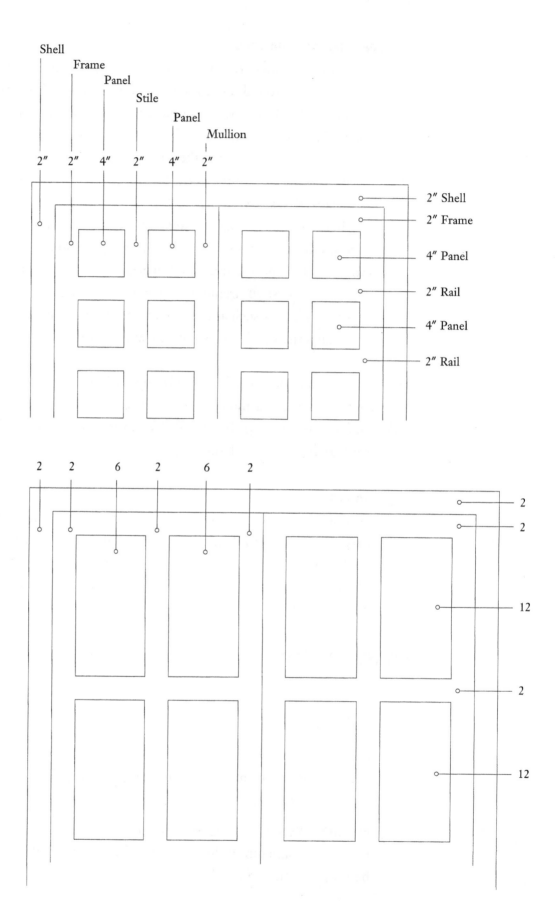

FRAMING—Anything within a frame belongs (or should belong), so the frame itself is symmetrical and adds order to the design in the limits it defines and the component shapes it surrounds.

Sizes by Adjacent Location

Another judgment call is comparing the specific size of a part to the whole, and to the other parts. Think of why the part is included and the function it provides.

ADJACENT—Contiguous components vie for attention. If one component is tiny, it becomes insignificant to the whole. It can stay small as a design element with some sort of demarcation, maybe standing proud, inset, with beveled edges, or something to show it is meant to stand on its own. Otherwise, shape-to-shape relationships might need to have more equality in the face width presented to the viewer. A small delineation separating two parts is known as a *quirk*. A quirk can be a narrow groove, fillet or channel that delineates a change and adds a design element to highlight an interesting component shape or treatment.

Maybe leaving these interior proportions or relationships a "judgment call" is the easy way out and shouldn't be left hanging. There are a few guidelines that might become a "standard" to follow or modify to suit your project. And therein lies the dilemma of specifying: If the top is 1″, the widest leg thickness should be 2″ and the apron, 3″. This may fit a normal approach, but your project may not be "normal." Play around with these proportions. Draw or cut patterns of candidate sizes from cardboard, and arrange and rearrange to compare the alternatives. You'll know when a piece is too slim or too massive for the design and will design accordingly.

To select optimum width and depth of the shell, begin with the proportions based on its target height. If you apply the golden rectangle to the proportions shown in the front view of the table, you could use the proportions of the golden shell, where the depth is equal to the height of the rectangle (which is also the major segment of the golden section). This is shown in figure 3-13 as a Worktable/Desk.

However, if you are designing an entryway or foyer table, this would be far too deep for the piece, so use the minor section as the designed depth, or go even shallower if the space and the design permit. When designing a round or square table, use the total section for the depth.

FIGURE 3-13
Planning Design Elements

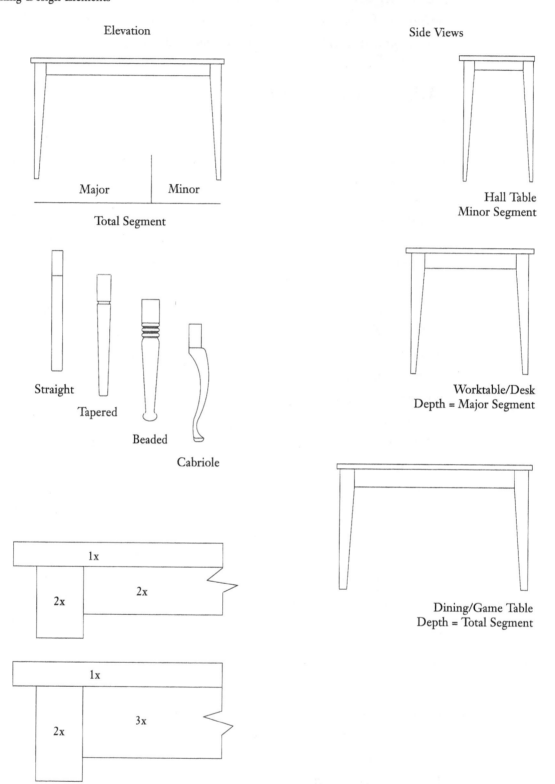

Elevation

Major | Minor

Total Segment

Straight

Tapered

Beaded

Cabriole

1x

2x

2x

1x

2x

3x

Side Views

Hall Table
Minor Segment

Worktable/Desk
Depth = Major Segment

Dining/Game Table
Depth = Total Segment

If the piece is long and narrow, the legs and any aprons and stretchers should be on the scant side. Look at the narrow-end view to establish the pleasing thicknesses of the pieces. Transfer this over to the elevation view to determine whether the chosen thicknesses may be too scant for the expanse. If they could be beefed up a bit, compromise on a thickness that complements both views. Where the design includes other elements, such as a drawer in a hall table, the drawer facing height may dictate the apron thickness. The side view might continue this dimension around. If the look is too heavy on the end view, consider undercutting the apron with an arc or some other treatment to lighten the look of the apron, but only if it goes with the piece.

The worktable designed to the proportions of the golden shell will be larger and heavier in mass, and can be outfitted with slightly thicker legs and apron.

The square (or round) tabletop design can, but not necessarily must, accommodate larger components. Part of the design exercise is to determine the clearances required for comfortable dining or game playing before arbitrarily assigning a dimension to the apron. The tabletop thickness can be upscaled proportionally as well, but unless the success of your design depends on a heavy slab top, stay with standard milled-lumber thicknesses for economy of materials and ease of fabrication. A wider piece of trim or molding along the apron could be added around the periphery to give a heftier look.

Casework has been described in detail elsewhere, so it won't be repeated here. But the same relational sizes apply to the overall mass and the sizes of the components encased by the shell.

Regarding leg design, an inside taper is the leg style shown in figure 3-13, but any other type chosen should follow the same thickness adjustments. These tapered legs could be four-square or turned on a wood lathe. Another option is to round the legs with six or eight facets—again only if this detail would be compatible with the design.

Bridging Shapes—Transitions

Along any plane, consider how the pieces making up the run will come together—tangential, butt, inset or flush. Consider both the elevation and quarter views, envisioning offsets, when planning how one piece goes into another.

In turnings—design definition includes proportion and transition—lathe work is like carving. Think round, think tapered, think flat, and design accordingly. A flare that has no relationship with any other form on the turning may not belong. Design them as crisp shapes, with natural and clean transitions to the next, preserving an adequate average thickness to meet the assigned task.

In your turnings, all diameters should be contained within an overall envelope. Envision a straight cylinder or tapered cylinder, and no part should extend beyond that theoretical envelope. There are exceptions, such as cabriole legs or custom design features, but a huge ball at the end of a tapered turning can spell a design disaster. Shanks should be substantial enough to support vertical loads (weight). Feet of the turned spindle should look capable of supporting the weight without appearing to pierce or penetrate the floor.

While some examples in figure 3-14 are round turnings, think two-dimensionally for purposes of this discussion. Spindles or balusters exhibit a profile designed to be pleasing. Their spacing also forms a profile of negative shapes. In small railings, maybe for a bookshelf atop a desk, consider the profile of both the positive form and the area in between a row of spindles. These would normally be spaced farther apart than shown, and as the spread increases, perception of the defined space between spindles becomes less obvious.

Any repetitive pattern that is to be carved, applied or decoratively painted should begin with geometric shapes. Scallops (if they are in your future) should be patterned from full circles drawn along the cut line. These can be connecting circles or spread out, but still begin with aligned, evenly spaced circles.

When connecting arc segments with adjacent circles, be sure to keep all connecting arcs tangent to the adjoining form. Tangent arcs touch lightly, and flow smoothly and naturally through the same point of the two arc segments being connected.

If you want to abruptly terminate an arc by squaring off a run-out, maybe for a broken pediment or at the apron-to-leg juncture, your layout should extend the arc or curve beyond the location of the cutoff so the curve flows naturally all the way to its terminating point.

If a skirt or apron is contoured, make it symmetrical about a decorative center design or around an undelineated centerline. Any carved or painted embellishment should flow with the lines of the cut contour and remain

FIGURE 3-14
Symmetry and Transitions

Consider both positive and
negative space where shapes
are repeated

Form serpentine about
adjacent circles

Wave form patterns are
tangent to arc segments

Aprons and skirts are
symmetrical within envelope

Carvings, inlays and painted
motifs stay inside defined
margins

FIGURE 3-15
Sample Turnings

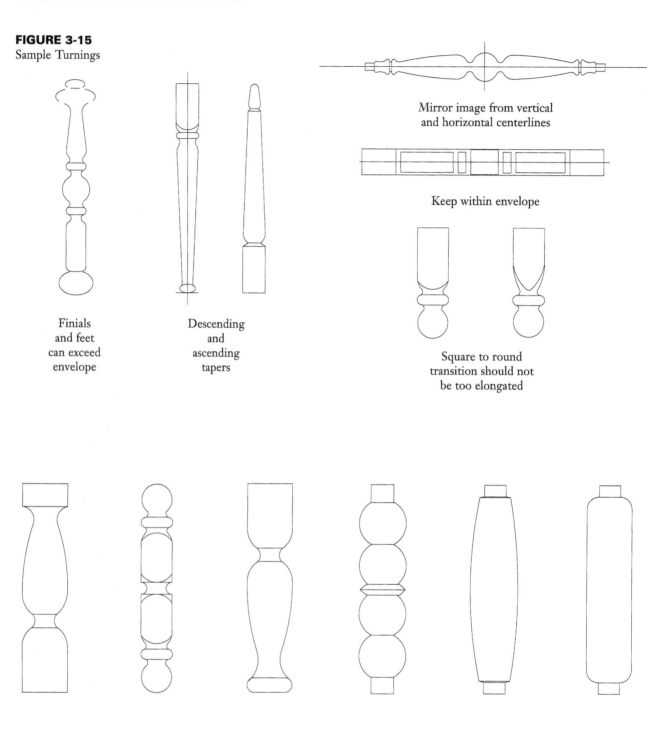

Finials
and feet
can exceed
envelope

Descending
and
ascending
tapers

Mirror image from vertical
and horizontal centerlines

Keep within envelope

Square to round
transition should not
be too elongated

within the confines of an imaginary border conforming to the cut contour.

Lathe work not only bridges shapes in the two-dimensional plane, but obviously in the third dimension as well. Since most turnings are symmetrical, they take on the third dimension when viewed off-center, sighting along the form. Your turned shapes and transitions between those shapes take on varying forms with each viewing angle.

There are a few turning truisms to keep in mind when carving away anything that isn't the blanket rail you are turning:

1. Spindles should be symmetrical and reversible, that is, a mirror image on each side from the centerlines.

2. No shape should extend beyond an envelope (your turning blank) within the length of the turning, except . . .

3. A mushroom cap or a finial can be wider in some designs, or a bun or ball foot could be oversize, piercing this envelope.

4. Turned leg shapes can fill parallel sides, or fill an envelope tapering from top to bottom in descending diameters, but should visually define a shape that comprises the turned pattern.

5. Spindles, balusters and bedposts may be within a parallel envelope or tapered toward the top, again making an overall form.

6. The transition from square to round elements of a turned post forms an interesting arc on the flat of the square being cut. This is soon exaggerated to produce a severe shape that may be unlike any other profile of the turning. Design the cuts to net pleasing shapes that exhibit a sense of belonging, in the same family, and on the same turning.

7. Decorative turnings are usually structural members as well, so transitions between shapes should not be severely undercut to the point the piece is, or even appears to be, incapable of supporting its weight.

There are a few classic shapes that can be taken from our predecessors, and some should be followed to the letter when making a replica of turned furniture.

If there is a single ball or a series of round beads, we can elongate the ball into an egg, a tulip, a vase, an onion dome as a finial, an elongated bead, a flattened bead, a bun, a bell or a mushroom, or go back to a square or rectangle.

Transitions between shapes are as important to the design as the shapes themselves. Beads can be lathe-turned to a common diameter between the equidistantly spaced beads, or a V-groove cut (parting tool or skew) is good when delineating this design series, as well as most other adjoining shapes. A U-groove (round-tip or gouge) will form a more gradual transition between dissimilar shapes, such as going from a tapered vase into a flattened bead, or going from a square leg top into a sphere, into a long tapered leg, and again at the end to form a foot or knob.

Lighting and Texture

Lighting and texture is a study of the effects of lighting on standard frame-and-panel treatments. This applies to whatever furniture you design, for the look will change with a change in lighting conditions. The most dramatic effect occurs between the extreme spot and the softer flood. Daylight hours may provide a natural cycle of lighting reaching the piece of furniture, but your control comes with the type of artificial lighting you elect to use.

Another aspect of lighting to consider, in addition to how the piece itself is lighted, is a task light for the user. The user needs a task-light source opposite their favored hand, or at least centered so the backhanded curl of us lefties doesn't cast a shadow on what we are writing or drawing.

A gooseneck light can be positioned for optimum lighting if it fits the style. A built-in light should be shaded from the user's eyes to prevent direct glare, and a spot- or floodlight shouldn't create a hot spot or bounce off paper or shiny surfaces.

Models, Mock-Ups and Miniatures

If you want to see how your concept looks in three dimensions, or to better visualize how it might fit in with the new surroundings, make a scale model of your design and whatever else you may want to visualize.

If you're unsure how the piece will physically fit or look in place, make a full-size mock-up, or maybe just the part of your design in question.

MODEL-MAKING OBJECTIVES

Do you want to visualize three-dimensionally what you envision in your mind's eye? Miniature furniture is a standard $\frac{1}{8}'' = 1'$ scale, or you can use the size in your assembly drawings, which is acceptable for modeling purposes. Your copy center can enlarge or reduce the drawing to a more convenient scale. Your assembly view can be cut apart from a copy and pasted onto a precut block, or glued to tag board and become an open shell.

Build up in a block-to-block relationship, or work out specifics using a more detailed "real-time" approach to the model to verify the stretcher, the wainscot or whatever addition is planned for the final piece.

The paper mock-up suggested in the proportion discussion may be all that is needed to help visualize your design if the piece is for personal use. When designing a commissioned piece, however, a more complete model

FIGURE 3-16
Relief and Texture

TONES, TEXTURES AND LIGHTING

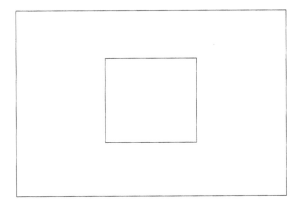

Light shapes blend in with light environs

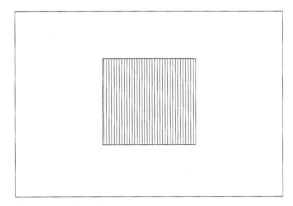

Textures add midrange tones

Dark shapes appear slightly smaller

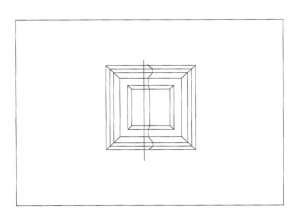

Relief adds tone under floodlight

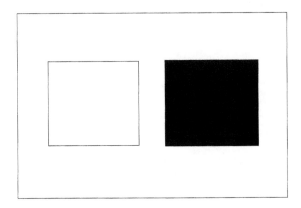

Used together, dark is prominent

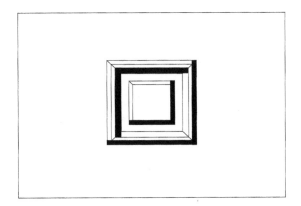

Relief adds shadow under spotlight

FIGURE 3-17
Approaches to Miniatures, Models and Mock-ups

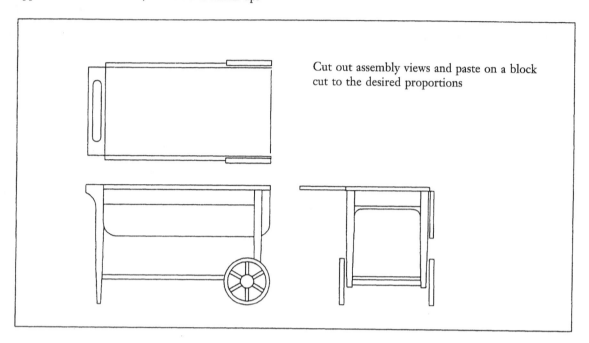

Cut out assembly views and paste on a block
cut to the desired proportions

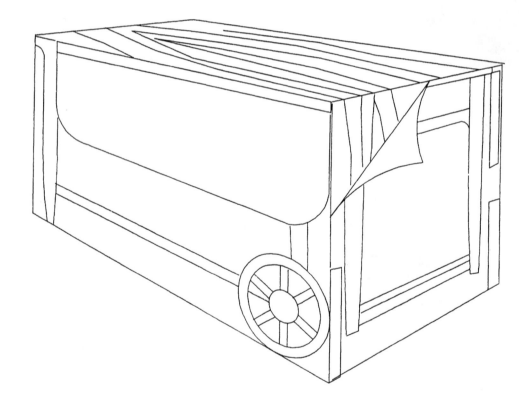

is an excellent visual aid to communicate your concept to the client. The best time to communicate the results of your developing design approach and the product you envision is before launching into a full set of detailed drawings (described in the next chapter). The drawings or sketches that resulted in your being selected for the task may have been interpreted differently, using different assumptions, when based only on vague sketches or verbal description.

An assembly drawing can be used in much the same way the proportion model was made, except here you have more detail, a more complete scaled rendition showing parts and pieces. Cut out and glue a copy of your assembly drawing to a wood block cut in scale and to the proportions of the piece.

There is seldom a need to build a replica in a scaled miniature, but if you do, the accepted scale for miniature furniture is usually $\frac{1}{8}'' = 1'$.

Mock-ups can be helpful for questionable part or piece relationships, or to perhaps block in what you envision in place.

Draw Standards From the Past

The chronology shown in chapter one's Furniture Time Line offered little editorializing on the why and wherefore of past styles, and chapter two, Defining Scope, highlighted the more popular styles in search of their endearing qualities applied to today's furniture. Contained below is a suggested method to take these forerunners and apply them to your furniture project.

What is it you like about furniture style that is pleasing to you? Any of the attributes could apply: simplicity, detail, size, finish, feel or look.

Contemporize

Play around with some concepts here. Instead of traditional spindles of crisply defined shapes, maybe suggest these forms in shallow relief, or treat what was normally a rounded form as a four-, six- or eight-sided cylinder cut on your table or band saw.

Look at the Craftsman style, with four legs square to the floor. What happens if this becomes a rocker, or a sliding swing, or a Giverney-type bench?

Personalize

What is your furniture hallmark? Do you finish edges on the sharp, break them slightly or give them a full bull-nose treatment? Are you into veining, tapering or inlays? Look at the task at hand and put your mark on it.

Standard Construction Methods

Material sizes and physical characteristics are described in more detail in the next two chapters, and chapter two discussed some standard joinery techniques to help define the scope—that is, how complex a project you want to undertake. For purposes of what may be considered "standard" construction, we look at how these may be joined and assembled for the style you're designing.

Construction materials have logical standards. For example, the majority of construction-grade lumber is milled for standard construction: in 8' lengths, or multiples of 8, which is the standard residential joist height for framing. The framer places these studs 16' on center, so the wallboard or paneling, 4' by 8' sheets, will extend from floor to ceiling on the length, and the width will butt, and fasten, centered on every fourth stud. This standard results in economy of materials.

A designer/craftsman, like the framer, keeps standard dimensions in mind when designing furniture. Size of lumber and wood products might vary slightly by mill run, but are generally standard.

Select matching stock—species, color, figuring (grain) and thickness. End grain is a window on the cut of the lumber. It may be flat-sawn or quarter-sawn, each producing different physical properties, such as hardness, grain lift and how well it takes a finish. These properties are described in chapter five.

Summary

In chapter three, you:
- applied dimensions to proportions
- revisited environs for influencing comparable size, shape and form
- integrated functional and aesthetic objectives into an efficient shape and size

- divided that size and shape into its component parts—shell case, drawers, doors, legs, sides, base and top
- assigned component proportions, relationships and transitions between shapes
- planned for efficient and economical use of materials
- considered using a model or mock-up to confirm that your concept will satisfy your design objectives

Regardless of how far you take the concept, whether only in your head or full-blown miniatures to full-size mock-ups, your objective in this phase is to lock in your design concept. In chapter four, this concept can be committed to paper and made ready for your own or someone else's construction.

Committing Plans to Paper

The creative process doesn't end with a clear vision of your concept or a practical look at your capabilities and capacities. The physical properties of the materials and the mechanics of the piece must also be considered when converting your vision to plans.

Some design elements come from conceptualizing, and many of the details come from resourcefulness—a process of refining and developing, defining and redefining to capture a workable concept. Making do with what you have, many times, results in a truly unique design or improvement on the characteristic style that meets all the design objectives described earlier. Innovation is a continuous process that can happen in the shop or in the shower.

Muster this type of detailed planning early, at the drawing board, and lock in the design details before you begin making sawdust. That is not to say changes won't occur later when you wonder "Why did I want it this way?" Working out details can be a conscious exercise, or sometimes your subconscious will mull over some unclear or troublesome aspect of the project for later revelation. But solutions result from concentrating on detail.

Just how much of this detail you formally commit to paper depends on who will be using the drawings. If you are the designer and craftsman, as well as the draftsman, maybe sketches, notes and cryptic memory joggers will suffice. Any builder other than yourself will need more detailed drawings and instructions in order to translate your concept into reality.

In this world there are two types of custom-furniture builders. Those with a kit-making bent will need specific information in the detailed drawings and notes. The opposite type, the ones who work out the details on the fly, should still be given all of the basics and enough detail on paper to ensure lists of stock, part sizes and quantities are complete and accurate.

The preplan/precut types will (and should, if the designer is not the builder) dimension all parts, including tenon dimensions; the latter type may just assume a tenon is required and include the extra lengths in the materials list.

Adapting Published Plans

The easiest approach to building a piece of furniture is to assemble precut parts from a kit. Second easiest is to follow a complete set of plans that have been created, prototype-tested and published for readers of magazines or books, or from mail-order offerings. It is easy to personalize published drawings to suit the tastes and needs of the user. If custom changes are minor, mark up the plans, or you might redraw the more complex parts to work out your changes or figure how to approach the joinery.

If you see what you want to build in a photo or illustration, whether pictured in an advertisement, catalog or book, there are a number of ways to translate a photo or drawing into construction plans. Orthographic drawings presented in three views are easy to follow. If your source is from photographs or perspective drawings, you'll want to find the proportions. Included in this chapter is a discussion on overlaying a perspective grid to determine widths, lengths and heights in what may be a foreshortened projection.

When using source drawings or photos from the historical archives, keep in mind that the stature of the population of yesteryear was somewhat smaller than it is today, so the standard bed of yore was shorter and narrower than we're accustomed to.

Making Orthographic Drawings

Orthographic drawings are representations presented two-dimensionally on a flat plane facing the viewer. These are usually shown in three views: an elevation view (face on), a side view (only one if sides are identical) and a plan or top view.

In conventional drafting practice, the elevation view is usually the key view, with the plan view drawn above and rotated up and toward the viewer. The end view is drawn to the side and on the same baseline as the elevation view. In the side and plan views, the common lines are adjacent, as if the

FIGURE 4-1
Orthographic, Three-
View Plans

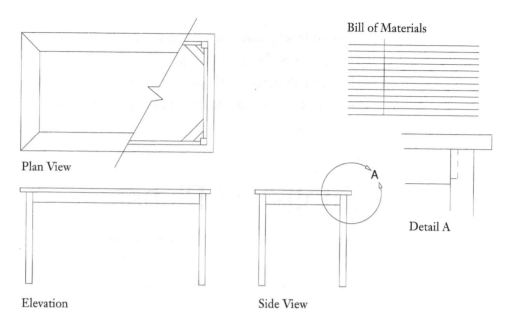

Bill of Materials

Plan View

Detail A

Elevation

Side View

object was rotated along an axis of the nearest common edge.

By drawing these views to a common scale, it is possible to measure part lengths and distances to record the assembly and details of the components. Drawing to scale is a good second check of your shop math as well. Enlarged details of more complex joinery, fits and shapes will clarify design detail, allow the dimensioning of parts used when preparing the materials and cutting list, and guide in the construction.

Personalize a Published Drawing

The thought process here should be to revisit your design philosophy, your decisions on style, space, scale and proportion of the piece, and the amount and type of detailing that fits the style of the piece and your custom signature.

Bring together the results of your conceptual design, your experience and your design philosophy applied during the concept phase. Only now, plan and record every design detail in shop drawings to ensure your objectives are conveyed on paper and met in the shop.

Basic furniture size is fundamental. What you design to fit such an envelope is expression. I guess a Louis XIV dining room set could be the source of proportions and construction methods in modern furniture, but finding plans or photos that come close to what you are designing bypasses the extra efforts of eliminating the more obvious adjustments for style.

Convert Photos, Drawings, Pieces

Whatever the source of your idea, determine what you especially like about the piece and why you want to design and make something similar. Equally important, identify those things you want to change or alter, then look again to see if the charm you initially saw survives these changes.

Scaling on Grid Paper

You can draw the assembly in scale, using engineering (decimal), architectural (fractional) or metric measure. You'll find a protractor and a pair of dividers come in handy, and a circle template is helpful both at the drawing table and in the shop. Or, draw a grid on the piece to enlarge or reduce the same number of squares onto butcher paper to record the shapes, such as arcs, curves or ogees.

An alternative to redrawing would be to take the view to the local copy center or a blueprinter for an enlargement to a workable scale and maybe an enlargement to actual size for a part or portion of the design for use as a pattern.

Proportional Scaling

Proportioning is adjusting the relative sizes to a reduced or enlarged set of values. The relationships of parts to the whole remain constant; only the physical dimensions change proportionally.

An example would be enlarging or reducing a square. Draw a diagonal through two corners of the square. Lines drawn parallel to the existing sides from any point on the diagonal—inside or outside the original square—will resize the two equal sides. Applying this same method to a rectangle, the sides will be reduced or enlarged proportionally, and the sides will remain in proportion to the original rectangle. Any element drawn within that square or rectangle will be resized in proportion to the whole.

One aid used in printing/graphic arts is the proportion scale, a circular scale with an outer and inner ring, both calibrated in inches (which can be read as feet or centimeters or whatever). Values on the outer ring represent the original size, and the rescaled value is read on the inner ring. There also is a window that shows the percent reduction or enlargement, and this can be your first parameter if you know the dimension should be reduced

FIGURE 4-2
Grid Enlargement

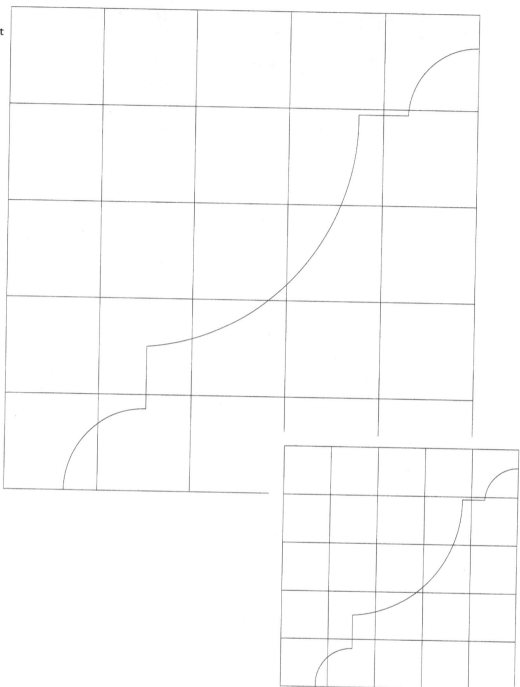

by 10 percent. This is essentially a circular version of the nearly extinct slide rule, which was replaced by PCs and powerful handheld calculators.

THE PROPORTION SCALE CAN BE USED TO QUICKLY:

1. Change known shell dimensions by the percentage of enlargement or reduction: If the height X is to be reduced by 20 percent, the Y and Z

dimensions are changed by the same percentage as shown on the wheel.

2. Calculate widths and heights of components: If the apron height is 3″ within a 30″ table, reducing the table height by 10 percent to 27″ will reduce the apron height to 2.7″.

Shop math can do the job as well. A ratio between two known dimensions can be applied to a second ratio where only one dimension is known. To bring the table height from 30″ down to 27″, if the original apron is 3″, the reduced apron dimension would be x, expressed as:

30	:	27	=	3	:	x
(Original Height)		(Reduced Height)		(Original Apron)		(Reduced Apron)

Or remember your algebra, and cross multiply the fractions:

$$\frac{\text{Original Height (30″)}}{\text{Reduced Height (27″)}} = \frac{\text{Original Apron (3″)}}{\text{Reduced Apron (x)}}$$

$$\frac{30}{27} = \frac{3}{x}$$

$$30x = 27(3)$$

$$30x = 81$$

$$x = 2.7$$

So the reduced apron is 2.7″.

(And you thought you would never use algebra.)

PICKING DIMENSIONS OFF DRAWINGS

Where the source drawing is a two-dimensional orthographic view, just measure as drawn. If it is a quasi-three-dimensional *isometric drawing*, the height and width of the planes you want to capture were most likely drawn to scaled proportions. The isometric view may have been drawn as an *isometric projection*, foreshortened for a truer visual representation of its proportions. If the drawing is not dimensioned, or you want to change the values, you can divide the width into as many units as needed.

Extend the outermost lines either above or below the drawing to a working area. Place a scale diagonally between these limits, with zero on one side and the number representing the number of divisions you need aligned on the opposing side. Tick off that scale on the diagonal, then project these lines down to a baseline on the plane. If the number of demarcations equals the desired width (say 5′), then the distance between each line would be 1′. Simple enough. If you are targeting for a 65″ desk, each line would equal 13″.

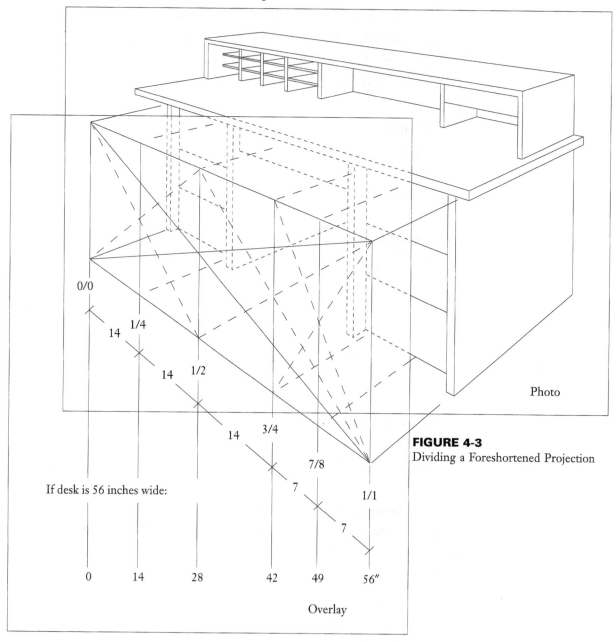

Photo

FIGURE 4-3
Dividing a Foreshortened Projection

Overlay

Dividing a Foreshortened Projection

If your source illustration is a perspective drawing or a three-quarter-view photo, planes will be shown at a diverging angle and foreshortened by

perspective. You could eyeball the divisions of foreshortened planes to esti-
mate component widths.

For more accurate results, use diagonals to divide the face or plane (see
Figure 4-3). To do this, place an overlay of vellum or tracing paper on top
of the image. Outline the plane being bisected, then draw a pair of diagonal
lines connecting opposite corners. At the point these crossed diagonals
intersect is the center of the foreshortened plane. Draw a vertical line
through this point to bisect the plane into two divided planes. Draw two
more sets of diagonal crosshairs in each of the divided areas, and add vertical
lines where these diagonals intersect to divide the whole into four lengths.
Continue the process by dividing each of the four spaces (yielding eights),
or just bisect the areas that contain the detail you want to capture.

Furniture catalogs, gallery brochures, etc. usually provide overall dimensions in the description. If not, assign a width to the desk, maybe determined
by a known dimension, such as its proportion to the height. Remember that
the vertical height in the photo or drawing may be foreshortened as well.
Hypothetically, if the height is 30″ and the width is 60″, each of the divisions
would represent 15″ when divided into fourths, and 7½″ when further divided
into eighths.

Photo images may suffer from a condition known as *parallax*, or *keyston-
ing*, where lines that are supposed to be parallel appear to curve or taper.
This is an effect caused by lens distortion based on the camera's location
relative to the subject. The table legs do not really converge (or so we hope);
therefore, assume the distance between legs at the floor is the same as it is
at the apron (after accounting for any taper or flair of the design).

Analogy on Perspective

Imagine you are standing in one end of a room-sized shoe box opposite the
item being viewed (see Figure 4-4). The top of the box is at eye level (which
is the horizon line). A clear pane (called a picture or projected plane) is
between the viewed object and the viewer. Everything in view within the
box is below the horizon line.

Perspective Elements

The *ground plane* is the box bottom, on which both object and viewer stand.
The *station point* is the height of the eye viewing the object through the
projected plane.

FIGURE 4-4
Perspective Elements

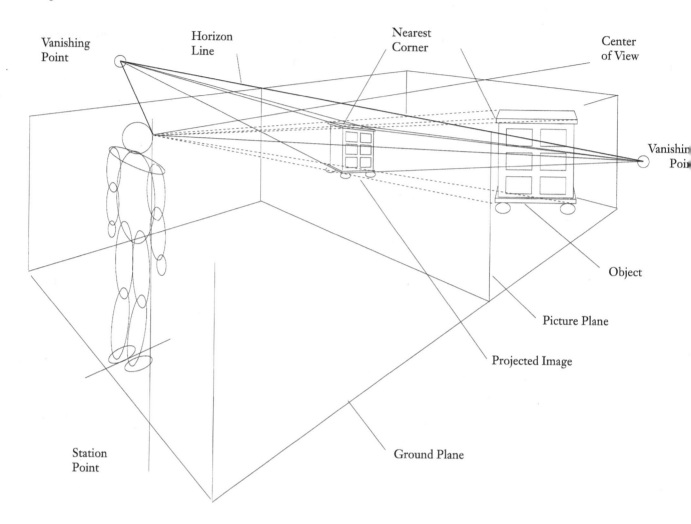

The *horizon line* is between two *vanishing points* established where the outermost lines, beginning at the nearest corner of the viewed object and along the same plane, converge with the horizon line. All horizontal lines, when angled in projection, converge on the left or right vanishing points.

It is *two-point perspective* when the vertical sides of the image appear perpendicular to the horizontal line and parallel to each other, and the line of sight is perpendicular to the projected plane. If the station point is well above or below the viewed object, the vertical lines also converge to a third vanishing point above or below the object, and you have *three-point perspective*.

The *picture plane* is your drawing surface. In the reality of optics, the image is seen inverted by the eye, as it is in a camera, but our brain conveniently flips this back to terra firma.

On paper (or the picture plane) the three-dimensional image is captured on a two-dimensional plane. The nearest corner appears largest, the farthest smallest, and everything between in the taint ('tain't biggest, 'tain't smallest) remains between the diverging lines that lead to the vanishing points at the horizon line.

If the closest corner is seen dead-on, the perspective is *parallel*. Lines of both sides diverge at the same angle; both vanishing points are positioned the same distance left and right from the center. Move the station point to either side of this nearest corner, and the perspective becomes *angular*.

Same Item, Different Views

Figures 4-5A and 4-5B illustrate a cube, such as a game table or butcher block, to show how these sides are equal when the drawing is in parallel perspective, and how one becomes shorter and one longer when viewed from the side or angular perspective. The trick in picking up dimensions from such drawings is to determine where the viewer (the camera or illustrator) is positioned relative to the object.

In perspective drawing, certain limits are imposed to result in a natural view. The eye's field of view can extend beyond 45° into the peripheral vision range, but what we perceive on the retina (the eye's picture plane) is focused within this 45° range, therefore, vanishing points are typically set no greater than 45° from the station point.

Measuring points differ from vanishing points in that measuring points are located at the distance from the vanishing point to the station point, set along the horizon line (see Figure 4-5). With some understanding of how the measurements were constructed in perspective, you can re-create the construction lines on a photo or perspective drawing.

The measuring plane along the ground line is divided in equally spaced increments from both sides of the nearest corner. When the object is viewed straight on, the increments on the vertical measuring line along the nearest corner are at the same spacing as on the horizontal measuring line (as shown by the radii drawn from the horizontal to vertical measuring lines). These vertical measures will shorten as the viewing angle widens either above or below the object.

An isometric view differs from perspective in that fixed angles, usually 30°/60° of inclination, replace the converging lines. These dimensions are usually scaled to size (isometric drawing), but may have been foreshortened for a better visual representation (isometric projection).

FIGURE 4-5
Same Item, Different Views

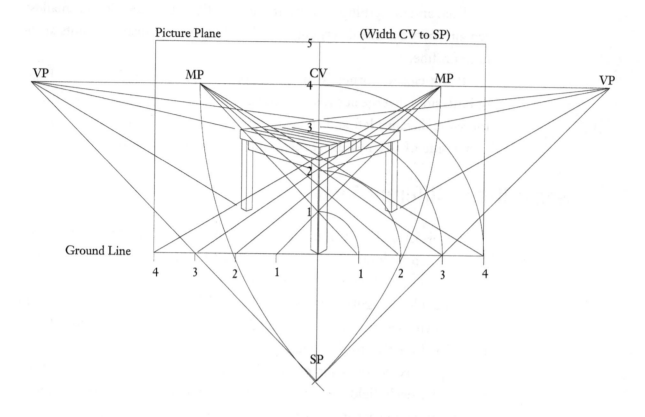

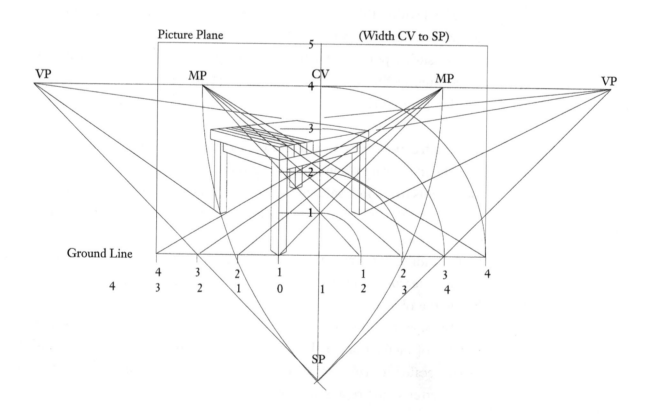

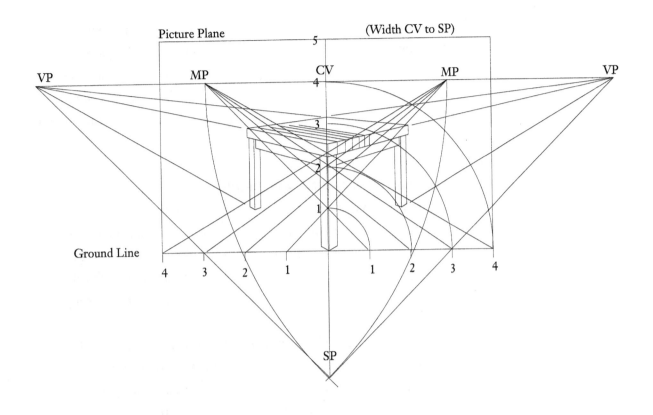

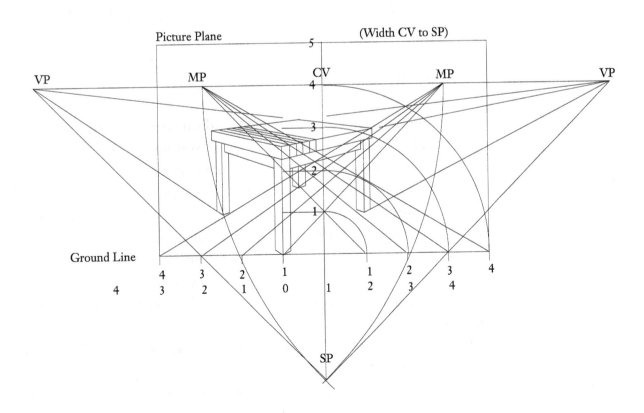

Diagonal Scaling

In the early stage of preliminary design or a first look at a source drawing, deal with concept, not fractional accuracy; when dividing spaces, work in whole, evenly divisible numbers. A quick method is to angle a scale across the extreme limits of the shape being measured, aligning an even number of units between opposite sides. This simplifies finding the centerline and blocking in component widths.

PROPORTIONALLY ENLARGING AND REDUCING

If the subject in your source drawing or photo has the desired proportions, you can rescale the shell size by drawing a diagonal line connecting two opposing corners of each plane—the top, side or face (see Figure 4-6). Draw a line parallel to one edge. Where this line intersects the diagonal, draw a right-angle line parallel to the adjacent side of the orthographic projection.

The illustration also includes drawing a diagonal on a perspective view, for which you extend two diverging lines of a plane to their point of intersection. This is the vanishing point for that plane, and all lines parallel on that plane originate from that point. On this type of representation, draw the diagonal in perspective, find the vanishing point and project the desired proportion off the diagonal.

Dividing Into Compartments

Chapter three contains various methods to divide areas into equal or diminishing progressions. In translating concept to plans, these spaces need to be looked at more closely to design the components that fill the area.

Casework, not to be confused with what social workers do, is the shell or carcass surrounding the facing. Rails are the uppermost and lowermost cross members within the case. Rails are also known as bearers when dividing drawers or other supported members. Stiles are the vertical members.

Where a tier of drawers will fill the case, your design considerations include both the position of the drawers' face plane relative to the surrounding case and the subdivisions within the face plane.

The face could be set in with a reveal, or set flush with the case, or stand proud of the case and lap the case frame.

Where each drawer face butts to the next (allowing for clearance) the

FIGURE 4-6
Diagonal Scaling

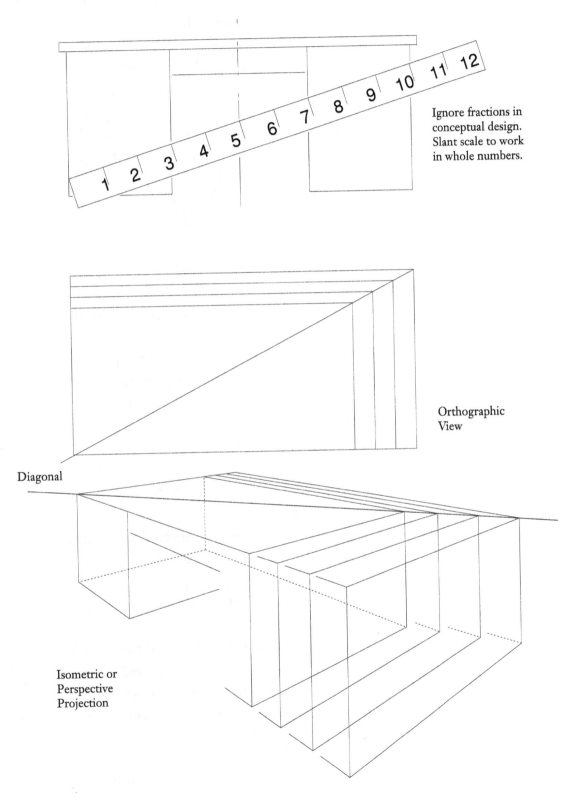

Ignore fractions in
conceptual design.
Slant scale to work
in whole numbers.

Orthographic
View

Diagonal

Isometric or
Perspective
Projection

bearing surfaces are along the side guides inside the shell.

Front horizontal bearers could frame individual drawer spaces. When front bearers are used, drawers may be positioned:

- Inset or flush, each in an individual compartment
- Half-lapped, where two adjacent edges lap and hide the bearer face
- Partially lapped, leaving some bearer face exposed

And drawers located between bearers may be guided by:

- Shims separating the bearer and drawer sides for alignment and to protect against wear on the bearer
- Center track guides attached above or below each drawer
- Side tracks, as if there were no bearers

If you set in each individual drawer between bearers with some reveal, it might appear you forgot to add stopblocks to align the drawer faces. If the bearers are inset as well, the design plane is defined. In some designs, however, individual reveals might be within the context of the whole.

First decide whether each drawer face will be separated by an exposed bearer, butted with no bearers (designing side runners for the drawers) or fully lapped (hiding the bearers). Such details need to be worked out early in your design to set the location of components within the area, and later to prepare the cutting list and bill of material.

1. When dividing a casing to be filled in with drawers, doors or shelves, whether equally spaced or in progression, first subtract the aggregate widths of all casings, bearers and rails, including the amount of clearance you intend to provide around each interior member. The remaining value is the dimension to be divided into equal or diminishing parts—that is, the area to be filled.

2. Recheck clearances, allowing for any tolerance buildup over the height or width being calculated.

3. If your plans include metal slide hardware for drawers or pullout work surfaces, buy it first, or at least select the model and get the specifications required for your design. The prerequisites for some drawer guides are specific, dictating minimum/maximum lengths, stock thicknesses and required clearances.

A couple of approaches can be used to divide spaces within a case.

For equally spaced drawers with hidden or no bearers, divide the height and width of the inside area into as many spaces as there are drawer or door divisions for face heights and widths.

Where the full thickness of the bearers, or any portion, are exposed to the face, reduce the dimension of the open area by the aggregate thickness of all separators, then divide the remainder by the number of openings (drawers) planned.

EXAMPLE: Five drawers with four ¾" separators within 28" would be

$$[28 - (¾ \times 4)] \div 5$$
$$= [28 - 3] \div 5$$
$$= 25 \div 5$$
$$= 5'' \text{ height per drawer face.}$$

This fills the area of the opening only, without consideration of the top and bottom rail thicknesses.

For diminishing heights, whether based on Fibonacci numbers or the Hambridge Progression (see the discussion in chapter three), the opposite approach should be taken. That is, add the heights of each diminishing drawer to determine the overall height of the case.

WHERE TO PLACE THE BEARERS: If the defined openings share the thicknesses of cross bearers, you can design the bearer to center on the theoretical division, then calculate the space between bearers. Or you can select where each of these thicknesses will share the dimensions that make up the progressive sizes—at the bottom or at the top. If the distances calculated are inside the dimensions of the casing, one of these areas will be either larger or smaller than the mathematical value. A solution, if this is a problem, is to include the face of the case rails when calculating the area to be divided.

Drawers

Dovetailing is an expected touch in fine furniture. A dovetail joint provides an extremely strong bond between drawer faces and drawer sides, the point of maximum stress over years of use. Design these as hand-cut or routed using a dovetail template.

Either way, include this detail if drawers are in your future. Materials specified should be a facing of the same woods used for the shell, with grain orientation running horizontally. Drawer sides can be thinner ash or alder, and the bottom ⅛" Masonite. For heavily laden drawers, design a more

FIGURE 4-7
Hambridge Progression Encased

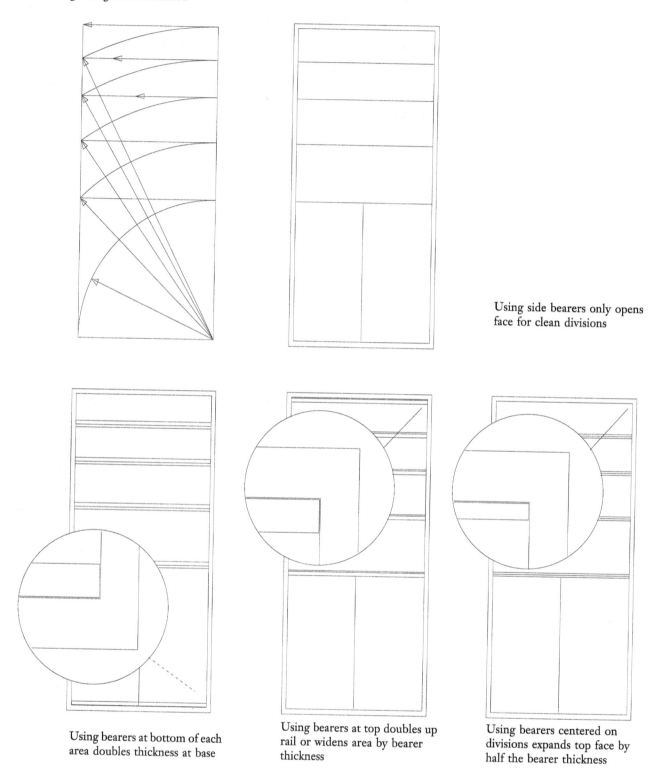

Using side bearers only opens
face for clean divisions

Using bearers at bottom of each
area doubles thickness at base

Using bearers at top doubles up
rail or widens area by bearer
thickness

Using bearers centered on
divisions expands top face by
half the bearer thickness

substantial bottom, maybe with a bevel at the front for getting into the face. Drawer sides power-stapled to the face may be functional (or expedient) in kitchen cabinets, but not in furniture you custom craft.

Doors

Consider how you'll fill an opening. Lapped mullions on overlapping doors produce a more finished look and seal the cupboard better than butt joints. With seasonal variations in wood size, the overlap lets you increase clearance to relieve stress without a gap during the shrinking cycle of wood.

Whether you glaze furniture doors yourself or have your local shop assist, you need to consider how the muntins will be formed and how deep and wide you will set the rabbeted edges to accept the glass.

The physical size of the door(s) and the weight of the glazing material will be factors in the designed width of the rails and stiles, and the quantity and size (strength) of hinges. Sheet material dimensions are discussed (beginning on page 52) as a guide to optimizing stock from standard sizes and to designing to the standard thicknesses.

Seats

Following the style or designing in context with the style, look into what's required to accept a solid, flat seat of a country chair, a shaped seat of a Windsor, a woven rush seat for a Shaker, caning for a Bentwood or an upholstery platform for a Sheraton, Hepplewhite or Queen Anne. Here you must design the frame for the seat. A rung frame of a Shaker or Carver chair can be woven into a rush seat; a flat-faced frame can accept rush for a Spanish stool. For caning, route a groove around the top opening of your Bentwood seat frame to insert and bead the caning in place. When forming a saddle seat or other conforming indentations on a solid plank seat, a la Windsor, draw the plan view and critical cross sections to indicate the depths and contours you want.

If you digress to Danish or other woven webbing applications, design an inner cleat for the hole pattern to hold the webbing that holds the cushion. For upholstered seats, design corner brackets in the frame so the seat bottom can be screwed from beneath after the platform has been upholstered, or rabbet a lip to receive the upholstered seat blank.

Tabletops

Square or rectangular tops and circular tops, with or without drop leaves, are easiest to plan, measure and fashion. If building ovals or breakfront tops, a little more design preparation is required for the planning and execution of the form. Be familiar with molding-knife profiles that produce a unique drop-leaf joint, and whatever table extension slides are needed for adding table leaves.

Legs, Rails, Spindles and Posts

Lathe work is a rewarding part of shop work. There are certain standards to be applied, including positive-negative space relationships, transitions of beads, squares, etc. Some general guidelines are given in chapter three.

At the drawing board you can detail a profile, or half spindle, from which a template could be cut to guide the turning of the shape.

Capturing Cross Sections and Profiles From Plan Views

Begin with a clear idea of how much relief you plan for your design. When forming something round, you need to think roundness. Likewise, when routing or carving a pattern in relief, you need to specify the desired depths from one plane to the next. The deeper the relief, the more pronounced the detail will appear, especially when displayed under direct lighting or side halo light.

Reliefs may be shallow (bas-relief), medium (mezzo-relievo) or deep (alto-relievo), depending on the style and the look of the design. Capture the cross-section attributes of rosettes, raised panels, moldings and other embellishments so the shape is clearly in the mind of the craftsman (most likely yourself) when the task is eventually tackled. Carved or routed rosettes, shell motifs or other embellishments can be profiled on the orthographic (two-dimensional) drawing in this manner.

Covings and moldings should be proportional to the adjacent pieces. A wider overhang on a top or base dictates the use of wider molding, such as coving. Thicker stock, regardless of the amount of overhang, similar to a mantelpiece needs heftier molding or coving for visual compatibility. Select optimum proportions, and maybe draw a cross-section detail to guide in preparing your materials and cutting lists. Also design within the limits of

FIGURE 4-8
Tabletops

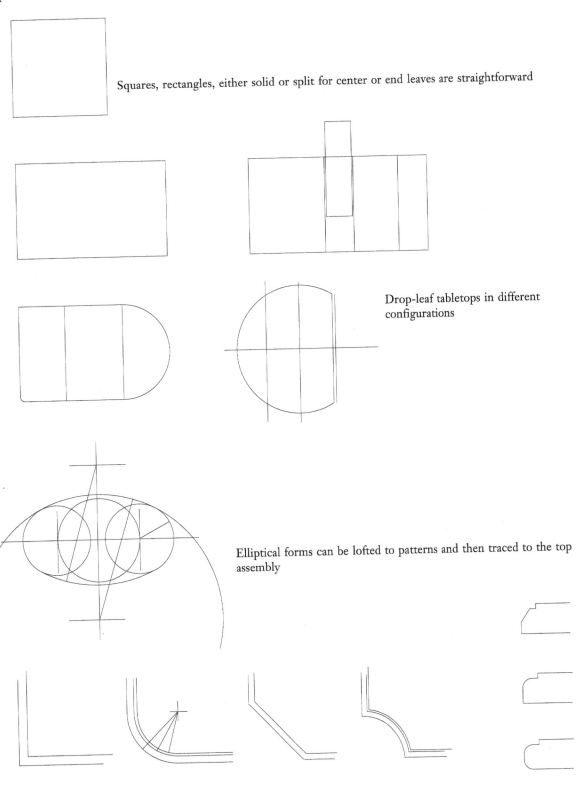

Squares, rectangles, either solid or split for center or end leaves are straightforward

Drop-leaf tabletops in different configurations

Elliptical forms can be lofted to patterns and then traced to the top assembly

FIGURE 4-9
Capturing Profiles on Plan Views

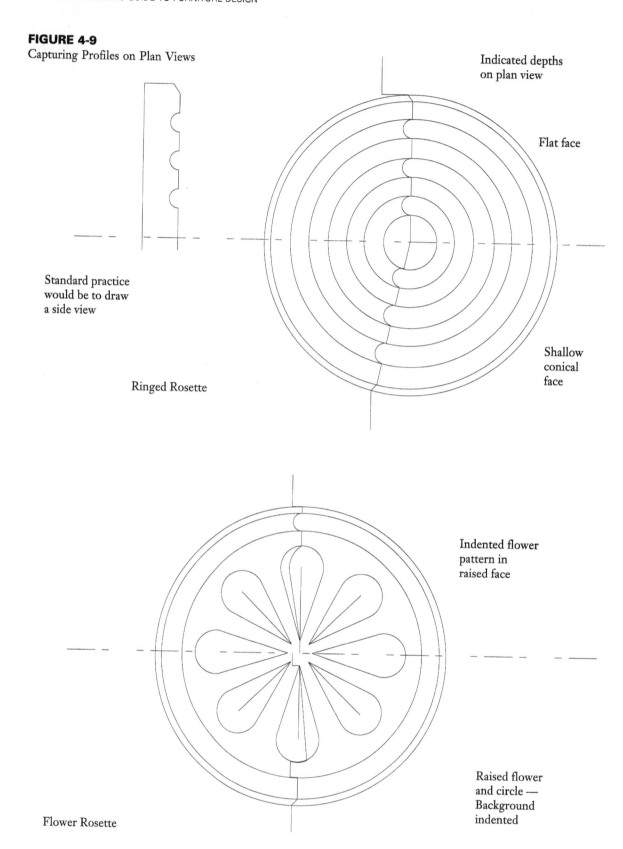

Indicated depths
on plan view

Flat face

Shallow
conical
face

Standard practice
would be to draw
a side view

Ringed Rosette

Indented flower
pattern in
raised face

Raised flower
and circle —
Background
indented

Flower Rosette

what is available commercially or doable with the available router cutters in your workshop.

Building up relief for a raised or applied panel in frame (as in frame-and-panel construction) may be a matter of selecting the right thickness of adjacent parts.

After designing the frame thickness and indicating the type of joints at junctions, design the cross section of the frame or the applied molding to serve as a transition to the frame—to the molding—to the panel, and how best to capture the panel.

The distance the molding stands proud of the frame, the amount of reveal of the panel to the molding (or rabbeted directly into the frame), and the thickness of any applied inner panel all make up the degree of relief, planes and transitions, and how prominent the assemblage will be.

Reveal is also achieved by the amount of offset used when designing leg-to-apron, side-to-base and side-to-top, drawers-to-case, and so on. Detail views are a place to exhibit these offsets. In the elevation view alone, offsets are not discernible, but the plan view clearly shows the position. This placement affects material sizes of the piece itself, as well as the lengths of adjoining pieces. This reveal can also be forgiving of cuts that may not be spot on.

If a table leg starts with a $2'' \times 2''$ square at the top, decide on the placement, flush or proud of the adjacent apron. This includes providing enough exposed corners for whatever edge treatment you plan as a design detail—veining, beveling or bull-nosing.

Leg dimensions and their installed positions will factor into the lengths of aprons and any tenons you plan. Placement also impacts lengths and angles of internal braces or brackets used to stiffen the piece.

Patterns for Larger, Complex or Repetitive Pieces

The design of a single breakfront desktop can be drawn and eventually scribed on the assembled part. But consider using a full-size pattern for any repeated element, or at least show on the drawing the method used to construct the shape.

Ovals can be lofted (drawn full-size) using a trammel point, the same way you draw to scale using a compass. Symmetrical cuts about a centerline can be drafted to a half-side only, and a pattern lofted to folded paper. When the paper is unfolded for tracing, both sides will be identical. For

**SKETCHPAD 4A
CAPTURING PANELS
IN FRAMES**

The thickness of the frames
and that of the panels being
captured, as well as the
amount of relief you are
looking for in your design,
will dictate how best to
capture the panels for the
thicknesses specified.

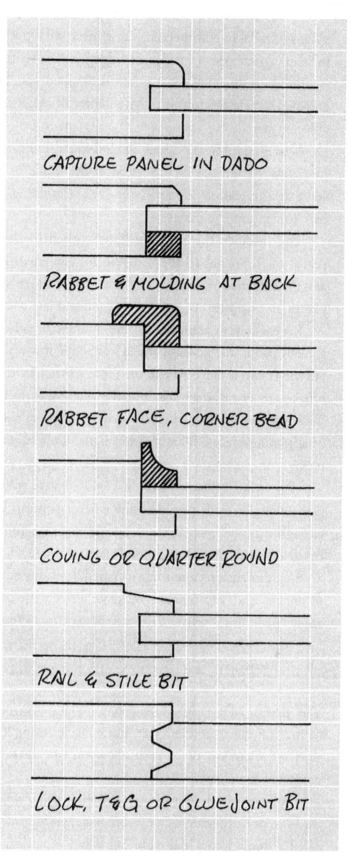

CAPTURE PANEL IN DADO

RABBET & MOLDING AT BACK

RABBET FACE, CORNER BEAD

COVING OR QUARTER ROUND

RAIL & STILE BIT

LOCK, T&G OR GWEJOINT BIT

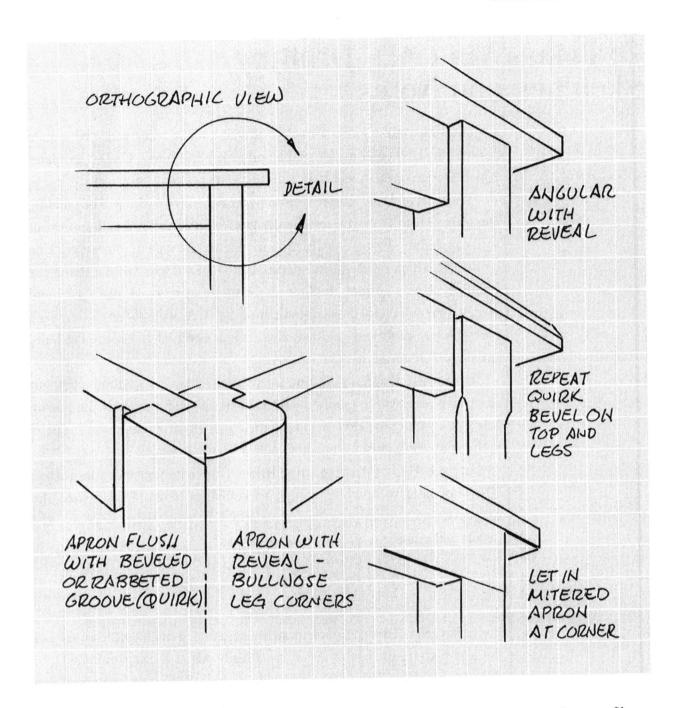

ORTHOGRAPHIC VIEW

DETAIL

ANGULAR WITH REVEAL

REPEAT QUIRK BEVEL ON TOP AND LEGS

APRON FLUSH WITH BEVELED OR RABBETED GROOVE (QUIRK)

APRON WITH REVEAL – BULLNOSE LEG CORNERS

LET IN MITERED APRON AT CORNER

SKETCHPAD 4B QUARTER VIEW STUDIES

Envision what you've designed from different angles to select the best positioning and relationship of the parts.

ogee coving or other complex transitions, be sure to provide a profile or show the tangent point of the arc or circle and dimension the center points from which the arc is drawn.

Drawings Via CAD, Drafting, Sketches and Notes

Committing your plan to a napkin, sketch pad, butcher paper or vellum while at the kitchen or drafting table, or using a full-blown CAD (Computer Aided Design) system will help to bring your concept into reality.

The level of detail you provide on paper depends on who will be building the piece. Most likely you are the designer/builder and will call upon your own capabilities during construction to execute the type of joinery, sticking or details, which need not be specified. If someone else will be doing the building, assume nothing. Include all the minutiae to avoid misfit parts and pieces. This amount of detail doesn't imply any lack of ability on the builder's part; it is just a cautious approach that includes every detail needed to build the piece you envision.

Even when designing/drafting for yourself, there is a minimum amount of workup necessary to ensure the bill of materials and ultimately the cutting lists will be accurate. This includes figuring all physical dimensions of parts within the whole, whether or not each is drawn to scale.

And speaking of drawing, the plans need not be reproduction quality. They just need to be clear enough to verify and communicate sizes and shapes. Careful attention to scaled assembly drawings, parts drawings and details will guide you on the road to success.

CAD

If you haven't used a computer drawing program, a major project may not the best place to learn. But if you are already adept at using AutoCAD, or their PC version, Autosketch, or maybe CorelDRAW, you are aware that these aids can be put to good use in the design/drafting process.

More and more software is being produced to assist in visualizing things around the home. These are spinoffs of commercial and industrial software used in the trade by architects, design engineers, interior designers and any other discipline earning a place in the commercial world.

Titles such as "Design Your Kitchen" or "Landscaping," may soon be joined by a "Design Your Custom Furniture" offering, or maybe a virtual reality desk designing program.

PC-based draw or paint programs not specifically loaded with clip art for cabinetwork or joinery can still be put to good use. Even simple programs offer a menu of basic objects that can be combined to capture or help to create your design. Straight lines, boxes, rectangles, circles, arcs and polygons can be combined, moved, scaled, rotated and otherwise edited to your form. Freehand is also a feature of most drawing programs, but combining geometric shapes is the best way to create your drawings. Freehand lines are easily drawn but difficult to modify. Annotation, for adding dimensions, call-outs and notes, is available in most drawing programs.

Some drawing options include *snap*, which directs the cursor to the next designer-specified increment; *rubber band*, where a line segment can be pulled between two endpoints; *stretch* allows a line to be increased or reduced in length or in arc; *ortho* limits a line to vertical and horizontal orientation only.

PC-based draw programs include Windows Draw from Micrografx, CorelDRAW from Corel Corporation, Autosketch from Autodesk and another, more complete program from Micrografx named Designer. Corel-DRAW offers three-dimensional capability in version 6.0 for use with Windows 95, but version 5 and earlier still simplify the drafting process. This information will soon be outdated, so investigate the newest, latest, fastest drawing programs that best suit your application.

A few of the more powerful programs will accept a scanned image that you can then edit—good for starting with a concept you wish to improve on. You can also use an ASCII file for text or call-outs you want to add to the drawing.

Drafting by Hand

When drafting or drawing by hand, you can be as formal as you wish. If preparing a package for publication, such as submitting your idea to Betterway Books, check with the publisher to see if they prefer author-generated art or if they usually redraw, and what guidance they offer. Such decisions occur down the line, since you will probably start with a query, including a synopsis of the proposed article and photos of your handiwork.

For your own use, however, or to job out the construction, make the drawings clear and complete enough to do the job. Do the math and scale the parts to work out, and double-check quantities and dimensions. Chapter five, Converting to Parts, presents thoughts on parts listing and cutting lists, but as a designer, you need to include as much information as necessary to check your own work, and provide a parts list that can be used to buy and cut the stock.

Drafting to Which Scale

The scale you select depends on the size of the object and the sheet size of the paper. For more complex designs use detail drawings of the critical areas. It is best to draft as large as practical for the object you are designing. There is no reason why an office ruler cannot be used, assigning a scale to each increment (i.e., ⅛″ = 1″ or 1′).

THE BENEFITS OF USING DRAFTING SCALES:

Fractions (architect scale) are in increments of eighths or finer, which are readily converted into feet, inches and fractions of an inch.

Decimals (engineering scale) are divided into tenths, hundredths and thousandths of an inch. The metric scale reduces the meter by tenths (decimeters), hundredths (centimeters) or thousandths (millimeters). Both of these scales are suited for the machine shop, where a surface is milled down 0.01″, or a tolerance is ±0.002.

Furniture design falls somewhere between these standard scales. When you are working with fractions, you must begin calculations by reducing all fractions to a common denominator and converting back to whole numbers and remainders. With decimals, summing tenths and hundredths of an inch results in the aggregate total without further conversion of fractions to whole numbers.

Use whatever scale you are most comfortable with. Avoid any eventual conversion from one scale to another, which invites mistakes—or at least adds steps.

Drafting scales contain a selection of calibrations. The architectural drafting scale has one side divided into 12″ with ⅟₁₆″ increments, another with ¼″-½″ scale and one with ³⁄₁₆″-⅜″ scale. Engineering scales are usually 12″ divided into tenth increments. Scaled reduction options are "20"—10 half-size demarcations within 24 segments—and "40," which is double the number of segments. The "30" and "50" scales divide that same 12″ into 30 and 50 decimal increments.

Strength, Sizes and Reaction of Materials

You don't need to get too detailed in your drawings. Work out the math, plan the joinery and commit details to paper for those components and fits that warrant this level of documentation.

Bending and Forming Wood

When planning some of the arcs, remember that wood has its own inherent qualities, so your drawn shape may be altered by the structural characteristics of the materials. Arcs traced from bowed battens will take on a natural flow, with or without detailed design sketches. Allowing materials to take their natural form will result in pleasing shapes.

Arcs to be cut may be lofted by compass (or if larger, from a trammel point) or scribed using a bowed batten. If laminating duplicate shapes, such as chair frames made from thinly resawn stock, you may want to cut a forming fixture on which to clamp and build up the thin laminates. Although the thicknesses and elasticity of the wood being bent will form its own shape for a solitary piece, don't rely on the wood's characteristics to net duplicate pieces. You might make a note to that effect, and also consider cutting thinner battens or steaming the wood to conform to the arc as drawn.

Margin of Safety

A little engineering might be necessary for a few parts of your project. Drawers, for example, obviously can't be longer than the shell that houses them, but they may need to be considerably shorter (or stopped shorter) for the designed base or legs to provide the needed support, with all four legs remaining on the floor while extending a drawer (or drawers) filled with paper. Design a shorter drawer length within the counterbalance weight and footprint of the shell. Pullout work surfaces should receive similar consideration.

Obviously furniture bases must bear the weight of stacked members: either chest-on-chest, a two-piece secretary or a Welsh dresser. And, as mentioned earlier, they need to *look*, as well as *be* adequate for the task.

Chapter five also contains typical working characteristics of wood by species, which can be used in calculating stress, deflection and margins of safety.

For a person standing on a library ladder, consider the deflection and stress this structure must withstand. Let in the ends at least half the thickness of the member, or capture long tenons from the tread into the closing side. This added depth will increase the gluing surface holding the weight.

Without going into full-blown stress analysis, provide substantial thickness, and supporting cleats and stiffeners if necessary, to stay on the conservative side of the required strength. Give such parts a good margin of safety. Should the required thickness appear too great for the target design, taper the facing edge, or design a step (tread) of thinner material and add a cleat or stiffener below, behind and out of sight.

Tread depth and consistent risers are as important on a small library ladder as they are on a flight of stairs. Provide an ample platform for climbing and standing, and design all risers, beginning with the floor to the first riser, to a constant dimension. No surprises!

Design in a safety margin of at least twice the anticipated load for anything built to support a standing figure. For chairs and beds, the same weight is distributed over a greater area, and the stress and deflection are not concentrated.

Sheet Dimensions—Plywood, Glass, Grilles

You can do a lot to ensure the efficient use of materials if you design with standard sizes in mind.

PLYWOOD

Plywood in fine furniture is relegated to shells or carcasses, drawer bottoms and so on, but some veneered sheets may be used with good results in some designs. Panels, as in frame-and-panel construction, come to mind. Where a large piece of furniture would be too heavy if built from solid, edge-joined lumber, thinner veneer ply might be a good substitute.

Plywood is a dimensionally stable material with little warpage, shrinkage or expansion, and isn't subject to the changing characteristics of solid woods. By the time the ply or solid core is constructed of thin sheets peeled from the circumference, and with that unnatural grain orientation laid up alternating 90°, there is little opportunity for the wood to move, much less to shrink and expand.

Plywood is available in full 4' × 8' sheets, half sheets and quarter sheets in thicknesses of ³⁄₁₆" (door skins) to ¼", ⅜", ½", ⅝", ¾", 1", etc. Like today's hardwoods where 4/4 isn't always 4/4, the ply manufacturers (especially imported wares) sometimes shave a bit off the top to improve their bottom line. Domestic manufacturers aren't guaranteed to be true to net sizes either, but the extra price of domestics will buy you extra quality in ply construction (adhesives, allowable voids), and therefore durability.

Know the thickness you will be designing for and plan around standard sheet sizes or half/quarter sheets. Lay out parts on a cutting plan. If you have any latitude on panel sizes, maybe by adding widths to the frames or reducing the amount the panel is let in, stick with even multiples of these ply sheet sizes to net the maximum number of parts.

In addition to solid and ply core, improved manufacturing methods have opened the use of some composition wood-product sheets, including MDF (medium density fiberboard). Some veneered sheets are on MDF as well as plywood.

Standards apply to the percent of allowable voids in the interior plies, and how many voids can be filled at the surface.

Cabinetmakers know about Medite, its exterior counterpart Medex and MEL (Melamine) made of MDF which is available in $4' \times 8'$ sheets (actually slightly over), and in ¼", ½" and ¾" thicknesses. Melamine is prefinished on either one or both sides, and is available in white, almond, gray and black. It is not intended for what we think of as fine furniture, but we build other things, and this is an excellent material for built-in task centers and workstations. Cut edges can either be mitered as you would any ply, or the exposed core edge can be sealed and painted or covered with a glue-impregnated facing ironed in place. Similar to veneer edging, the width can be trimmed back to the sheet edge with a sharp matte knife and lightly sanded.

All MDF is brutal to sharp saw blades. Carbide tips will stand up to the abrasive characteristics of MDF better than conventional steel blades. In either event, plan a trip to your sharpener soon thereafter.

SPECIFYING PLYWOOD GRADES

LETTER DESIGNATIONS—A-D indicates the good side (A) is backed with a bad side (D) and is probably not suitable for even the deepest, darkest corner of your project. In A-B, the B side has flaws that have been filled with dutchmen, but is a suitable side for applying veneer.

GLUES—ABX indicates an exterior glue has been used on interior ply. This is not Marine Grade, which uses waterproof glue, or even an exterior grade, which should have fewer internal voids. It is an expedient shortcut by manufacturers, since the glue pot is mixed up for their exterior anyway.

VENEERS—Based on your design, ready-made veneered plywood or even wall paneling in standard thicknesses is available, or the builder can apply a wood veneer to the shell.

GLASS

If your design project includes glazing, sheet size isn't a factor, since we would be using only a portion of a manufactured sheet. However, thickness is important. Glass is available in single strength ($\frac{1}{16}''$), double-strength ($\frac{1}{8}''$) and up to $\frac{1}{4}''$, which is also recommended for the best quality mirrors. Where a beveled edge is specified, use no less than $\frac{3}{16}''$ for this effect. Make sure to design the muntins and the doorframes to capture a standard glass thickness. Leaded glass channel, if in your future, is extruded for the lighter thicknesses, in different cross-section profiles; again, design and specify accordingly.

When glazing doors or other framed openings, design (and cut) the sheet size $\frac{1}{8}''$ shy for both horizontal and vertical dimensions to "float" in the receiving frame (or *muntin*, as it is called in window parlance). This allows for dissimilar movements (expansion and contraction) of dissimilar materials without breaking the sash, the glass or both.

Fail-Safe Cutting List Preparation

The surest way to ensure an accurate cutting list is to produce accurate scaled drawings and details. Enough care should be taken when preparing the plans to enable you to make up a parts list and cutting list from assembly and detail drawings.

Given that, still double-check the as-drawn size with the math to verify lengths, which can then be converted to linear feet or to board feet. A board foot is a length $1'' \times 12'' \times 12''$, or 144 cubic inches. So any combination—$2'' \times 6'' \times 12''$, $1'' \times 8'' \times 18''$ or $2'' \times 8'' \times 9''$—equals one board foot of lumber.

A board foot is a good measure when pricing lumber or defining how much lumber is on a barge or in a boxcar, but not too helpful in calculating the quantity of wood needed for your project. Do your workup in linear feet of each desired width and thickness. Gang and group pieces to net the most from standard lumber widths.

Know Your Net Thicknesses

In the previous section was a review of standard mill cuts and especially thicknesses available from the yardman or from your own stock earmarked for this project. Where possible, work from "knowns" when drafting and when calculating what will be needed in the way of lumber.

How much usable lumber you plan to net from these sizes depends on the cut of the wood, and whether you pay a little extra for S3S (surfaced three sides) so the builder begins with a straight milled edge as a rip guide. Lumber surfaced four sides (S4S) may be expedient for edge-joining boards into a solid planked top, but the widths will probably need to be cut down, so why pay the extra fee?

Rely on yourself, or whomever is selecting the lumber, to see firsthand what can be netted from the chosen pieces. You can't foresee all of the choices available at some future time of purchase.

Orientation

Orientation refers to the direction of the wood grain. When selecting boards, be reminded of the reaction of wood, and how best to capitalize on its positive attributes while avoiding its negative characteristics. Chapter five covers the best use of flat and straight grain cuts, grain direction for the size and application and when to avoid reaction wood that may twist or cup with time.

Common Dressed Lumber Sizes

NOMINAL SIZES	1 × 2	1 × 4	1 × 6	1 × 8	1 × 10	1 × 12
Actual	¾ × 1½	¾ × 3½	¾ × 5½	¾ × 7¼	¾ × 9¼	¾ × 11¼
Linear bf	0.167	0.333	0.5	0.667	0.833	1.0
Nominal Sizes	2 × 2	2 × 4	2 × 6	2 × 8	2 × 10	2 × 12
Actual	1½ × 1½	1½ × 3½	1½ × 5½	1½ × 7¼	1½ × 9¼	1½ × 11¼
Linear bf	0.333	0.667	1.0	1.333	1.667	2.0

Composite Sheets of Plywood or MDF

You can diagram the cutting plan as the designer, or wait until you change hats to craftsman to work out the details. Figure 4-10 shows an example of the planning process to net the required number of pieces from the smallest standard ply sheet or segment. If you have no need, or no room to store an extra half sheet for future projects, demand, plead, beg your supplier to sell only a half sheet, in this example cut lengthwise. Remind him he can sell the remainder as four $2' \times 2'$ or two $2' \times 4'$ panels at a nice markup.

If utilizing composite sheets for substrates, for a painted piece or for an unfinished shell to be veneered later, ply orientation is unimportant. Where a preveneered ply is being used, however, your cutting pattern must take into account the sheet sizes and the parts you can net with the proper figuring orientation.

Listings—Manageable Logic

The drawings you produce need to be supplemented with working lists. These include bills of material, a cutting list and cutting diagrams where appropriate. The dimensions should be checked and rechecked for accuracy. In fact, the process of listing is a check of the drawing accuracy.

It may help to have your drawings reproduced and use a copy to mark off each part as it is listed. It is even more helpful, but not necessary, to prepare an exploded drawing of the assembly.

Even though your parts/cutting list will not be prepared to some stringent government specification, it helps to have a guideline, a logical sequence, to avoid overlooking parts and to retest the lengths required.

Assign a part number for all pieces. This can be done sequentially if the project is not too complex. As the number of parts grows, consider using prefixes to identify subgroups—top, legs, drawers, doors—followed by a sequential number for each piece within that group. On the list include the part name, material, quantity and dimensions in nominal thickness, width and length.

When preparing the parts list, use "nominal" widths and thicknesses, but actual lengths. For the cutting list (and your earlier design drafting) work in physical sizes. A listing for a $1'' \times 4'' \times 27''$ is actually $\frac{3}{4}'' \times 3\frac{1}{2}'' \times 27''$.

A typical parts/cutting list for the drawing shown in Figure 4-11 groups

FIGURE 4-10
Cutting Plan for Veneer
Ply Grain

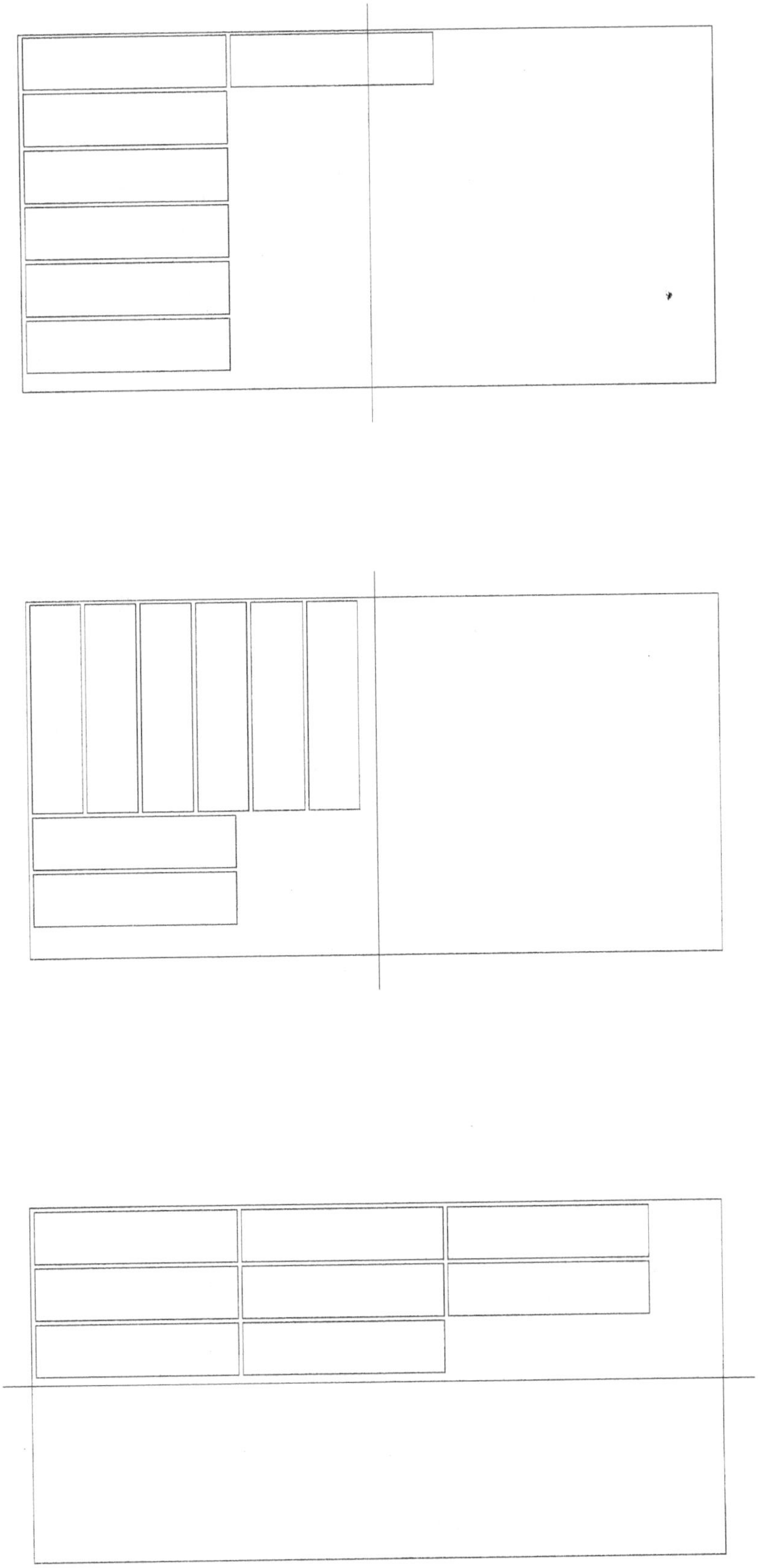

Assume you'll need eight
panels, 7″ by 28″

$48 \div 7 = 6.86$
$48 \div 28 = 1.71$
1×6 nets 6

If veneering later, or
painting or using MEL,
direction doesn't matter

Net 6 plus 2 cut crosswise
within 48″

To maintain grain
direction, ask if the yard
will sell half sheets cut
lengthwise

$96 \div 28 = 3.43$
$24 \div 7 = 3.43$
3×3 nets 9

157

FIGURE 4-11
Sample Exploded View

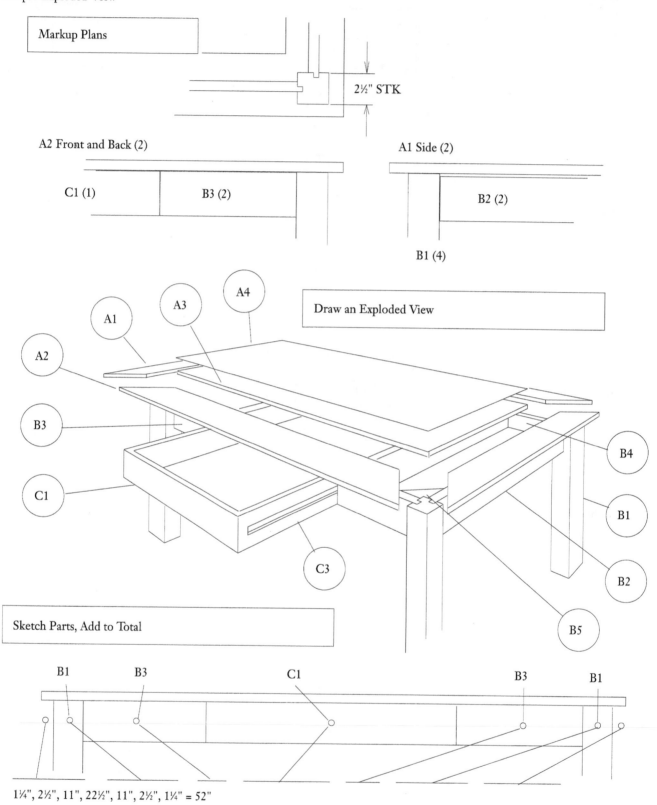

Markup Plans

2½" STK

A2 Front and Back (2)   A1 Side (2)

C1 (1)   B3 (2)   B2 (2)

B1 (4)

A4
A3
A1
A2
B3
C1

Draw an Exploded View

B4
B1
B2
B5
C3

Sketch Parts, Add to Total

B1   B3   C1   B3   B1

1¼", 2½", 11", 22½", 11", 2½", 1¼" = 52"

Sample Cutting List

ITEM	MAT'L	QTY	T	W	L
A—Top					
A-1 Sides	Walnut	2	¾	4	36
A-2 Front/Rear	Walnut	2	¾	4	52
A-3 Substrate	Plywood	1	⅜	33	49
A-4 Insert	Formica	1	⅛	32½	48½
B—Leg Frame					
B-1 Legs	Walnut	4	3	3	27
B-2 Apron—Sides	Walnut	2	¾	3	30½
B-3 Apron—Front	Walnut	2	¾	3	11
B-4 Apron—Rear	Walnut	1	¾	3	45
B-5 Corner Brace	Walnut	4	2	3	6
C—Drawers					
C-1 Face	Walnut	1	¾	3	22½
C-2 etc.					

parts by location. For a desk, you could consider all parts the top comprises to be "A," and the listing might appear as above.

Rechecking Your Lists

Check your component lengths by reassembling to the whole in a math table:

Top Width		<u>52</u>
Rear Apron 45—(¼ tenon × 2)	=	44½"
Legs 2½ × 2	=	<u>5</u>
Subtotal		49½
Overhang 1¼ × 2	=	<u>2½</u>
Total		52

When compiling the buy list, lay the parts out on paper, selecting optimum widths to hold spoilage to a minimum. It is your option whether to net four pieces of 3″ stock from two lengths 6″ wide, or four lengths 3″

wide (allowing for kerf thickness and dressing the edges).

Keep your options open when visiting your local lumberyard. Maybe the 6″ stock isn't as straight and true as you would like, or doesn't have the figuring you're looking for, so opt for the better looking but narrower stock. Stay loose and recalculate for the best stock selection.

Regarding lengths, obviously you'll inspect the boards for end checks and splits, but go well beyond the length you need to net so you can square cut the ends well inside any migrating flaws. Also, length of stock for planking applications should include a generous allowance for squaring and cutoff after joining. Go long.

Mechanics of the Piece

Here are some thoughts to consider during the design/drafting phase that will bring the concept into the real world of fabrication.

CANTILEVERS—Any overhang, such as a keyboard rack, drawer, pullout work surface or even the distance of a table edge back to the supporting legs and aprons, needs to be identified here, and designed within a workable range. If someone sits or leans on a table's extended edge, the supporting leg frame must be close enough to that cantilevered edge to provide support, not a fulcrum point for a tilting table.

BASES—Common sense dictates a base design that will adequately accept and support whatever is on top, but this must also appear visually adequate for the task. It may be prudent to increase the thicknesses, or the width and length, to provide the optimum relative sizes of the support to the supported.

HEIGHTS—Just as with bases, a shell can appear too tall if the footprint is too small, too narrow or too shallow. If building a freestanding, thin display cabinet, be sure the base, be it flush or overlapping, is adequate to maintain the vertical position.

FRAMES—If you plan to overlap door mullions, you'll want to present equal widths to the face, which means the backside member needs to be wider.

SLIDES AND GUIDES—Get the specifications early and design to the chosen mechanism, or study trade-offs and select a more suitable slide.

HANGING HARDWARE—Select hardware that will fit the facing and thickness of the scantlings.

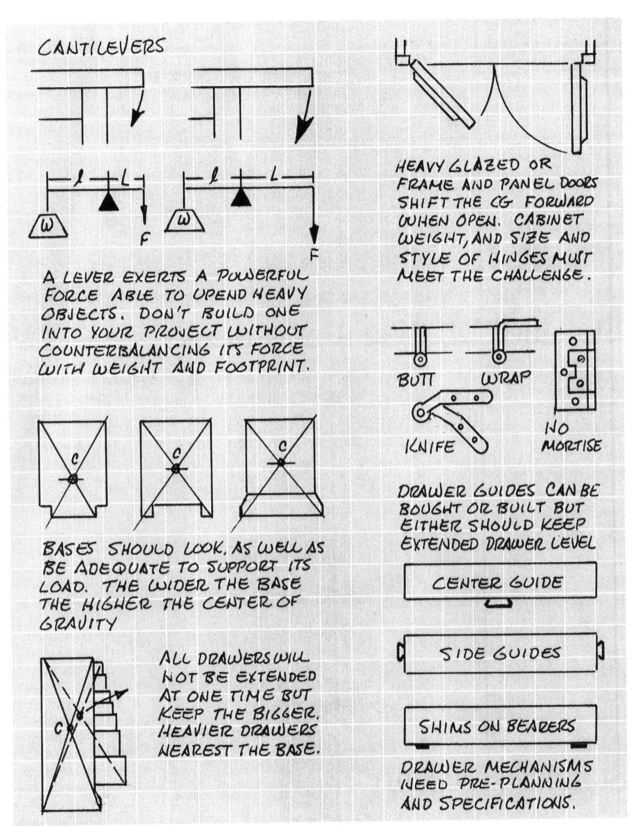

CANTILEVERS

A LEVER EXERTS A POWERFUL FORCE ABLE TO UPEND HEAVY OBJECTS. DON'T BUILD ONE INTO YOUR PROJECT WITHOUT COUNTERBALANCING ITS FORCE WITH WEIGHT AND FOOTPRINT.

BASES SHOULD LOOK, AS WELL AS BE ADEQUATE TO SUPPORT ITS LOAD. THE WIDER THE BASE THE HIGHER THE CENTER OF GRAVITY

ALL DRAWERS WILL NOT BE EXTENDED AT ONE TIME BUT KEEP THE BIGGER, HEAVIER DRAWERS NEAREST THE BASE.

HEAVY GLAZED OR FRAME AND PANEL DOORS SHIFT THE CG FORWARD WHEN OPEN. CABINET WEIGHT, AND SIZE AND STYLE OF HINGES MUST MEET THE CHALLENGE.

BUTT   WRAP

KNIFE   NO MORTISE

DRAWER GUIDES CAN BE BOUGHT OR BUILT BUT EITHER SHOULD KEEP EXTENDED DRAWER LEVEL

CENTER GUIDE

SIDE GUIDES

SHIMS ON BEARERS

DRAWER MECHANISMS NEED PRE-PLANNING AND SPECIFICATIONS.

SKETCHPAD 4C
MECHANICS AND MECHANISMS
Be aware of the physical requirements you might be imposing with your design, whether from size, shape or proportion, or some commercial part that must fit just so.

Hinges
- *Butt hinges*
- *Trap hinges*
- *SOSS hinges*

Latches and catches
- *push/pull*
- *magnetic*

Templates to duplicate placement

Stress calculations

Trapezoidal length

Louvers, spindle screens

Standard Drafting Accessories

In order to produce accurate exploded drawings, elevation drawings, orthographic drawings or drawings from photographs, you need to have the proper tools to do the job. These items will also give you more guidance and accuracy than those original concept drawings done on a napkin. You don't need to go all out to get good drawings, but quality tools will ensure accuracy. If you know your geometry well enough, all you really need is a compass and a straightedge, but each of the following will help you in creating your design.

- Scales—engineering, architectural, metric
- Grid paper
- Triangles—30°/60°, 45°
- T square
- Straightedge
- Compass
- Protractor
- Proportion wheel

Standard Measure

A foot, including the toes, was once a unit of measure, and a yard was once the distance from the king's nose along an extended arm to his fingertip. We still use hands as a unit of measure for the height of horse haunches,

FRACTIONS					TO DECIMALS	TO MILLIMETERS
				1/32	0.03125	0.794
			1/16		0.0625	1.588
				3/32	0.09375	2.381
		1/8			0.125	3.175
				5/32	0.15625	3.969
			3/16		0.1875	4.763
				7/32	0.21875	5.556
		1/4			0.25	6.35
				9/32	0.28175	7.144
			5/16		0.3125	7.938
				11/32	0.34375	8.731
		3/8			0.375	9.525
				13/32	0.40625	10.319
			7/16		0.4375	11.113
				15/32	0.46875	11.906
1/2					0.5	12.7
				17/32	0.53125	13.493
			9/16		0.5625	14.288
				19/32	0.59375	15.081
		5/8			0.625	15.875
				21/32	0.65625	16.669
			11/16		0.6875	17.463
				23/32	0.71875	18.256
	3/4				0.75	19.05
				25/32	0.78125	19.844
			13/16		0.8125	20.638
				27/32	0.84375	21.431
		7/8			0.875	22.225
				29/32	0.90625	23.019
			15/16		0.9375	23.813
				31/32	0.96875	24.606
1					1.0	25.4

but most others have since been standardized into U.S. units of measure (while the rest of the world converts to metric).

Common length measures of U.S. units and their equivalents in metric units divide the:

yard into 3 feet, 36 inches or 0.9144 meters

foot into 12 inches, 0.333 yards or 30.480 centimeters

inch into 0.083 feet, 0.027 yards or 2.540 centimeters

So you won't have to look elsewhere, an equivalency chart dividing the lowly inch is presented on page 163.

The metric system is an efficient measure for shop work. There is no conversion from decimal to fraction or reduction of fractions to their common denominator, which can create a breeding ground for error.

meter	1
decimeter	0.1
centimeter	0.01
millimeter	0.001 meters

CHAPTER FIVE

Converting to Parts

Construct, fabricate, fashion, craft—whatever term you apply to transforming your design into reality—the moment of truth is at hand.

The look you want from your custom-crafted furniture design will most likely be achieved from a combination of the physical size and shape coupled with the construction methods and materials. The design, made in the fabrication process chosen during the development phase, now must be translated into parts for assembly.

Some questions to consider when converting plans to pieces include the following.

WHICH WOOD IS MOST SUITABLE FOR THE DESIGN? Determine which variety will meet the majority of your most critical objectives. Desired characteristics may include color, grain (pattern and figuring), hardness, strength and workability.

WHAT IS THE BEST WAY TO JOIN THE PIECES? Considering the construction method selected, what can you expect from the fit of the joint and its gluing surfaces, and when should joints be augmented with tenons, dowels or biscuits for added strength?

WHICH GRAIN ORIENTATION IS MOST SUITABLE? Considering machining, strength, seasonal expansion and shrinkage, which cut will expose the hardest surface, most impervious to abrasion and wear, and which cuts are preferred for different purposes?

WHAT IS THE BEST MACHINING SEQUENCE? How can I maintain a guide edge until all critical cuts have been made? Which feed direction is most likely to produce the smoothest surfaces, and what precautions can be taken against splitting or blown-out fibers?

WHICH GLUES ARE BEST? Considering the intended location and use, suitability, strength and bond life, what measure should you take to prepare and control its application?

WHAT ARE THE BEST FINISHING TECHNIQUES? What are the best finishes, sanding sequences, coloring pigments, filler agents, sealers and overcoats?

Answers to these questions will differ based on the mission and the construction technique you've selected.

Determine Which Construction Method— Frame and Panel, Solid or Ply?

You had different options to choose from when selecting the construction method for your design. Among these were planked edge-joined, frame and panel or veneer plywood shell; pegged chair or table legs vs. the addition of an apron. The desired look or style of the piece should have dictated the best method of fabrication.

Whatever was committed to paper in the previous chapter now needs to be transformed into parts. Part sizes and shapes will differ depending on the type of joinery you employ.

Joinery should follow the visual style and must provide the required strength for the piece. You designed the joinery for indoor or outdoor use and for the best joint to suit the style of chair, table leg, bedpost, stool, desk or whatever it is you're building.

Choose Materials—Woods: Solid, Ply, Veneer or MDF?

You can bend tradition and seriously consider using the woods you like to work with and that your shop is equipped to produce. This is just another reminder that real-world limitations can result in innovative and imaginative uses that extend beyond the standard applications.

Nearly every species of wood in a variety of milled forms has been used in custom furniture. Select the species that best suits the structural requirements, the look you want and the construction realities of the piece.

Trees and Their Growth Patterns

Trees grow in two distinct ways. The tuberous types, yucca and palm, generate new growth from inside the core, pushing the older growth outward. These aren't good for much except coconuts and dates. Banded-trunk varieties grow in a more structured cellular pattern, adding new growth—new cells dividing in the area between the cambium layer and the bark—with each growth cycle.

The cross section of a banded-trunk tree comprises:

BARK, made up of live inner cells and dead outer cells, forms a protective cover to combat pests, fire, moisture and heat. As the tree adds girth, the outer bark often sloughs off.

CAMBIUM LAYER is the area of new growth—new cells from which nutrients are transmitted throughout the structure.

SAPWOOD is the outermost portion from just inside the bark layer toward the center, extending just into the dormant and dead cells. Its newest cells transmit nutrients from the soil to the leaves, while the older cells begin to harden and fill.

SPRING WOOD (EARLYWOOD) develops during the rapid growth cycle as the tree is given its first shot of mild weather and warmth, and awakens from a winter's rest. These new cells are thin-walled to maximize the amount of nutrients transmitted from the roots to the pores and the leaves.

SUMMER WOOD (LATEWOOD) has thicker cell walls, darker in color in some species, that develop as the growth cycle plateaus, readying itself for winter.

HEARTWOOD becomes denser and stronger with age, adding more weight and substance to the pores and forming the armature of the tree.

PITH is the center core of the trunk, limb or branch, and is the center core of all appendages.

RAYS are radial cells carrying nutrients to the live but dying cells between sapwood and heartwood. These horizontal pores also store a reserve of nutrients to transmit vertically as needed.

FIGURE 5-1
Microscopic View of Wood Composition.

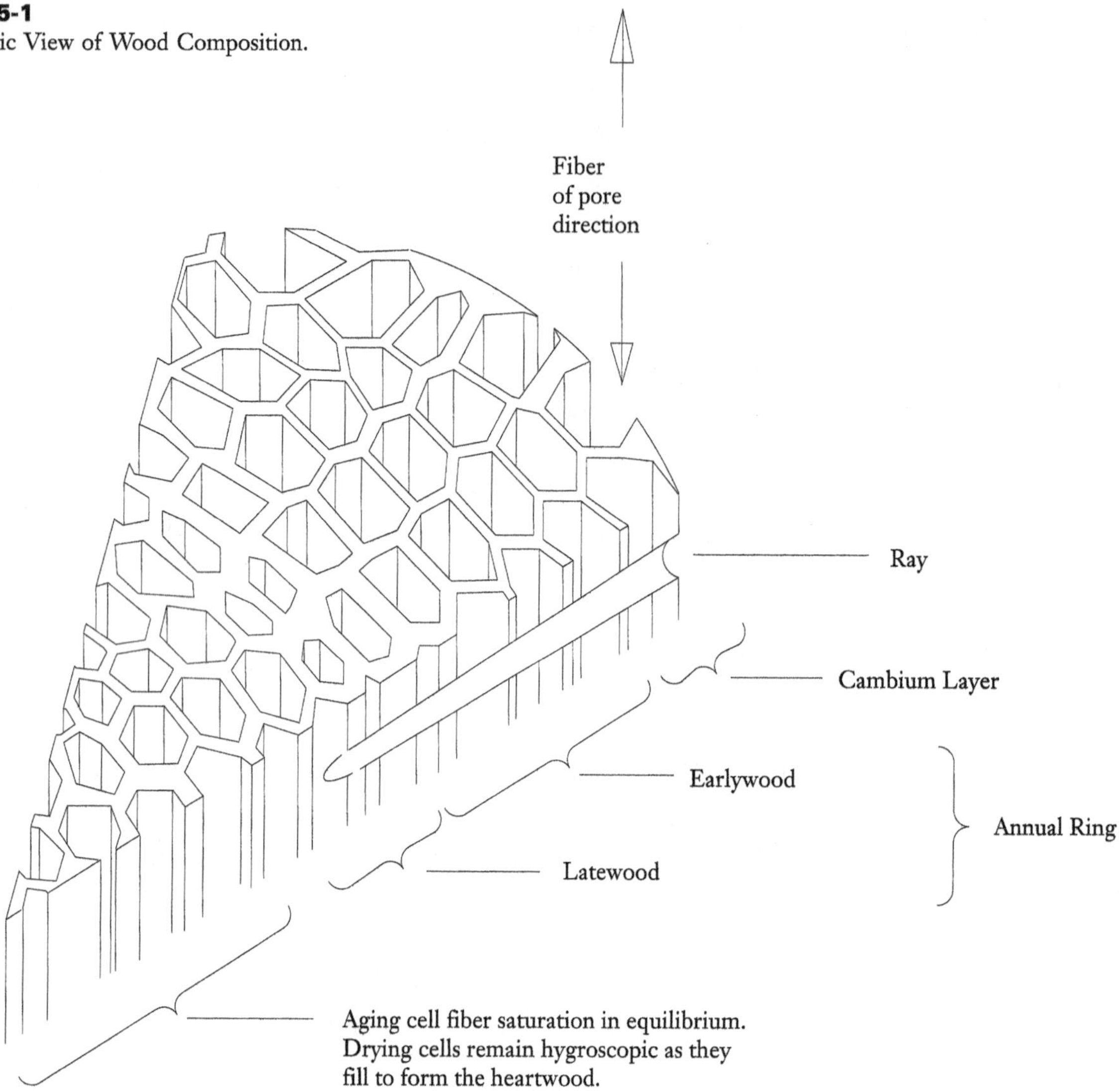

Fiber
of pore
direction

Ray

Cambium Layer

Earlywood

Annual Ring

Latewood

Aging cell fiber saturation in equilibrium.
Drying cells remain hygroscopic as they
fill to form the heartwood.

ANNUAL RINGS are readily discernible in ash and oak, whereas maple and birch show little demarcation, but both sets of examples produce fairly homogeneous lumber, with little density difference between spring- and summerwood.

From the "who cares" file: In 1906, astronomer A.E. Douglas was one of the first to record age-dating of trees by their growth rings. He was looking for confirmation of his theory of an eleven-year cycle of sunspots, and used trees to prove his theory by the rate of growth evident in the thickness of the growth rings.

Defying Classification

Hardwoods and softwoods are classified by their leaves. Broadleaf trees are classified as hardwoods. These are the deciduous varieties that lose their leaves each year except in very warm climates. Softwoods are from the family of conifers (trees that produce cones) with needles or scale-like foliage, such as pines and cypress. Under this classification, balsa and basswood are hardwoods. The terms have little correlation to the actual hardness of wood.

Because of some variation in densities between spring and summerwood, the material is neither uniform nor resilient enough to use standard hardness tests without scratching or poking holes in the surface. The wood industry records the pressure required to penetrate a ¼″ ball bearing into the surface to gauge hardness. This is a destructive test and of little help to the designer/craftsman. However, the density, or specific gravity of the wood, is a good indicator of its hardness properties.

From visual analysis of the wood you can deduce that a medium- to high-density lumber cut from heartwood will provide the most homogeneous surfaces, especially when quartersawn (vertical grain). The plain-sawn, tangential grain exposes wider areas of differing hardness of the spring- and summerwoods. This difference is magnified when the cut is taken through sapwood that has not had time to fill and become more dense.

Tangential grain in softwoods has the propensity to separate between the layers of spring- and summerwood. This seldom happens in premium hardwoods, and you don't want separation to occur in the middle of your project. There is further discussion on recommended mill cuts for various applications later in this chapter.

You can enjoy working with richly figured, premium hardwood, and ultimately appreciate furniture that showcases its traditional beauty. You can also take a medium to its limit and try something different. Also, look at any of the composition boards used as an underlayment for flooring or insulation: What would happen if these sheets were cut and layered to form a piece of sculpted furniture? Standard applications can be expanded beyond their common uses to challenge the craftsman.

A Look at Hardwood Grades

The hobbyist visually inspects the hardwoods on hand and selects pieces for the article. But if the project is more expansive, or if the yard must order what you want, here are the standard grades you might want to specify.

FIRSTS AND SECONDS

- Random widths, but minimum is 6″.
- Minor blemishes and stains, but no splits and no knots over most of the board.
- Will take natural finish.

SELECT

- Random, minimum width should be 4″.
- Most of the best surface is free of splits and knots. Backside may contain knots and stains, but board must be free of rot.
- May take natural finish.

NO. 1 COMMON

- Random, minimum width (for common) is 3″.
- Larger areas front and back may be blemished, but good painting surface.

NO. 2 AND NO. 3 COMMON

- Random widths, minimum is 3″.
- Increasingly larger areas of blemishes permitted.

There is no need to buy top-grade firsts and seconds or select lumber if the work is to be veneered or painted, or when duplicating cottage style furniture. For the latter, you might want a few flaws to add to the charm. Select the grade that best suits the design and the look you want to achieve.

Choosing Materials

The list of objectives for selecting wood is a mix of "likes, wants, needs and musts," including:

- Continuing the established precedent for the style of your design—what follows tradition?
- Indulging yourself with a personal preference—which woods do you enjoy working?
- Matching an established theme or style to fit a decor.
- Mismatching that theme for some contrast or effect.

Compatibility and workability in machining is of vital importance. Sticking, turning, carving or other processes in your design will come off with more success if met with suitable characteristics that allow the wood to be milled smoothly or carved nicely.

In fact, historical periods labeled as the Age of Oak, Walnut and Mahogany were so identified from the processes that characterized the style. Craftsmen in those eras used the most suitable wood to execute a particular style of furniture; e.g., heavy dark furniture, ornately carved furniture or highly figured wood.

It is important is to use a wood that you enjoy working. Nothing dampens a woodworking project more than selecting a wood that can't be worked with satisfaction and that won't be appreciated later in its finished form because it's devoid of richness and beauty.

Wood selected based on its appearance and workability, however, needs to be reviewed for its structural properties. The properties must provide adequate strength in the designed thicknesses and for the intended use. Will the parts and the whole be strong enough to last under the task?

Selecting the Mill Cut

After checking off your objectives and selecting a wood with the best qualities to meet the majority of your needs, you can still do more. Maximize the physical properties of the wood by selecting the best mill cut for the pieces and the purpose. Not only does the figuring of the material differ with location and orientation of the mill cut, so do the physical properties including seasonal changes in size, surface hardness, color and finishing.

Many terms are used for different cuts of wood, depending on whether it is a hardwood or softwood.

In Hardwood Family	*In Softwood Family*
Plain-sawn, aka tangential	Flat-sawn, aka slash grain
Quartersawn, aka radial	Edge grain, aka vertical grain
Rift-sawn—45° to growth rings	

Plain-sawn hardwood (flat-sawn/slash grain in softwood) is milled tangent to the growth rings (perpendicular to the radial rays of the log). This is also known as tangential. Quartersawn (edge grain/vertical grain) is cut perpendicular to the growth rings (parallel to the rays, or radial).

End grain is a window to the cut of the board. Annual rings angled 0° to 45° to the width is plain-sawn, 45° to 90° is quartersawn. As a general rule, plain-sawn (flat/slash grain) has more figuring and color variation than quartersawn (edge/vertical grain). The quartersawn board presents a more homogeneous, more abrasion-resistant surface because any variation in density between springwood and summerwood is exposed in their minimum thicknesses. Tangential wood exposes more of each growth period at the surface.

Swells in Summer/Shrinks in Winter

Unless you are logging for personal use, the shrinkage factor from green to seasoned lumber of 15 percent is of little consequence. Properly air-dried logs and rough mill-cut lumber will lose its free water, that is, water contained in the open capillary pores of the tree when harvested. Hardwoods may be kiln-dried under high heat conditions to further reduce the water content absorbed into the cell walls.

Kiln drying can control the drying rate to minimize checking, splitting or warping caused by sudden reductions in moisture and rapid changes in its cellular elasticity. Some cuts containing random grain reaction wood, or weak cellular structure, might not survive the process. It's better you know before that piece becomes a part of your project.

Even after thorough drying, cell walls remain hygroscopic and will reabsorb moisture from the humidity in the air, only to expel it again when the ambient humidity drops. All wood changes in weight and in physical size with the seasons.

When using green or air-dried lumber, you need to plan for the inevitable shrinkage. The moisture level present at the time you assemble and apply the finish will also determine the level of moisture sealed in.

Wood will stay sealed for a short time, keeping moisture in equilibrium, but the natural porosity of wood will soon break down the barrier and allow moisture to evaporate and be absorbed. When in equilibrium, the cell walls contain as much moisture as they can hold without being supersaturated. This is their fiber saturation point. Winter-to-summer changes can affect size by 1 percent for every 3 percent increase in absorbed moisture. This change varies by species and mill cut.

Plain-sawn boards cut from the outer, softer portion of a log will take in and let off less water than the denser boards cut from heartwood (the armature or supporting structure of the tree). Although this wood is more dense (open cell walls have thickened and filled), it tends to absorb more moisture in its somewhat denser cells. Therefore heartwood changes size in a greater proportion than the more open cellular structure of sapwood.

Cuts containing reaction wood cut through a crotch or burl will swell and shrink at different rates, which makes these cuts susceptible to splitting.

Standard Wood Cuts

Figure 5-2 shows the origin and nomenclature of mill cuts. The plus and minus symbols indicate in which direction the seasonal change will occur, and which orientation changes to a greater or lesser amount.

Mill cuts made tangent to and those made through annual rings produce different coloring, figuring, surface hardness and uniformity that affect appearance and finish.

Fiber direction oriented longitudinally with the grain is the board's strongest direction. Tenon shoulders should be cut cross-grain, and tenons should be an extension of the longitudinal fibers for maximum strength.

Random grain (from burls and crotches) is preferred over straight-grain lengths for gussets, knees and braces used to support your assembly.

When planking with plain-sawn boards, alternate boards with rings arcing up, then down, to prevent further compounding the effect of cupping across adjacent boards.

Grain should be oriented with the lengths of rails and other horizontal frames to minimize the seasonal change in piece lengths, and consequently door width. Vertical-grain stock will change less than tangential grain.

Panels (of wood, glass or whatever) should be designed undersize to "float" in the receiving frame. This allows for expansion and contraction of different materials or structural orientation. This is especially critical when combining dissimilar materials. If inserts made from something other than a like wood are to be fastened, slotted holes should be used to relieve the stress and prevent compression or tension from building up in the assembly.

What to Expect From Lumber Standards

In lumber for the construction trade, a *board* is anything under 2″ in thickness, *dimension* lumber is over 2″, and *timbers* are 5″ thick and better. Standards for hardwoods are expressed in quarters, where 8/4 stock is 2″ net. Hardwood

FIGURE 5-2
Standard Wood Cuts

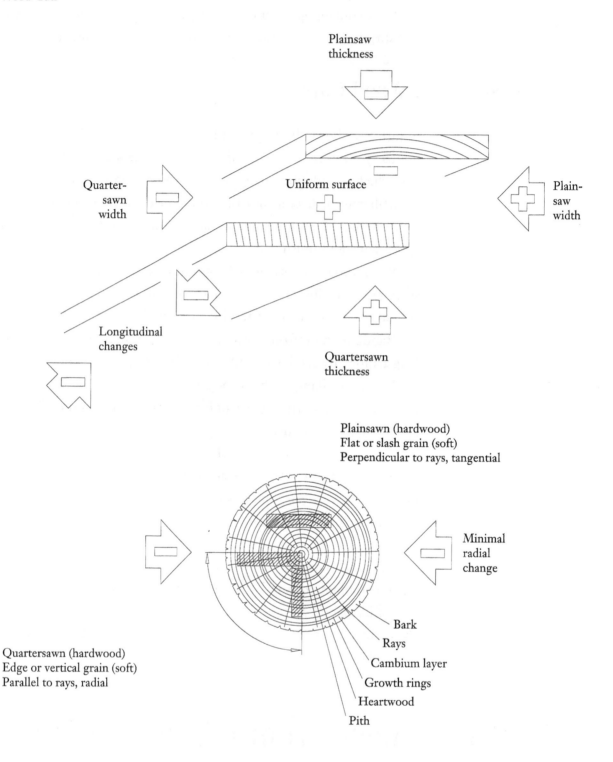

Plainsaw
thickness

Quarter-
sawn
width

Uniform surface

Plain-
saw
width

Longitudinal
changes

Quartersawn
thickness

Plainsawn (hardwood)
Flat or slash grain (soft)
Perpendicular to rays, tangential

Minimal
radial
change

Bark
Rays
Cambium layer
Growth rings
Heartwood
Pith

Quartersawn (hardwood)
Edge or vertical grain (soft)
Parallel to rays, radial

trade associations have since adopted a new standard, however, more closely aligned to those for softwoods.

It seems to me, when premium hardwood was specified in quarter-thickness increments, stock sizes were milled to net the specified thickness. Now hardwood providers are adopting common lumber standards where a 4/4 board is milled to $^{13}/_{16}$″, an 8/4 board to $1\frac{3}{4}$″, etc. So, the standard has changed from specifying and delivering net thicknesses, to up-sizing in order to net the design thickness.

NOTE: Dimension lumber in hardwood parlance refers to finished sizes and cross sections direct from the planing mill ready to pop into place.

Standard Thickness of Milled Hardwoods

In Inches

Rough:	Surfaced:
$^{3}/_{8}$	$^{3}/_{16}$
$^{1}/_{2}$	$^{5}/_{16}$
$^{5}/_{8}$	$^{7}/_{16}$
$^{3}/_{4}$	$^{9}/_{16}$
1	$^{13}/_{16}$
$1\frac{1}{4}$	$1\frac{1}{16}$
$1\frac{1}{2}$	$1\frac{5}{16}$
$1\frac{3}{4}$	$1\frac{1}{2}$
2	$1\frac{3}{4}$
$2\frac{1}{2}$	$2\frac{1}{4}$
3	$2\frac{3}{4}$
$3\frac{1}{2}$	$3\frac{1}{4}$
4	$3\frac{3}{4}$

See page 176 for a list of some candidate woods with their physical characteristics and possible applications. You already have your favorites which you enjoy working.

Unless your shop is equipped with an industrial-size thickness planer, it might be worth the additional pennies to buy surfaced lumber. This way you can select for the figuring and coloring you want for your project. Boards planed on the wide sides are surfaced two sides (S2S). Buying S3S lumber planed on a third side, the one guide edge, makes life easier when cutting pieces to length (at a right angle to a finished edge) or ripping, using the planed edge against your rip fence.

Premium Woods

SPECIES	COLOR, FIGURE	HARDNESS, POROSITY	STYLE
Alder	Cream, minimal	Minimal, closed	Modern, country
Ash	Gray, moderate	Maximal, closed	Federal
Birch	Light, moderate	Moderate, closed	Country
Butternut	Light brown, soft	Moderate, closed	Shaker
Cherry	Pink, moderate	Moderate, closed	Period
Hickory	Light, distinct	Maximal, closed	Baseball bats
Mahogany: Philippine	Brown, minimal	Moderate, open	Arts and Crafts
Honduran	Red, minimal	Maximal, closed	Craftsmen
Maple	Light, moderate	Maximal, closed	Provincial
Oak: Red	Light, moderate	Moderate, open	Palladian
White	Light, moderate	Maximal, closed	Modern
Poplar	Green, moderate	Moderate, open	Shaker
Satinwood	Light, moderate	Moderate, closed	Sheraton
Teak	Brown, highly	Moderate, closed	Garden
Walnut	Dark, highly	Moderate, closed	Queen Anne

If you have a jointer/planer, you might prefer or be forced to true one guide edge yourself. In this case, start with the cupped, concave edge, snap a line, rip, then flip and rip the opposite side, which is planed to form a guide edge.

Consider Mechanical Properties

Since we're not building a subfloor to support heavy equipment, arched trusses to hold a roof in place, a cantilevered deck or a room addition for the projects discussed in this book, you won't need reams of calculations on those mechanical properties critical in construction safety. There are mechanical properties the custom designer/craftsman needs to consider, however, when designing and building furniture.

Respect Properties of Wood

Every custom-furniture project should be approached with a respect for the coefficient of materials, that is, the different rate of expansion and contraction or initial shrinkage. Then select the best variety and mill cut for the application. This involves orienting fibers and cells to minimize the effects of seasonal changes. As the Flemish and English discovered long ago, massive furniture might hold together better if built in the frame and panel style.

Each project should include an adequate thickness of its components for rigid construction, and should be capable of resisting deflection under years of normal use and withstanding the inevitable knocks of time. A desktop is a good example of a substrate—strong enough to resist a leaning elbow, and maybe even a standing figure if the desk becomes a convenient platform to fix a curtain or to bag a bug, or just serve as a stacking platform during a move.

More Critical Properties

Furniture designed to be sat, climbed or stood on should undergo some stress analysis (either by eye or mathematics) to verify that the structural properties are adequate for the design. This begins with the wood's strength in the thicknesses designed to support, span and join a structure capable of carrying the weight of a person. This is especially critical where all of the weight is concentrated in a small area, such as library steps or a ladder to an upper bunk bed. Here you want to design and build on the conservative side using a safety factor of 1½ to 2 times the strength required.

Your experience and common sense will result in a design that meets or exceeds the margins of safety required. Most furniture is not subjected to extreme stresses requiring compression tests, rupture or shear-strength analysis—unless the scantlings are slight or the structural integrity of the wood is inherently weak. No one will, or best not, subject your piece to its rupture failure point, so many of the stress-analysis tests do not apply in furniture building. What is needed is a good margin of safety in the strength provided, for the safety of the user and to ensure the longevity of the piece.

A three-step library ladder and a nearly vertical ladder leading to a top bunk bed have similar characteristics and safety considerations.

A flight of stairs or a ladder form a right triangle where the rise and the run meet (see figure 5-3). The sloping side is the hypotenuse of this triangle, and its length can be found using:

$$\text{sloping side} = \sqrt{\text{rise}^2 + \text{run}^2}$$

FIGURE 5-3

A Look at Ladders and Stairs

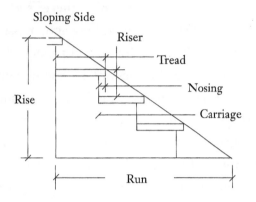

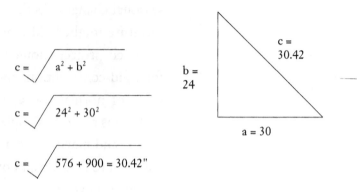

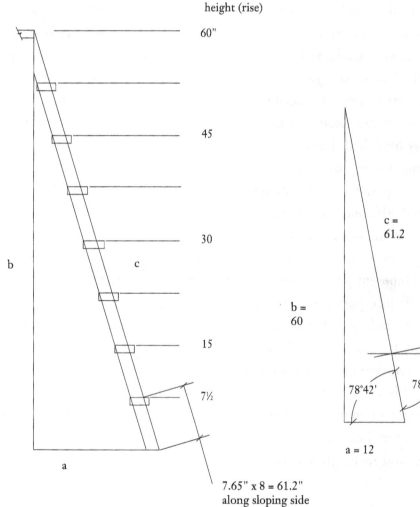

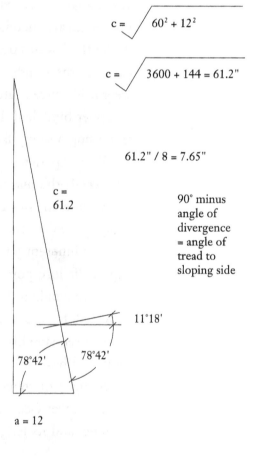

The hypotenuse is equal to the square root of the sum of the squares of the sides, remember?

Stair risers (height between stairs) should not exceed 8″, and are more comfortable at a 6″ rise. So a landing 24″ high (a rise of 2′) could be three treads at 8″, four treads at 6″, or six treads at 4″ each. With a base of 30″ by 30″, you would solve for the slope length using:

$$\text{sloping side} = \sqrt{24^2+30^2} = \sqrt{576+900} = 38.42''$$

A comfortable rise for a ladder is 10″ between rungs, but for a child's room, maybe 8″ is better. Here you have a height set by the upper bunk rail. Let's assume the ladder will hook at the rail at 5′. So the rise equals 60″. The run could be zero (vertical), but probably safer if designed at an angle. The ladder base should not project too far into the room, so assume a run of 12″. Therefore:

$$\text{sloping side} = \sqrt{60^2+12^2} = \sqrt{3600+144} = 61.2''$$

The upper bunk rail, located 60″ off the floor, is considered to be the uppermost rung location. Therefore 60″ (target rise) divided by 8 (number of steps) equals 7½″ between treads along the vertical rise. To determine the spacing on the slope, divide the length of the hypotenuse (61.2″) by the same number of divisions (8), yielding 7.65″ rung spacing.

There is one more bit of information you'll need: the angle of the tread to the slope. You want to keep the tread horizontal so the angle of the tread to the slope will equal the angle of the ladder to the floor. Unfortunately, unless you want to guesstimate with a protractor, this angle is determined through mathematical formulas that require the use of a table of tangents, sines and cosines (see *Machinery's Handbook*) for given angles, or a calculator. In fact, you will need a scientific calculator, or at least one that can figure out tangent, sine and cosine.

To figure out the angle of the ladder to the floor, you need to determine the tangent of the angle (B). This is simply defined by the relationship of the rise to the run. The formula is tan B = rise/run. Now, just plug in the numbers you know: tan B = 60/12. So we know that tan B = 5. To determine angle B, you need to press *5* on the calculator and then press the *inverse* or *second function* key and then press the *tangent* key. This should give you an angle of about 78.69°.

For both safety and appearance reasons, you will want all riser heights to be identical throughout the flight, including the floor to the first tread, and the top tread to the destination.

A short library ladder should be designed with an ample tread of at least 8″ from the front edge, or nosing, to the riser at the back. The top step can be a minilanding, deeper than the ascending treads, to be used as a standing platform. Ladders can have shallower tread, which are more comfortable fdsgon the feet than rungs or rails, but the treads must have adequate depth and clearance for the feet.

THICKNESSES—Treads supported by boxed risers (library steps) can be thinner than the rungs spanning the closing sides of a ladder. In this example, the treads are subjected to many stresses known to man: bending, stiffness and shock. The area of section (cross section) of a spanning member, the distance spanned and the joinery at the supporting ends combine to make up the strength.

The cross section of a single board 1¾″ by 8″ (2 × 8) would represent an area of section equaling 14 square inches (see figure 5-4). After determining this is adequate for the projected loads but too heavy for the style, the target cross section (and therefore strength) can be achieved by designing a tread of 1¹⁄₁₆″ × 8″ (1¼ × 8 nominal), augmented by a 2″ × 2¾″ support under the tread to total 14 square inches. Where a riser is added, even thinner stock can net the same 14-square-inch cross section, by designing a ¹³⁄₁₆″ × 8″ (1 × 8 nominal) tread, a ¹³⁄₁₆″ × 6″ riser, and a ¹³⁄₁₆″ × 3¼″ lower support.

CAPTURING LADDER SIDES—The method you design to attach treads to the closing sides is your preference of what best suits the piece. Ladder treads should be let into the closing sides as far as possible without compromising the integrity of the vertical sides, maybe ⅜ to ½ the thickness of the vertical members. A dado can be augmented with a cleat to add more supporting surface under the tread, which also provides a means of fastening the tread from below. Through dowels or plugged screws might fit the design if you elect to fasten through the outside of the closing sides. Also, any stringers can be locked into the cleats to increase the rigidity.

Select the Best Grain Orientation

Wood should be selected for the desired look, feel, color and finish. There are also physical properties that need to be considered, which can be enhanced by the cut you select.

FIGURE 5-4
Capturing the Tread

Stiffness

Area of Section

1¾ x 8 = 14 sq in.

1¹⁄₁₆ x 8 = 8.5 sq in.
2 x 2.75 = 5.5 = 14 sq in.

Bending Strength

¹³⁄₁₆ x 8 = 6.5 sq in.
¹³⁄₁₆ x 6 = 4.875
¹³⁄₁₆ x 3¼ = 2.641
Section = 14.02 sq in.

Shock Resistance

Area of section can be a
single board, or built up of
tread, brace and riser

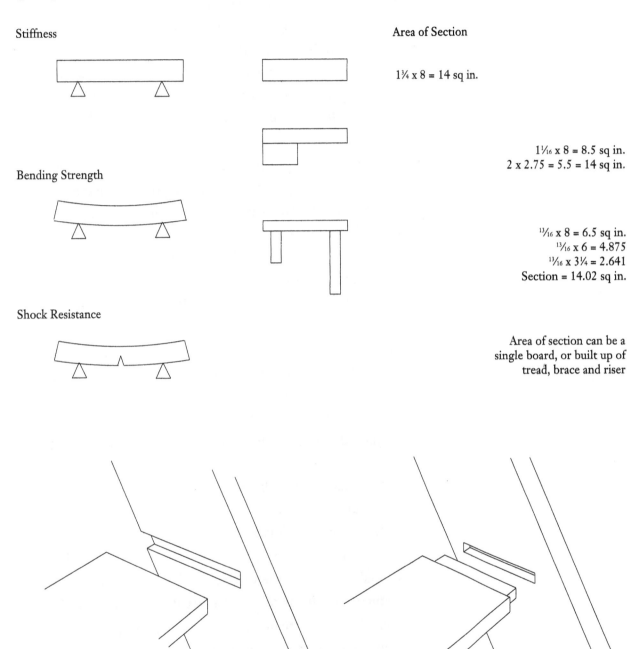

MATERIALS—Choose flat-grain stock over vertical grain for this application because it presents a stronger interlocking network of longitudinal fibers which are less likely to fail along the shear line. The shear line occurs where the nosing of a tread stands proud of the riser plate below, or without a riser plate in ladders. The vertical grain, so highly touted in the next paragraph for its mar-resistant qualities, would present its weakest face along the highest stress line, where the fibers could roll over each other and break down a little with each climb.

Vertical grain will provide a mar-resistant surface to hold up better throughout its life. For example, edge grain will resist penetration better than a flat-grain board. Consistent hardness is an important attribute for a writing surface. Ladders and steps are trodden on, but have more important considerations that overrule this premise, as described above.

With all these characteristics considered, the selected wood must be workable. To use ironwood or lignum vitae for its hardness is self-defeating. These are difficult to carve into a saddle seat or bend in an arc.

If softer woods are preferred, or if they are the traditional materials for a style such as Shaker or Windsor chairs, the mill cut you select can maximize the characteristics desired. When producing your own molding, a homogeneous wood of a medium density will machine easily and consistently. Longitudinal grain, either plain or quartersawn, can be run through the milling heads satisfactorily for successful sticking. Reaction wood, or boards milled on the diagonal, or slope-grained, can produce areas where you'll cut against random cells and fibers, which can affect the smoothness of the cut and the finish.

Orientation of wood fiber normally runs with the length of the stock. Short lengths should be cut so the direction of the grain maximizes joint strength and reduces the effects of seasonal expansion and contraction.

Whether you select the more highly figured pattern of plain-sawn wood, or the more homogeneous quartersawn vertical grain, be sure the board was cut aligned closely with the grain direction. Slope grain can weaken a board by as much as half the normal strength of a straight-grained cut where fibers are at a severe angle to the run of the board.

Use the fiber direction to your advantage when cutting pieces to length. Mortise and tenon, dowel and biscuit joints are strongest when the mating parts are aligned with the grain. If the shorter members are cut cross-grain, there is a chance of failure between cell walls or of the fibers rolling over

FIGURE 5-5
Grain Orientation

Relative Strength:

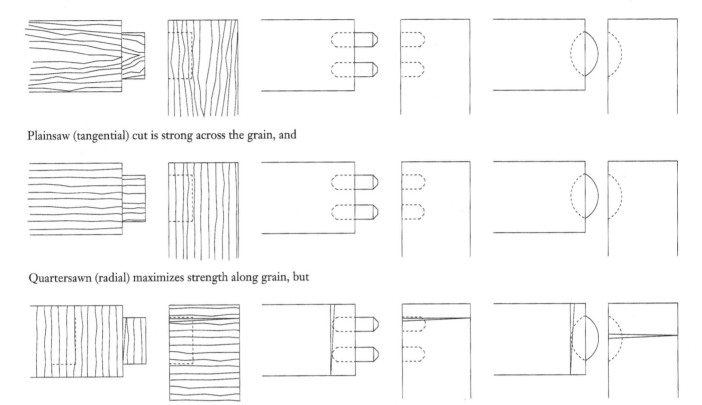

Plainsaw (tangential) cut is strong across the grain, and

Quartersawn (radial) maximizes strength along grain, but

Quartersawn may fail sooner if grain is perpendicular
to the length

Amount of Shrinkage and Expansion:

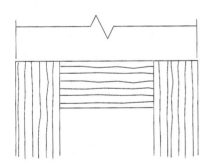 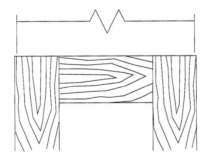 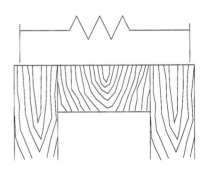

Quartersawn
changes size a
lesser amount
across the grain

Plainsaw
changes size
across the grain
more than
quartersawn

Maximum change
occurs when
all joined pieces
are plainsawn and
oriented
crossgrain

each other (rolling shear stress) when they run perpendicular to the length of the member and in the normal stress direction.

Another plus for running the grain with the length of the piece is that seasonal changes have almost no effect on wood in the longitudinal direction of the fibers. It is the cross-grain direction that changes most with the amount of moisture absorbed. And again, plain-sawn wood will change more than quartersawn in the cross-grain orientation.

Reaction wood has random grain, usually occurring in and around a branch or crotch or burl. In softwood, the area of reaction wood is under the branch and is considered to be in compression. In hardwoods, this area occurs above the branch causing stress in tension. These cuts, if they have survived air drying, and possibly kiln drying, are good candidates for corner gussets, brackets and braces, since there is no single direction of weakness as you might find in straight-grained wood.

Direction of the grain is also to be considered when machining wood parts. *The Encyclopedia of Wood* reminds us that reaction wood, especially in stress as is typical of hardwoods, can pinch the saw blade during cutting, as the wood in stress could relieve that stress by closing around the saw blade. Rate of feed and blade type can overcome this action.

There are some species of trees that do not grow straight, but rather have more of an interlocking and irregular grain. Among those you might have used in the past, or may plan to use in your next project, are apitong, laurel, lignum vitae and rosewood.

Figure 5-6 shows how best to rip and plane parts and pieces, normally with the grain. A board that has been mill cut parallel to the fibers should feed successfully in either direction. A close look for any blown fibers along a cut edge, or more roughness felt in one direction than the other as you run your fingers along the cut, will indicate which direction is with the grain. If you still can't tell, feed direction does not matter.

Any slope-grain stock you may have acquired should be cut, planed and milled with the run-out of the fibers trailing, not leading. If planing end grain, do not plane the full width of the board without first undercutting the run-out edge with the jointer/planer. When the piece is reversed and fed in the opposite direction, the first cut will provide a relief for the cutter blades and prevent splitting of the end as the cutter blows out from the run.

FIGURE 5-6
Feed Direction

Joint/Planer Direction — Edges

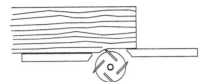

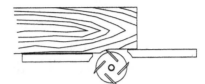

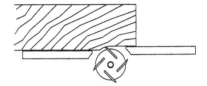

Parallel grain
feeds in either
directions

Plainsawn
grain direction
should trail

Slope grain
should trail
as well

Direction — End Grain

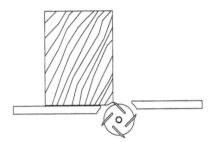

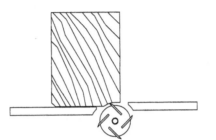

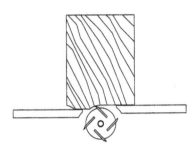

Notch trailing
edge

Reverse and
feed toward
notched
corner

Undercut
should prevent
splitting and
blowing out

Splitting is assured without undercutting trailing corner

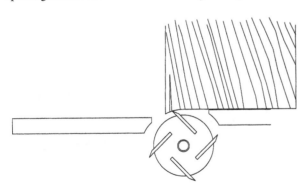

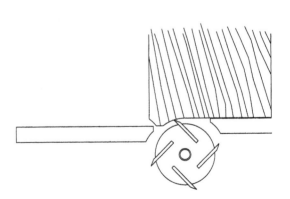

Bonding and Adhesives

There are numerous factors that make up a strong, lasting glue joint. Physical properties (strengths) of materials and optimum gluing conditions are controlled by your selection and timing.

Bonding strength of an adhesive can be further enhanced by your design of the joinery. Take a close look at the percent of bonded area to the pieces being bonded and increase for the amount and type of stress the furniture will withstand.

Adding Bonding Area to the Joint

Where a straight butt joint represents a 100 percent gluing surface bonding to an adjoining piece, more complex joints provide more gluing surfaces, as shown in Figure 5-7. For example, a simple butt block will augment a gluing surface by whatever size block you elect to use.

CORNERS

For corners, a miter joint adds about 40 percent more area to the gluing surface over a butt joint. A mitered spline increases that gluing surface by the area of the spline, which could be another 80 percent, so a mitered spline joint could present a 220 percent gluing surface when compared with a straight butt joint.

A rabbeted joint adds the area equal to the depth of the rabbet times the member width. So if the rabbet is one-half the thickness, it would add 50 percent to the bonding area. A mitered rabbet is just for the corner appearance, since it adds only 10 percent more gluing surface to the joint.

A lock miter not only adds gluing area, but uses the strength of the wood to prevent pullout in the direction of a drawer face to drawer sides.

Finger lap joints that are set in the thickness of the corner materials will add 100 percent to the area glued. The dovetail, a fancy finger lap configuration, relies more on the interlocking shapes and the strength of the wood to produce a lasting joint. However, the added gluing area increases its integrity while preventing pullout from side loads.

EDGE-JOINED PLANKS

Edge-joined planks can be strengthened by increasing the area with a tongue and groove. Or use a gluejoint bit to shape the mating edges into

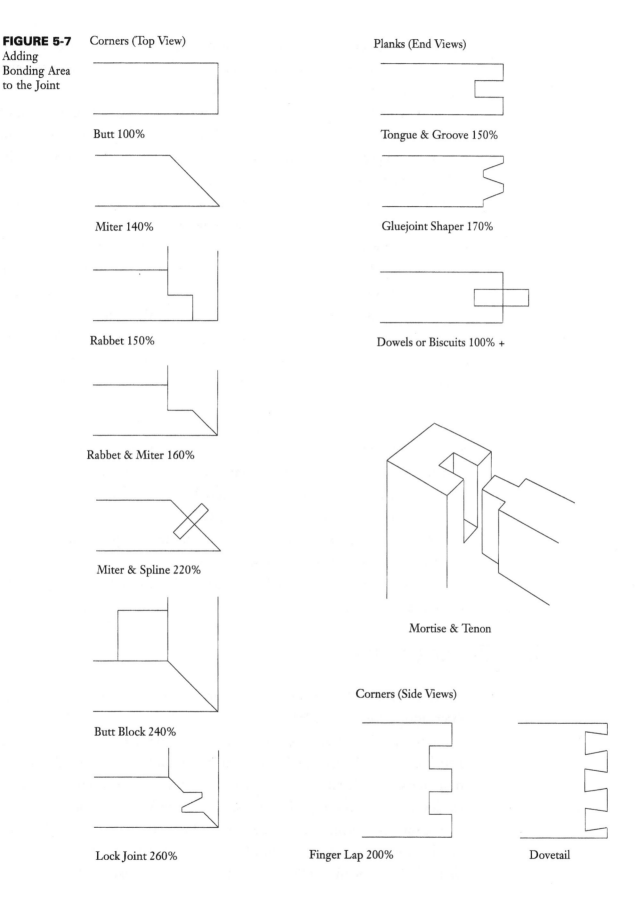

FIGURE 5-7
Adding
Bonding Area
to the Joint

Corners (Top View)

Butt 100%

Miter 140%

Rabbet 150%

Rabbet & Miter 160%

Miter & Spline 220%

Butt Block 240%

Lock Joint 260%

Planks (End Views)

Tongue & Groove 150%

Gluejoint Shaper 170%

Dowels or Biscuits 100% +

Mortise & Tenon

Corners (Side Views)

Finger Lap 200%

Dovetail

187

a reversible pattern, one in which the profile reverses top to bottom to match up the thicknesses of the planks. The glued surface is increased and the interlocking tongues prevent vertical lift.

Mortise and tenon joint strength is a factor of the depth and height of the tenon. The use of tenons or splines will increase gluing area and augment the structural properties of the joint. Tenons, splines, dowel pins or biscuits add the structural properties of their own materials to the joint.

Bond strength is further ensured through adequate surface preparation.

Fits should be snug but should not squeeze all the glue from the joint. Leave room for the adhesive to penetrate and bond the parts.

Cuts should be smooth and free of any residue, but not overworked. "Distort not the straight cut" (as some wise person must have said) and leave some tooth to the material for linking with the glue.

Glue joints involving end grain, such as miter joints, usually require more glue to migrate into the open cells. A double application of glue to end grain will penetrate and seal the cells and prevent wicking, which starves the joint of the needed glue.

You should always follow temperature ranges, clamping pressures and set times recommended by the adhesive manufacturer.

Mitered splines, dowel pins, biscuits and metal fasteners all contribute the inherent strength of their own materials to the joint.

Increased gluing area can add strength, but that is just a part of the preparation. The adhesive you use must be up to the appointed task, be it outdoors where it must withstand wide temperature and moisture variations, or a friendlier environment indoors, but subject to high stress levels and heavy use.

Glue Characteristics

Before we launch into properties, preparation and product, a few general observations might be helpful.

Waterproof glues are resistant to heat and moisture, capable of holding their bond in boiling water for a few minutes. But because you don't plan to submerse your furniture, maybe you don't have to contend with the rigid, nonflexible adhesives, especially those that come in dark colors.

For outdoor furniture, consider some of the epoxy products. These are also suitable for laminating thin plies to form a mass or shape, especially when a balloon or fiber filler is added to close any small voids.

Water-resistant aliphatic resin glue for indoor use, when well sealed in high humidity climates, is an easy-to-use, easy-to-finish, translucent adhesive, capable of providing a good long-lasting bond between wood parts.

Contact cements and mastics have their place in the bonding scheme of things as well, such as bonding an inset top panel to a substrate. Surface preparation and application procedures are critical to a good bond. Yellow glues could be used for this application as well, if the materials are sufficiently absorbent for the glue to penetrate the materials.

Surface preparation is more critical to bond integrity in oily woods, such as teak, rosewood and lignum vitae. To promote better bonding, before applying glue, these woods should first be wiped along the gluing surfaces with acetone or lacquer thinner to remove the oils at and in porous cells near the surface.

NOTE: When using solvents, follow the manufacturer's recommendations and cautions. Warnings about flash points of flammable materials, possible irritation when in contact with the volatile material, proper disposal of rags, and so on, are to be seriously considered and heeded.

Mating surfaces should be planed smooth, but not polished. A slight tooth improves bonding by providing more area of microscopic crevices and pores to receive and lock the glue line.

Splines, dowels, biscuits and tenons should be snug, but not power-pressed into the mating part. This allows room for glue to coat and set on mating surfaces and to relieve stress during expansion and contraction. It should be noted, however, that in softer woods, pegs tightly wedged into a chair back have stayed in some seats for over one hundred years.

A glue comparison has been compiled from various sources, including manufacturers' data, as a guide to selecting adhesive for different types of projects. The following table presents some general characteristics of the basic glue types. Manufacturers' literature will be helpful in selecting the right glue for the task.

Tests conducted by the U.S. Forestry Service's Forest Products Laboratory (and published in *The Encyclopedia of Wood*) rated the strengths of several rigid thermoset adhesives fully exposed outdoors over an extended period. The resorcinols and phenols retained close to 100 percent of their original strength when exposed to the outdoor elements for eight years. During that test, Melamine lost approximately 25 percent of its original strength, and the urea-type glues failed halfway into the test. These are all

Attributes of Glues

TYPE	FAMILY	ATTRIBUTES
WATERPROOF	Epoxy	Two-part resin and catalyst
		Bonds similar and dissimilar materials
		Provides filler with fibers or balloons
		Translucent
		Withstands extreme environments
		Pot life and set time affected by catalyst content, volume of batch mixed and temperature
	Resorcinol	Two-part powder and hardener
		Dark red or purple in color
		Resistant to temperature and chemicals
		Withstands moderate environments
		Longer pot life, longer set time
		High-pressure clamping during set
MOISTURE RESISTANT	Urea Resins, Plastic Resins	Precatalyzed dry powder—water-activated(formaldehyde) or two-part resin powder/formaldehyde mix
		Amber
	Improved Yellow	One-part cross-linking polyaliphatic resin
		Translucent
		Strong initial tack
	Thermoplastic Resin	Heat gun applied
		Little penetration
		Fills and bonds
MOISTURE-SUSCEPTIBLE	Hide Glue	Natural protein
		Dry strength, wet release
		Slow set
	Original Yellow	Aliphatic resin
		Heat and moisture susceptible
		Cream to translucent
	White Glues	Polyvinyl acetate resin
		More pliable than moisture-resistant glues
		May give under continued stress
		Better for crafts than craftsmen
ELASTOMERS	Contact Cements	Applied to both surfaces, pressed or pressure-rolled
	Mastic	Tubes, applied by caulking gun

rigid glues, as compared with the vinyl acetate white and the aliphatic resin yellow varieties. Epoxy was not included in the test samples.

These samples were subjected to the most extreme conditions and certainly would not be typical of your project. But the tests provide some insight on the relative strengths and durability of these adhesives.

Glues are formulated for specific uses, and some trade-offs are made to meet market requirements. Brittle glues do not creep and are used where the laminate or joint is under constant load. Such a constant load will cause a softer glue to creep and fail, especially under high temperature. But brittle glues are less shock resistant, whereas the more flexible types will withstand an occasional jolt or jarring. You pay your money, and you take your chances.

Specialty glues have been developed (or touted) for their woodworking qualities: slow set for some applications, quick tack for others, high viscosity to eliminate run and drip and dark-colored glues for dark wood. Hide glue is favored as the antique-furniture repairer's glue for its strength, but ease of removal when softened with water.

Visit your glue purveyor and choose the right glue to meet the objectives.

Components: Cutting Lists, Plans, Patterns and Profiles

The fail-safe steps when going from plans to cutting list, detailed in chapter four, should be reviewed here. Cutting all parts beforehand can be a risky approach, but one that many craftsmen take in the interest of time and shared-use workshops. If this approach is preferred, an increased emphasis should be placed on the accuracy of your drawings and the math used to define and verify the widths, breadths and lengths of the piece's parts.

The materials list prepared from your drawings defines the bill of materials, giving you an idea of how many board feet or linear feet of material you will need of specific thicknesses and widths. Revisiting this work, or completing it now, should reduce the number of trips needed to the lumberyard and ensure matching stock is used throughout the project. This is no guarantee that all types, coloring and net dimensions will be the same, or that they will all finish exactly the same, but one-stop shopping improves the chances of selecting matching characteristics for use in a piece of custom furniture.

When going from the cutting list to the cutting table, your cuts must be right on. Recheck the dimensions. *Remember to measure twice, cut once.*

Duplicating Pieces

In your design you went to great pains to lay out what you want to see in the final article. Getting into a production mode is easier when you have some aids to guide the duplication process.

Flat Work

Some details may be easier to fabricate and duplicate if you work from a full-size pattern. Scrolls, corbels, arcs, mirror-image aprons, skirts and the like are candidates for lofting such patterns. Your alternative is to locate precisely the trammel point to strike a long arc the same distance from the stock being scribed in as many pieces as your plans call for. It is usually easier, faster and more accurate when tracing from a pattern.

Turnings

Lathe work for some people, myself included, is one of the more enjoyable processes in the shop. With a diagram of diameters and their locations, you can cut the blank to the various diameters along the blank as verified by a good pair of outside calipers. Then, with the aid of a cut profile guide, you can bring the turning into a duplicate spindle, spandrel, leg or bedpost.

A more traditional style might call for matching half-turnings. If so, temporarily glue the two halves of the turning stock with a single sheet of newspaper in between. After turning, finishing and removing from the lathe bed, a blow with a sharp chisel will split the newsprint, thereby separating the halves cleanly. Remove the glue/paper residue and the pieces are ready to apply to the furniture.

If your project includes some type of a raceway, perhaps for a lamp base cord or to route power to a computer desk—something integral to the furniture—you could prebore the center hole in oversize stock, then cut the stock square and concentric to the bore.

Where two longitudinal pieces will form the turning blank, dado a groove down the center of one or both facing planes before the halves are glued. Plug or cap the prebored hole for the drive spur and tailstock of the lathe.

Pantographs or other tracing aids can be used with a router or a lathe to duplicate parts from a model or first article. Lathe work can also duplicate longitudinal veining using a router jig over the lathe bed.

Selecting the Hardware

Choose the Right Fasteners

Whatever fasteners you buy for your project, don't scrimp on quality. Even though these will not be exposed (in most designs), use screws and bolts cut from quality metal. Nickel-plated wood screws properly sized to the parts being fastened through prebored pilot holes will eliminate assembly frustration and provide lasting holding strength.

Many new fasteners are on the market, including self-tapping, sharp cutting screws. Self-cutting, square drive screws may be used in some fine furniture applications, but not without first predrilling properly sized pilot holes. These screws were designed for construction in wallboard/common lumber, where the cellulose composition will compress. This is not the case in seasoned premium hardwoods.

In premium hardwoods it is still best to use wood screws and glue to fasten bases, gussets, braces and cleats using high-quality standard wood screws and predrilling matching pilot holes.

Standard screw heads include:
- Flathead chamfered with slot drive
- Flathead Phillips
- Flathead with square drive
- Oval head, chamfered (with or without washer)
- Round head, flat bottom (with or without washer)

For all such hardwoods, where gussets are glued and screwed or bases are attached, control drill lengths using a collar or a visual stop mark just long enough for the size of the screw being used to prevent distortion, or worse, penetration through exposed surfaces. Specify on the drawing (or just remember) to drill pilot holes for the screw size. The screw designation can be $1\frac{1}{4}''$ #8, or #10 × $1\frac{1}{4}''$ where the # designates the wire gauge and the

FIGURE 5-8
Fasteners—Putting It Together

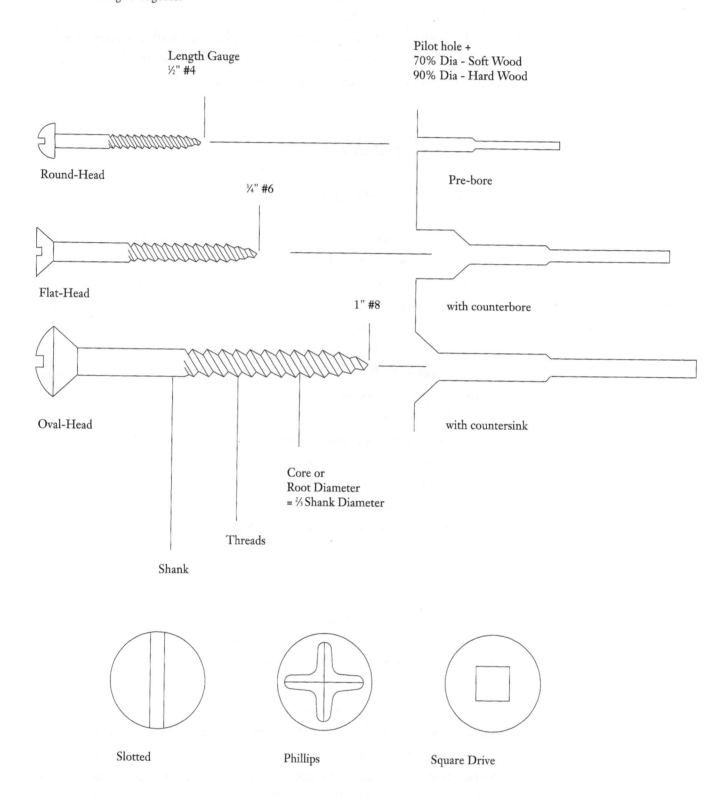

Length Gauge
½" #4

Pilot hole +
70% Dia - Soft Wood
90% Dia - Hard Wood

Round-Head

Pre-bore

¾" #6

Flat-Head

with counterbore

1" #8

Oval-Head

with countersink

Core or
Root Diameter
= ⅔ Shank Diameter

Threads

Shank

Slotted

Phillips

Square Drive

Pilot and Counterbore Hole Sizes

Gauge #	2	3	4	5	6	7	8	9	10	12
Shank Size	.086 5/64	.099 3/32	.112 7/64	.125 1/8	.138 9/64	.151 5/32	.164 11/64	.177 11/64	.190 3/16	.216 7/32
Pilot Hole Soft	.047 3/64	.047 3/64	.063 1/16	.078 5/64	.078 5/64	.094 3/32	.094 3/32	.110 7/64	.110 7/64	.125 1/8
Hard	.056 3/64	.071 1/16	.078 5/64	.090 3/32	.096 3/32	.108 7/64	.116 7/64	.123 1/8	.126 1/8	.155 5/32
Counterbore Hole	.172 11/64	.199 7/32	.225 1/4	.252 1/4	.279 1/4	.305 5/16	.332 11/32	.358 3/8	.385 13/32	.438 7/16

other the length. Diameters for the range of gauges are presented above.

Combination bits are designed for each specific screw diameter and length. These bits usually provide a pilot hole equal to the root or core diameter between the screw threads and the actual shank and head diameter. Some bits are length-adjustable.

Whether you use a combination bit or multiple bits, preparing the holes for the right screw size makes driving easier, is kinder to the wood and will hold fast. If you plan to use a power driver, test the first hole by hand to determine how much torque is required to drive the screw home. Too much torque can cause splitting, even when holes are offset from a common line to prevent such occurrence. If the screw has too much resistance, increase the pilot or shank diameter for a snug, but not an ultratight fit where you could turn the head off the screw.

Recommended screw lengths by aggregate thickness of joined pieces:

1/2″ + 3/4″	1″, 4
3/4″ + 3/4″	1 3/4″, 6
3/4″ + 7/8″	1 1/4″, 8

Screw length should ideally be twice the thickness of the board being attached, but should extend no more than three-quarters of the way toward an outside exposed face. Fastening a board through its thickness into a board on-edge can apply the double thickness rule. Longer screws are recommended for fastening into end grain.

When choosing hardware, the designer/craftsman should consider the variables that affect holding strength. Each combination of materials, joinery, clamping pressure and duration will net a different holding strength. Some of the alternatives you might consider are:

Holding by orientation

- *Straight into various grain orientations*
- *Angled into same*
- *Counterbore depth*
- *Plugs—button, round, flush*
- *Countersinking*
- *Exposed—half-round, oval with finishing washers*

Holding in wood

- *Species*
- *Density*
- *Integrity*

Holding by mill cut

- *Direction of fiber*
- *Edge grain*
- *Flat grain*
- *End grain*
- *Slope grain*

Holding by fastener

- *Screw material*
- *Screw length*
- *Screw diameter*
- *Thread diameter*
- *Prebore length*
- *Prebore diameter*

Joint in stress

- *Bearing weight*
- *Bearing angle*

Adhesive

- *Glue integrity*
- *Bonding strength*
- *Bond life*

Whatever combination of physical parts and preparation, one important tip is to never rely on the screw alone to bring pieces together. Clamp firmly before fastening.

Accessorize in Context

Match metals, certainly throughout the piece being built, and also any theme or pattern already established in its new environment. Don't select Southwestern hardware for your Hepplewhite cabinet. This is ridiculous to mention, but it is equally ridiculous to mix styles, which spells disaster for your design efforts.

Select hardware for the look you like, for the style you're producing and any special mechanism or application. Some of the many specialty outlets carrying quality, special-purpose hardware are listed in the resources appendix on page 202.

Size is as important as style in the hardware for your design. You can choose the "perfect" complementing knob or hinge, but if it is out of scale, either too small to function properly or too small or too large for the proportions of the furniture, you can unravel the design and the positive attributes you've preserved throughout the project. Hardware should complement the design, which may have been influenced by some detail earlier, after some preliminary legwork in finding and maybe even buying the right hardware.

Finish to Complement Form, Materials and Environs

The design process continues in your selection of how the piece will be finished. Select a finish that suits a number of considerations, including location, style, wood and years of use and abuse. Consider the surrounding environs—room color, amount of light, matching furniture, etc. Select a finish that complements your design or typifies the style and era if building a replica. The function of the furniture also should be considered when selecting its finish. A matte finish could "powder" or "chalk" under hard use; a high-gloss finish might be harder.

Newly finished wood tends to look bright and new. Much can be done at the outset to tone down the wood, or you can be patient and let the sunlight, heat and ultraviolet rays mellow the finish. Darker woods lighten and light woods darken gradually over time.

Traditional furniture should be finished traditionally. Contemporary furniture has no precedent or preconceived format to be followed. Your goal is to protect the surface with a quality, long-lasting finish that can be maintained easily to retain the beauty. The finish coat can be high gloss, semigloss, matte or flat, or maybe oiled or waxed—whatever is most suitable for the article in its surroundings.

Too much color or pigment that hides the natural beauty of the fine hardwood you so carefully selected would be criminal. But in some designs, a clear natural finish might be out of character. If you intend to paint from the outset, select a wood based more on its characteristics and capacity to hold a good finish coat of paint, whitewash or antique finish.

Some wood species, such as red oak and some mahoganies, and different mill cuts will be porous. For these you might consider a sanding sealer or filler-type stain. Filler stains close open capillaries and provide a smoother base for the sealing coat.

If you will be applying a clear coat, you can use lacquer or varnish. The type of varnish or polyurethane you select is important. In the old days, varnish was formulated for the purpose. Known as short, medium and long, these terms applied to the amount of oil used per 100 pounds of resin. Short used only 5 to 15 gallons of oil, medium was 15 to 20, and long from 35 to 50 gallons of oil per 100 pounds of resin. A greater proportion of oil produces a softer, more elastic varnish, whereas more resin results in a harder, faster drying surface.

The synthetic resins, such as the polyurethanes, follow the same tradition. Most of the yellowing tendencies of the polyurethanes have been formulated out (we hope). It is best to test the product on a sample strip that has been sanded with the same smoothness as the furniture you're finishing, to check for color, reflection, marring and chalking before laying a brush to your work.

Some preparations, products and techniques you can choose from include:

NATURAL	STAINED	SEALER
Wax	Wipe-on	Shellac
Oiled	Antiquing	Lacquer
Clear	Aniline dyes	Varnish and
	Filler	polyurethanes
		Satin
		Matte
		Semigloss
		Gloss

A dust-free surface and a relatively dust-free environment are essential while brushing or spraying on the finish.

If using any type of antiquing, check for solubility of the undercoat in the overcoating material. Allow the pigmented undercoat to dry before applying the finish coat, and even then, work in one direction and continue moving on. Don't go back to try to fix a holiday (a blank or missed area) or a run in the initial coat. This could lift the pigment, thin it out or spread it around a bit. Fix it during an interim or final coat.

The reminders, cautions and suggestions contained in this chapter will hopefully serve as a memory jogger for the designer/craftsman to ply the trade. As in all media of expression, from music to art to building fine furniture, personal interpretation and skilled execution make the design unique, your signature, your mark.

Epilogue

The remaining pages contain some resources, although you may already have your network of favorite suppliers of tools, equipment and materials needed to fabricate your design. Your local providers are your best resource, but there may be some specialty hardware or precut parts that would add that extra spark to your project. This is your personal preference.

Your personal preference will be applied to the content of this book as well. Beginning with developing the initial concept, you have your own way of approaching a new project, and your way of completing it as well.

What we've tried to do is to put on paper the mental processes, the design decisions and the course you might take throughout the task. This book offered guidelines on standard sizes and shapes, on how to commit your ideas to paper, and finally a few thoughts on what might, or should, be considered in transforming these ideas into reality. Maybe we have averted a minor disaster, added a few new ideas and helped make your next project a more enjoyable one, from the first spark of an idea to the finished piece.

Bibliography

This bibliography contains literature cited, referred to, or thought to be of interest for further reading or reference.

Andrews, Edward, Deming and Faith, *Shaker Furniture* New York: Dover Publications, 1964.

Aronson, Joseph. *The Encyclopedia of Furniture*. 3rd ed. New York: Crown Publishers, 1965.

Burchell, Sam. *History of Furniture*. New York: Harry N. Abrams, Inc., A Times Mirror Company, 1991.

Ching, Frank. *Interior Design Illustrated*. New York: Van Nostrand Reinhold, 1987.

Sanders, Barry, ed. *The Craftsman, An Anthology*. Santa Barbara/Salt Lake City: Peregrine Smith, Inc. 1978.

Domenech, Rafael and Luis Perez Bueno. *Antique Spanish Furniture*. New York: The Archive Press, 1965.

Dormer, Peter. *The New Furniture: Trends & Tradition*. New York: Thames and Hudson, Inc., 1987.

Fiell, Charlotte and Peter. *Modern Furniture Classics Since 1945*. Washington, DC: Thames and Hudson, Ltd./American Institute of Architects Press, 1991.

Forest Products Laboratory, Forest Service, U.S. Department of Agriculture. *The Encyclopedia of Wood*, Rev. New York: Sterling Publishing Co., 1989.

Grotz, George. *The Furniture Doctor*. Garden City, NY: Doubleday and Company, Inc., 1962.

Joy, Edward. *Connoisseur Illustrated Guide: Furniture*. New York: Hearst Books, 1972.

Mang, Karl. *History of Modern Furniture*. Translated by John William Gabriel. Stuttgart, Germany: Verlag Gerd Hatje, 1978.

Moser, Thomas. *Measured Shop Drawings for American Furniture*. Edited by Michael Cea. New York, NY: Sterling Publishing Co., 1985.

Nutting, Wallace. *Furniture Treasury*, 8th printing. New York: The MacMillian Company, 1971.

Oberg, Erik, Franklin D. Jones, Holbrook L. Horton, and Henry H. Ryffel. *Machinery's Handbook: A Reference Book for the Mechanical Engineer, Designer, Manufacturing Engineer, Draftsman, Toolmaker and Machinist*. Edited by Robert E. Green. 24th ed. New York: Industrial Press, Inc., 1992.

Panero, Julius and Martin Zelnik. *Human Dimensions and Interior Space: A Source Book of Design Reference Standards*. New York: Whitney Library of Design, an imprint of Watson-Guptill Publications, a division of Billboard Publications, Inc., 1979.

Stone, Michael A. *Contemporary American Woodworkers*. Layton, UT: A Peregrine Smith Book published by Gibbs M. Smith, Inc., 1954.

Stoops, Jack and Jerry Samuelson (Cal State Fullerton). *Design Dialogue*. Worchester, MA: Davis Publications, Inc., 1983.

Resources

RESOURCES FOR WOODWORKING TOOLS, PARTS AND MATERIALS

Included here is a list of suppliers offering specialty woodworking tools and hardware. More generic parts, pieces and fasteners are available at your home-everything store, but you should strive for just the right hinge that has been well crafted from the finest materials.

In the design process, an early look at the woodworker's cache of fasteners, hardware, mechanisms and finishes might influence your design efforts on the next project.

MANUFACTURERS, SUPPLIERS

Finding resources of premium wood, dimension parts, power and hand tools, finishes and hardware can be solely a local exercise. You each have a favorite purveyor of the supplies you need to pursue your interests as a designer/craftsman.

And you are undoubtedly on many mailing lists for catalogs of woodworking supplies. In the event these suppliers have missed you, or you haven't ordered anything for a period of time and you have both forgotten one another, here is a list of the sources to contact to reestablish the relationship. Addresses and telephone numbers are correct as of mid-1996.

ADAMS WOOD PRODUCTS
974 Forest Drive
Morristown, TN 37814
Order Line   (423) 587-2942
Fax Line   (423) 586-2188
Adams Wood Products carries dimensioned parts, that is, precut/ready-to-use furniture products developed to meet past customer requests. Their catalog selection includes bedposts, rails, legs, bases and blank turning squares.

AMANA TOOL CORPORATION
120 Carolyn Boulevard
Farmingdale, NY 11735

Referral Line   (800) 455-0077
Fax Line   (516) 752-1674
Amana Tool Corporation specializes in cutting tools, including router bits, boring and drilling tools, saw blades and dado sets, shaper cutters and planer-jointer-molding knives and hand tools. Their products are available through retail stores in your area.

CONSTANTINE'S
2050 Eastchester Road
Bronx, NY 10461
Order Line   (800) 223-8087
Fax Line   (800) 253-WOOD (9663)
Constantine's is a fairly complete supplier of woodworker's supplies, including hand tools, aids, literature and specialty wood parts and inlay materials, woodturning supplies, adhesives, seating materials and specialty hardware.

CRAFTSMAN WOOD SERVICE COMPANY
1735 W. Cortland Court
Addison, IL 60101-4280
Order Line   (800) 543-9367
Fax Line   (708) 629-8292
Craftsman Wood Service Company is a furniture builder/cabinetmaker's resource for woods, veneering, dimension pieces, moldings, mechanical slides and guides, small power tools, hand tools and much more.

DAP, INCORPORATED
855 N. Third Street
Tipp City, OH 45371-3014
Corporate   (800) 327-3339
DAP, Incorporated is the maker of Weldwood waterproof and water-resistant glues, which are available through retailers. The corporate office offers guidance in glue selection.

FRANKLIN INTERNATIONAL
2020 Bruck Street
Columbus, OH 43207
Customer Service (800) 669-4583
Tech Service (800) 347-GLUE (4583)
Franklin International makes Titebond woodworking glues in specialty formulas for many general applications.

GARRETT WADE COMPANY
161 Avenue of the Americas
New York, NY 10013-1299
Order Line   (800) 221-2942
Fax Line   (800) 566-9525
Garrett Wade Company offers a complete line of general woodworking supplies including tools, parts and finishes.

GOUGEON BROTHERS, INCORPORATED
P.O. Box 908
Bay City, MI 48707
Corporate   (517) 684-7286
Gougeon Brothers, Incorporated develops, tests and manufactures West System, a complete line of epoxies for marine and outdoor furniture application which is available through retailers.

McFEELY'S SQUARE DRIVE SCREWS
1620 Wythe Road
P.O. Box 11169
Lynchburg, VA 24506-1169
Order Line   (800) 443-7937
Fax Line   (800) 847-7136
More than square drive screws, McFeely's carries clamps, cutting tools, drills, drivers, finishes, measuring aids, router supplies and dimension parts.

OSBORNE WOOD PRODUCTS
8116 Highway 123
North Toccoa, GA 30577
Order Line   (800) 849-TURN (8876)
Fax Line   (706) 886-8526
Osborne Wood Products offers turned table legs, Queen Anne cabriole legs, bedposts, bunn feet, spindles, balusters and newels, plus specialty hardware.

SEARS POWER AND HAND TOOLS
Sears Shop-at-Home Specialty Catalogs
Catalog   (800) 948-8800
Power and Hand (800) 377-7414
Tools
Parts   (800) 366-7278
Craftsman shares catalog space with the automotive hand tools. Sears offers a variety of power and hand tools for the woodworker under the Sears label and other brand names as well. If you prefer another

manufacturer, go directly to the company for information on product and purveyors in your area.

SHOPSMITH, INCORPORATED

6530 Poe Avenue
Dayton, OH 45414-2591
Order Line   (800) 543-7586
Shopsmith, Incorporated carries an esoteric product line of no interest unless you own, or plan to buy, their multipurpose machine for your space-constrained workshop.

TREND·LINES

135 American Legion Highway
Revere, MA 02151
Customer Service (800) 877-7899
Order Line   (800) 767-9999
Trend·lines is a diversified company warehousing and distributing woodworking tools and supplies (and golfing supplies), on the premise that the winter months are spent in the workshop and summer months on the links, so their warehouse is always full of what's needed for the season. They

offer a fairly full line of power tools (portable and bench type), hand tools, measuring equipment, wood parts, fasteners, etc.

WOODCRAFT SUPPLY

210 Wood County Industrial Park
P.O. Box 1686
Parkersburg, WV 26102-1686
Order Line   (800) 225-1153
Fax line   (304) 428-8271
Woodcraft Supply offers general woodworking supplies with an emphasis on tools, kits, finishes and woods.

THE WOODWORKERS' STORE

4365 Willow Drive
Medina, MN 55340-9701
Order Line   (800) 279-4441
Fax Line   (612) 478-8395
Technical Service (800) 260-9663
Rockler Industries operates a dozen retail Woodworkers' Stores throughout the U.S. and also sells via catalog from Minnesota. They offer a complete line of woodworking supplies, tools, literature and know-how for use in your next project. Special-purpose hardware is available for sewing cabinets,

blanket chests, drop-front writing cabinets, computer keyboards.

WOODWORKER'S SUPPLY OF COLORADO

1108 North Glenn Road
Casper, WY 82601

WOODWORKER'S SUPPLY OF NEW MEXICO

5604 Alameda Place NE
Albuquerque, NM 87113
Inside NM   (800) 321-9841
Outside NM   (800) 645-9292
Fax Line   (505) 821-7331
Woodworker's Supply of New Mexico offers cutting tools, abrasives, adhesives, air tools, clamps, drill bits, fasteners, hand tools, hardware, machinery, portable power tools and specialty woods.
Woodworker's Supply of New Hampshire, North Carolina or Wyoming may be closer sources.

These are just a few of the sources for everything from Forstner bits to Grecian table legs. Your local library has the *Thomas Register*, listing manufacturers of almost anything you would ever need. If just starting out, it might pay to research a source such as this to find out who has or does what you need for your project.

The home-everything stores, local hardware and lumberyards have, or can help you find, the needed item.

LOCAL HELP FROM LOCAL WOODWORKERS

Some resources you will need to ferret out in your locale. Are you new to an area and would like information on the local happenings? Try the local schools—high schools, trade schools, community colleges—to get a list of the who's who of local artisans and their suppliers. Find out where these people exhibit their work. This should be of interest as both a spectator, seeing what is being done, and a possible source for exhibiting your own work.

There may be a local woodworking association comprising tradespeople as well as artisans and hobbyists with whom you can rub elbows (or maybe bend an elbow on occasion), share your thoughts and experiences, and benefit from the lessons of others.

Glossary

aliphatic glue Generally the yellow family of woodworking glues.

annual growth rings A tree's growth pattern in rings comprising springwood (fibrous, faster growing wood) and summerwood (more dense, harder wood terminating at the end of the growing season).

apron Trim or structural member beneath projecting top or table surface, used as tie-in for leg or corner joinery.

auger bit Used for hand drilling using brace and bit.

backsaw A small handsaw with reinforced spine for rigidity. Also known as a miter saw.

banded-cell or banded-trunk Refers to the way this variety of trees is formed into a structured cellular pattern.

band saw Stationary saw using continuous cutting blade that rides over a drive wheel and tension wheel. Cuts thick stock, can scroll, resaw or cutoff, depending on the blade in use.

batten Cleat fastened across a series of boards, also any thin board used to mark curvatures.

bearers Horizontal rails dividing drawers.

bench grinder Motor-driven wheels ranging from abrasive to buffing cloth to perform a variety of sharpening, honing, cleaning and polishing of cutting tools and other metal.

bench plane term given to planes with larger footprints and wider cutter, e.g., smoothing plane, jack plane.

bevel (1) Any edge angle other than 90°, sloping away from a major surface plane. (2) An adjustable square to capture and angle for measurement or for marking the captured angle on the workpiece.

blind spline A spline inset in a blind dado, of a length that stops short of exposing either the dadoed groove or the spline that fits between the two joined pieces at the ends.

blind tenon A tenon fully enclosed by a mortise cut in mating member.

block plane Smaller planes, lower angle of cutter having bevel facing up for truing end grain.

brace (1) Structural member augmenting the primary member, usually oblique to the structure. (2) A driver for an auger bit, formed in the shape of a crank for rotating the bit (as in brace and bit).

brad point Twist drill with center point projection.

brad point (drill) A twist drill having a center spur to guide the bit in an advancing pilot hole.

break Woodworking an edge to remove the sharp corner.

bullnose (v) Mill edge to a half-round, convex edge.

bullnose plane Concave cutter for rounding edges.

butt joint Two square edges, sides or ends meet.

cambium layer Area of new growth between bark and sapwood in tree trunks, limbs and branches in banded-cell-type trees.

cantilevered Plank or beam fastened or supported only by a downward force at the captured end.

capitals Finales, tops or extreme ends of a column.

carriage Supports under stairs sloped to the run and rise.

C-clamp A C-shaped clamp with an open side large enough to span the parts being held by an acme-threaded opposing swivel end.

chuck Split sleeve tightened around a tool shank by a ring or collet as a drill chuck. A Jacobs chuck refers to a taper designed to hold the drill chuck more firmly on the spindle.

counterbore A deep depression for recessing the head of a fastener well below the fastened surface; may receive a bung or button to cover the fastener head.

countersink A shallow depression that sets the head of a fastener flush or below the surface of the piece being fastened.

chamfer Bevel or slant along board edge.

clamp A device to hold work in process.

combination bit Drill bit shaped to screw size, drills pilot hole, shank, chamfers and countersink in one operation.

compound angle A cut made from setting two angles, neither at right angle to the workpiece.

cove bit Convex flute to cut concave edge or groove.

coving Concave molding for a transition from vertical to horizontal.

cross-cut Cutting across wood grain.

cross lap Two members each notched to half the depth that receive the other flush with both top and bottom surfaces.

crotch (Crooks) random grain from tree branching areas.

dado (n) (1) A groove made by dadoing. (2) A tool for dadoing.

dado (v) (1) To provide with a dado. (2) To set into a groove. (3) To cut a rectangular groove.

dovetail Fan-shaped interlocking joint.

dovetail bit Specialty bit for interlocked joints.

dovetail key A fancy groove-and-spline configuration allowed to run out at the ends, comprising opposing dovetail slots joined by a dovetail-shaped spline. A slight interference fit will force the two parts (being joined) together.

dowel A cylindrical piece of wood with glue slots to strengthen wood joints or appendages.

dowel-pinned A joint or attachment press fit or glued where dowels provide the later strength between two joined parts.

dressed Lumber planed smooth during the finishing process.

drill press A drill head and motor mounted on a vertical column aligned with an adjustable worktable mounted on the same column. With a drill bit or router bit in the chuck, the drill press spindle is lowered into the workpiece by means of a wheel/ratchet track.

face plate Wood-lathe attachment to support turning block.

fair A smooth blending of pieces joined to form a curvature.

fay To fit or join tightly, such as timbers or boards.

fiberglass GRP, glass-reinforced plastic.

figuring Wood grain characteristics (see flat grain).

file Hardened steel tool in many configurations cut with ridges to abrade away material from the workpiece.

finger joint (or **finger lap joint**) Evenly spaced notches to receive fingers from joined piece.

fixture A device for supporting work during machining.

flat grain Lumber cut tangent to the annual growth rings, appears highly figured.

flat-sawn Lumber sawn with the flat grain exposed on the wide surface, i.e., sawn perpendicular to the radius and tangent to the annual rings of a log.

flight A series of steps without a landing.

flitch Thin flat-sawn sheet veneer gathered in the order sliced from a log prepared for resawing (which is also known as a flitch).

fluting Parallel patterns plowed into the surface of furniture members.

gluejoint bit One-pass profile for added glue area.

grain Usually refers to texture, porosity or figuring of wood.

groove Plow cut similar to dado except made with grain, usually near, but not on the edge of the wood.

gusset A triangular block to strengthen the joining of two members assembled at an angle.

half-lap One member notched to receive a thinner member flush with the top surface.

handsaw An open saw (one blade, one handle) with teeth cut into the saw for crosscutting (more points per inch), ripping (fewer points per inch) or a combination saw (somewhere between) for general work.

hardwood Wood from a family of deciduous trees (angiospermous).

heartwood Aged wood in the center of a tree trunk or limb.

holiday Areas void of paint or varnish unintentionally skipped during application.

honing Sharpening to a fine cutting edge.

isometric drawing Image drawn in three-dimensional form on a 30°/60°

axis using true-scaled dimensions along the axes.

isometric projection Same as above, except foreshortened to appear more natural as viewed.

jig A device to maintain mechanically the correct positional relationship between the work and the tool, or between parts for assembly.

jigsaw (or **scroll saw**) Converts rotary spindle to an up/down motion. Stationary jigsaws have both upper and lower chucks to hold a thin blade for fancy scrollwork.

joinery (joinerwork) Matching and mating woods to form intricate, tightly joined assemblies.

jointer plane Long footprint plane for smooth, even edge.

jointer/planer Rotary cutters (three or more blades, 4″ to 6″ in length) for power-planing squared edges for joining, rabbeting or beveling by adjusting the guide fence and depth of cut on the feed table.

laminate A glued build-up of thin layers of resawn wood.

lap joint Overlapping boards each cut to half thickness.

lathe A metal- or woodworking machine that holds a workpiece at both ends of a horizontal axis for shaping with cutting chisels.

lathe chisel Any of a variety of handheld woodcutting tools with sharpened metal blades in long wooden handles. Supported on a lathe's tool rest.

let-in Term for a housing joint accepting the edge of one board into another.

lockjoint bit 45° miter bit interlocks parts of drawer face.

loft (*v*) To lay out in a full-size drawing the lines and contours (typical in shipbuilding).

margins Edging or borders, sometimes extended for mill work.

measuring point In perspective drawing, the distance from two vanishing points along the horizon line equal to the distance of the vanishing point to the station point.

mill work Shaped or dressed surfaces through single or repetitive cuts.

miter joint Two edges joined at any angle of cut.

molding Decorative lengths of

recessed curves or rectangles intended to finish an edge or form a transition between two angled planes.

mortise (*n*) Hole, groove or slot into or through which another part passes or fits (as in tenon).

mortise (*v*) (1) To join or fasten securely (tenon and mortise). (2) To cut or make a mortise in.

mullions Center stiles of swinging doors or windows.

muntin Rails and stiles separating panes or panels inside a frame.

nosing Tread projecting beyond face of the riser.

ogee Molding with an S-shaped profile.

ogee bit Molding or margin with S-shaped profile.

parting tool Lathe chisel sharpened to a *V*, used for cutting, grooving or separating wood from turning.

perspective, angular View drawn to one side or the other from the nearest corner, creating different angles of divergence and foreshortening toward the vanishing points.

perspective, parallel View drawn with both sides flanking the nearest corner converging at the same angle and measuring the same distance toward the vanishing points.

pilot hole A prebored hole of smaller diameter drilled on center to guide a larger bit through the same center line. Also used to prevent splitting when driving nails and screws.

pipe clamp (or **bar clamp**) One end of the clamp jaws is attached to one end (the head) of standard metal pipe or bar stock, and the other (the foot) is cam-cleated or slipped into various slots. Pressure is applied by turning an acme-threaded swivel at the head end.

plain sawing (also flat cut, plain-sliced) Cutting one sheet after the other straight through the log.

plain-sawn Another term for flat-sawn.

plane (*n*) Any one of a bench plane, block plane, jack plane, rabbet plane with cutters designed for special cuts.

plane (*v*) To make smooth and even or level so a line connecting two points on the plane would lie on the surface.

quarter-round Convex molding of a 90° cross section.

quartersawn Lumber resawn from

quartered logs so the annual rings are nearly at right angles to the wide face of the board (see vertical grain).

quirk A narrow groove, fillet or channel which delineates a change and adds a design element to highlight an interesting component shape or treatment.

rabbet (rebate) (n) Channel, groove or recess cut out of the face of any body intended to receive another member, usually on the edge of the wood.

rabbet (rebate) (v) (1) To cut a rabbet in, (2) to unite edges or (3) to become joined (by a rabbet).

rabbet plane Edge plane for producing edge shelf for rabbet.

radial arm saw A motor and circular saw blade that moves along an overhead track, drawing the saw across the work. Blade may be rotated and locked in place for ripping.

rail When referring to paneled doors, the horizontal member above and below the panel.

rail and stile bit Rail-and-stile combination (reverse assembly) cuts profile, bevel, rabbet or dado.

rasp Hardened steel tool with many cross sections into which teeth have been formed by cutting away material leaving sharp toothlike edges to cut away the workpiece.

rays Storage cells in living trees used for nutrients, oriented horizontally, vertically or in pockets radiating from the center of a tree, crossing radially its growth rings.

reeding Raised parallel convex beading on furniture members.

resaw Rip with the grain parallel to the wide side.

reveal Sides of surrounding frame exposed by a panel or member set in from the outermost plane.

ribbon-cut (or plain cut) Wood cut on the quartersawn section forming alternating light and dark or other opposing patterned stripes.

rift-cut (or rift-sawn) Wood, including veneer, cut at 45° to the growth rings.

rip Rip saw in the direction of the grain, normally lengthwise and through the narrow side.

rise Total height spanned by steps or ladder.

riser Vertical front between steps or rungs.

rotary-cut Veneer sliced away from a cylindrical log by means of a knife blade forced against a revolving core that has been centered on a lathe.

router Ultra-high-speed motor with spindle and collet for inserting a variety of router bits to perform a variety of cuts from dadoing, milling, lettering and decorative designs.

router bit Any one of a number of special cutters.

run Horizontal distance occupied by a ladder.

saber saw Sometimes a "jigsaw" of the portable variety. Comes equipped with a number of accessories to allow cutting circles or scrollwork or guiding a cut along an edge. Blades are heavier than with a jigsaw and are held in one chuck only.

sapwood Area of new, live and dying cells of a tree.

scantlings Dimensions of the wooden members of construction.

scarf Lap joint over area greater than the width for joining long members end-to-end.

scribing (spiling) Transfer lines to replacement member or pattern using dividers or circle compass.

seasoned Wood treated in preparation for use, air-dried, kiln-dried.

shouldered tenon Reducing thickness to form a projection (tenon) some distance in from end or edge.

skew Wood-turning chisel with edge sharpened at angle.

skirt(ing) Molding or finishing board at the base of a piece of furniture.

softwood Wood from evergreen (coniferous) trees with a few exceptions in the deciduous family. Hard- and softwood designation does not equate to the wood hardness, however.

spade bit Flat woodworking bit for high-speed drilling of larger diameter holes. Width can be ground to non-standard diameter.

splat Thin piece of wood used in chair backs.

spline Thin piece of wood for (1) inserting in glue joint, and (2) a batten for bending into a fair arc or curve.

spring clamp Moderate tension (therefore multiple clamps may be needed) to hold parts between spring-tension fingers while gluing.

square, adjustable Bevel guide with locking nut.

square, carpenters Fixed 90° angle, long inside/outside square.

square, combination Adjustable head allows outside/inside angles, depth gauge, marking gauge level and 45° miter.

square, try Fixed 90° small square, inside/outside.

stainless steel Alloy of iron and chromium (also nickel and manganese) with low-magnetic qualities, rust resistant.

stand proud To extend beyond, to stand out.

station point Viewer position in perspective drawings.

stile In door panels, the vertical members in which the muntins are inserted or attached.

straight bit Single flute for grooving, double flute for grooving or cutting away.

string, closed Step ends captured by sloping planks.

string, open Steps cantilevered beyond carriage.

surface (v) To plane or make smooth.

table saw A machined worktable including guide slots, rip fence track, etc., surrounding a circular sawblade, used for precise cuts of small or large pieces fed into the blade for cutting off, mitering, ripping and milling.

tenon Inserted member of a mortise and tenon joint.

texture Density, or lack of, of the cellular structure of wood.

thermoplastic Glues that soften when heated, reharden when cooled.

thermosetting Glues that will not soften with heat.

through tenon Projection ending flush or proud of the thickness of member containing the mortise.

tongue and groove Mating edges cut with tenon and a receiving slot.

transverse Perpendicular to the center line.

tread Horizontal area of a step or rung.

truing (1) The act of making true, as in square, flat, concentric, balanced, or (2) to restore to an original shape.

twist drill A drill bit comprising a

cylindrical shank with helical flute to carry away the cut material. End is sharpened in a conical angle, forming cutting edges.

vanishing point Point where the lines of an item drawn in perspective converge. May be one-, two- or three-point perspective.

veining Grooves cut into workpiece.

veining bit Rounded flute for decorative routing, scrolling.

veneer Thinly sliced sheets of specialty woods for applying to the surface of common structural woods.

vertical grain Lumber milled so that a cross section of annual growth rings appear with the grain lines parallel on the face of the board (see quartersawn).

web clamp (or **band clamp**) Fabric strips with cam cleats to hold the clamped assembly, such as chair legs, in even compression while gluing.

whet Something that sharpens or makes keen.

wood-boring drill bit (or **spade drill**) A flattened piece of tool steel with sharp beveled edges flanking a brad point aligned with the round shank that fits in a high-seed drill chuck.

wood chisel Hand pressure or struck with a mallet, the chisel blade is a flat bar of tool steel sharpened with one side beveled and honed for surface penetration or carving.

wood-turning chisel *See* **lathe chisel.**

Index

CPSIA information can be obtained
at www.ICGtesting.com
Printed in the USA
FSHW022101160119
55082FS